21世纪高等学校专业英语系列规划教材

教育学专业英语教程

English for Pedagogy

董晓波　孙茂华　主　编
于银磊　韦　希　殷云菲　副主编
刘丽昀　冯　琦　赵有珊　陈亦麟　参　编

清 华 大 学 出 版 社
北京交通大学出版社
· 北京 ·

内容简介

本教程在内容编排上力图反映当代教育学的发展趋势与新特征，注重教育学专业知识与英语学习的有机结合，所包括的课文涉及当代教育学的主要方面，不仅注重英语能力的培养，也强调教育学专业知识的传授和技能的训练。

本教程除适合高等师范院校本科生、研究生使用外，也可供各级各类教育学院教育学、教育心理学、英语教学法等专业的本科生和研究生学习教育学专业英语之用。此外，对于大、中、小学教师了解教育学理论知识，提高教育学专业英语水平也是难得的参考书。

本书封面贴有清华大学出版社防伪标签，无标签者不得销售。
版权所有，侵权必究。侵权举报电话：010—62782989 13501256678 13801310933

图书在版编目（CIP）数据

教育学专业英语教程/董晓波，孙茂华主编．—北京：北京交通大学出版社：清华大学出版社，2015.2（2023.8重印）
ISBN 978-7-5121-2201-7

Ⅰ.① 教… Ⅱ.① 董… ② 孙… Ⅲ.① 教育学-英语-教材 Ⅳ.① H31

中国版本图书馆 CIP 数据核字（2015）第 027786 号

责任编辑：王晓春　田秀青　　　特邀编辑：孙晴霞
出版发行：清 华 大 学 出 版 社　邮编：100084　电话：010-62776969　http：//www.tup.com.cn
　　　　　北京交通大学出版社　邮编：100044　电话：010-51686414　http：//www.bjtup.com.cn
印　刷　者：北京虎彩文化传播有限公司
经　　　销：全国新华书店
开　　　本：185×243　印张：20　字数：426千字
版　　　次：2019年7月第1版第1次修订　2023年8月第7次印刷
书　　　号：ISBN 978-7-5121-2201-7/H•429
印　　　数：7 501～8 000册　定价：49.00元

本书如有质量问题，请向北京交通大学出版社质监组反映。对您的意见和批评，我们表示欢迎和感谢。
投诉电话：010-51686043，51686008；传真：010-62225406；E-mail：press@bjtu.edu.cn。

Preface 前　言

　　本教程是为高等院校教育学专业的本科生和研究生编写的，旨在通俗、系统地介绍教育学学科理论和教学实践的专业英语教材。

　　基于历史和现实的原因，英语作为国际语言，适用范围广、影响大，能更好地促进各个领域的交流和实践，尤其是在教育教学改革不断深入的当今社会，教育学作为一门研究人类教育现象和问题、揭示一般教育规律的社会学科，是广泛存在于人类生活中的社会现象，是有目的地培养社会人的活动。随着现代社会的进步以及现代教育实践的发展，为了有效地进行教育活动，人们对教育学研究以及教师教育提出更新、更高的要求。就教育学课程体系构建和教材建设而言，教育学专业英语教程的编写既需结合我国教师教育实际，又需满足基础教育改革对师资需求，进而有效地推动我国高等师范院校改革和发展新型的教师教育模式。因此，《教育学专业英语教程》将学习英语与了解教育领域内一些常见学科理论及教学实践，提高解决实际教育问题的能力紧密结合，即在学习英语的同时，使学生系统地了解教育学科学理论、专业知识和教学实践；在认识和走进教育领域的同时，学习和了解教育学科中一些常见的教育理论、观点（包括专业词汇、术语等）的英语表达，在巩固一般语言知识和运用能力的基础上进一步扩展学生的语言知识，提高学生的语言应用能力，将语言教学和专业教育融会贯通。

　　本教程选材广泛，信息量大，基本包含了当代教育学的主要方面。本教程文字浅显，结构严谨，行文流畅，语言地道。所有的文章均由英语国家教育学专业人士写作，在编选时，除极少数文章因技术需要略作删节外，力求保持原文风貌，避免一些同类教材用汉语材料译成英语的语言生硬的翻译痕迹，让读者享受纯正的教育学专业英语。在编排体例方面，为了方便读者提高阅读能力，本书增加了文章背景知识介绍，言简意赅地介绍文章基本线索，便于读者快速阅读和理解文章主旨；注释力求简单明了，方便读者了解教育学知识。词汇接近大学英语四六级难度，主要汇集教育学专业词汇，以降低阅读难度。书后附有练习答案，便于读者自学，自测学习效果。

　　本教程除适合高等师范院校本科生、研究生使用外，也可供各级各类教育学院教育学、教育心理学、英语教学法等专业的本科生和研究生学习教育学专业英语之用。此外,对于大、中、小学教师了解教育学理论知识,提高教育学专业英语水平也是难得的参考书。

本教程由董晓波、孙茂华任主编,于银磊、韦希、殷云菲任副主编,刘丽昀、冯琦、赵有珊、陈亦麟参编。在整个编写过程中,我们力求完美,但是限于水平及一些不可避免的因素,定不乏偏颇和疏漏,恳请广大读者朋友和同行不吝指正。

董晓波

2015年3月于南京

电子邮箱:dongxiaobo@163.com

Contents
目 录

Unit 1　Origin & History of Education　教育的起源和历史 ……………… (1)
　　Text A　The History of Compulsory Education in Europe ……………… (1)
　　Text B　A History of American Higher Education ……………… (6)
　　Supplementary Reading　The Origins of Distance Education ……………… (13)

Unit 2　Educational & Social Development　教育与社会发展 ……………… (17)
　　Text A　Open and Distance Education: a Better Way of Competence Building
　　　　　　and Sustainable Development ……………… (17)
　　Text B　Higher Education within a Knowledge-based Society ……………… (24)
　　Supplementary Reading　The Global "Imagined Community"—Global Civil
　　　　　　Society and International Education ……………… (31)

Unit 3　Education & People's Overall Development　教育与人的全面发展
　　　　……………… (35)
　　Text A　Role of Education in the Developmental Process ……………… (35)
　　Text B　Social Skills Development in Primary Education ……………… (40)
　　Supplementary Reading　Social Emotional Development: a New Model of
　　　　　　Student Learning in Higher Education ……………… (47)

Unit 4　Educational System & Educational Law　教育制度与教育法 ……… (50)
　　Text A　E-learning and Evaluation in Modern Educational System ………… (50)
　　Text B　Legislation and Equality in Basic Education ……………… (55)
　　Supplementary Reading　Major Continuities and Changes in the Basic

    Education Law …………………………………………………… (60)

Unit 5 Educational Justice 教育公平 ……………………………… (63)
  Text A Educational Justice in Schools ………………………… (63)
  Text B Efficiency and Equity of European Education and Training Policies
    ……………………………………………………………… (68)
  Supplementary Reading Educational Policy, Housing Policy and Social Justice
    ……………………………………………………………… (74)

Unit 6 Educator & Educational Thoughts 教育家与教育思想 ……… (77)
  Text A Disciples of Confucius …………………………………… (77)
  Text B Educational Thought and Teaching ……………………… (81)
  Supplementary Reading "Filling Bellies and Brains": the Educational and
    Political Thought of Frederick James Gould …………………… (88)

Unit 7 Educational Objective 教育目的 ………………………… (91)
  Text A Aims and Objectives of Education ……………………… (91)
  Text B Education, Basics of Education and Educational Objectives ……… (100)
  Supplementary Reading Knowing Your Learning Target ……………… (108)

Unit 8 Teacher & Student 教师与学生 …………………………… (114)
  Text A The Teacher, the Student and the Classroom ………… (114)
  Text B Teacher-Student Attachment and Teachers' Attitudes towards Work
    ……………………………………………………………… (124)
  Supplementary Reading New Teacher and Student Roles in the
    Technology-Supported Classroom ………………………………… (134)

Unit 9 School & Family 学校与家庭 ……………………………… (144)
  Text A School and Family Cooperation Models for Reducing Social Problems
    ……………………………………………………………… (144)
  Text B The Effects of Family, School, and Classroom Ecologies on Changes
    in Children's Social Competence and Emotional and Behavioral Problems
    in First Grade ……………………………………………… (154)

    Supplementary Reading Parent-Teacher Communication: Tips for Creating
     a Strong Parent-Teacher Relationship ………………………………… (161)

Unit 10 Moral Education 道德教育 …………………………………………… (165)
    Text A Education as a Moral Enterprise ………………………………… (165)
    Text B Moral Education of Youth in the Information Age ……………… (170)
    Supplementary Reading Moral Education and Improvement of Coexistence in
     Spain ……………………………………………………………………… (177)

Unit 11 Extra-curricular Activities 课外活动 ………………………………… (181)
    Text A Extra-curricular Activity and the Transition from Higher Education to
     Work …………………………………………………………………… (181)
    Text B Extra-curricular Physical Activity and Socioeconomic Status in Italian
     Adolescents …………………………………………………………… (189)
    Supplementary Reading Discussion and Conclusion of Correspondence
     Hypothesis ……………………………………………………………… (198)

Unit 12 School Management 学校管理 ……………………………………… (203)
    Text A What is School-based Management? …………………………… (203)
    Text B Comparative Case Study on School Management Practices in Two
     Schools in the United States and Turkey ……………………………… (212)
    Supplementary Reading Evaluating School-based Management …………… (221)

Unit 13 Teaching Methods 教学方法 ………………………………………… (227)
    Text A Refuting Misconceptions about Classroom Discussion ……………… (227)
    Text B Brainstorming: a Creative Way to Learn ……………………… (235)
    Supplementary Reading Learning Styles and Teaching Styles …………… (242)

Unit 14 Materials & Test 教材与考试 …………………………………………… (247)
    Text A Materials and Media ……………………………………………… (247)
    Text B In Defense of Teaching "Outdated" Material ………………… (255)
    Supplementary Reading Using Examinations and Testing to Improve
     Educational Quality …………………………………………………… (262)

Unit 15　Educational Evaluation　教育评价 ……………………………… (271)
　　Text A　Integration of Technology and Educational Assessment ………… (271)
　　Text B　Sustainable Assessment and Evaluation Strategies for Open and
　　　　　　Distance Learning ……………………………………………… (278)
　　Supplementary Reading　Broadening Our Approach to Teaching Evaluation
　　　　　　………………………………………………………………… (285)

Keys to Exercises　练习答案 ………………………………………………… (292)
References　参考文献 ………………………………………………………… (302)

Unit 1 Origin & History of Education
教育的起源和历史

Text A The History of Compulsory Education in Europe

导读：义务教育，是根据法律规定，适龄儿童和青少年都必须接受的，国家、社会、家庭必须予以保证的国民教育。其实质是指政府有义务运用公共资源保障所有适龄儿童接受的教育。义务教育又称强迫教育和免费义务教育。义务教育具有强制性、免费性、普及性的特点。凡是适龄儿童都有强制接受教育的义务，并且教育对象没有阶级或是出身的限制，此外还必须是免纳学费的。1717年，普鲁士王国开始实施义务国民教育，是全世界第一个实施义务教育的国家。《世界人权宣言》第26条第一款指出："人人都有受教育的权利，教育应当免费，至少在初级和基本阶段应如此。初级教育应属义务性质。"现代多数的国家和地区都实施了义务教育，但年数和成效不一。

In the past few years, there has been a high-profile anti-truancy publicity campaign aiming to send out a clear and tough message to the community, particularly the parents of truants—that truancy will not be tolerated. Thousands of press released from LEA have been fed to the national and local press generating adverse news and stories about the fining and jailing of truants' parents, who are regarded as shamefully irresponsible by failing to stop their children truanting.

Picking up any local newspaper, one would easily find the headlines that slam the "irresponsible parents" whose children are skipping schools. These press headlines on truancy have undoubtedly reinforced the fear that truancy levels have reached a crisis point. They have also given people the impression that the perceived newly-emerged "irresponsible parents" are one of the modern days' social phenomena that are seriously threatening our compulsory education system and, therefore, our civil society.

However, nearly 500 years ago, Luther (1530) was already able to observe three equivalent groups of "irresponsible parents" who were most likely to neglect their parental duties in sending their children to school. Most "irresponsible parents" at that time were those who might not understand what Luther thought as their God-given responsibility, others might not be suited for the duty, "... for they themselves have learned nothing but how to care for their bellies" (Luther, 1530).

A third group of parents was those who did not have the opportunity or the means to educate their children. Luther observed that these parents placed their children's material comfort above their spiritual needs. He argued in his address to the lawmakers that the civil authorities were under obligation to compel the people to send their children to school:

"Dear rulers... if the government can compel such citizens as are fit for military service to bear spear and rifle, to mount ramparts, and perform other material duties in time of war, how much more has it a right to compel the people to send their children to school, because in this case we are warring with the devil, whose objective is secretly to exhaust our cities and principalities of their strong men." (Luther, 1524)

One of the hallmarks of the Renaissance movement, which was reaching northern Europe in the sixteenth century, was the rebirth of learning. The Christian Reformation activists tirelessly advocated universal education as an important means in producing responsible citizens. In his open letter to the councilmen, Luther (1524) urged them to have a vested interest in education for a city's best and greatest welfare, safety and strength consist rather in its having many able, learned, wise, honorable, and well-educated citizens than in mighty walls and magnificent buildings.

However, in the early sixteenth century, there was no state education system and most education activities were conducted in monasteries, cloisters and other religious institutions run by the Roman Catholic Church. These institutions very often lacked minimal resources and did not enjoy parents' trust because of the corruption and abuse among the clergy. Many parents were increasingly reluctant to send their children to the training institutions run by the Catholic Church.

Luther (1530), therefore, wrote an open letter to the parents to convince his "beloved Germans" that the spiritual well-being of their children was more important than their physical comfort. Luther based his arguments for parental responsibility firmly on the Bible, citing several texts as proof. One quoted by him is Psalm 78:5-7, on how God commanded our fathers to teach (His laws) to their children; that the next generation might know them... and arise and tell them to their children, so that they should set their

Unit 1 Origin & History of Education 教育的起源和历史

hope in God, and not forget the works of God.

Another is Deuteronomy 21:18-21, the stories of rebellious youths being brought by their parents to the elders for corporal punishment. In Geneva another Protestant reformer, John Calvin (1536), was similarly making a case for compulsory schooling where all children were to be instructed in the "true faith" and "in the languages and worldly sciences" which served as a necessary preliminary for such instruction. Like Luther, Calvin was supremely confident that his possession of "the truth" gave him warrant to override the wishes and desires of parents who did not share his beliefs.

As a result of a Protestant reformers' campaign in the state of Gotha, the world's first primitive form of state schooling was established in 1524. It soon spread to Thuringia, Saxony, Wurttemberg and other German Protestant states. In 1559, the duchy of Wurttemberg ordered the introduction of a school attendance register and for the first time in educational history, levied fines on the parents whose children truanted.

However, the elaborate version of compulsory education as we see today did not emerge until the beginning of the nineteenth century when the Kings of Prussia established a system of state-controlled compulsory schooling and forcefully discouraged voluntary education. A minister of the interior was appointed to supervise the running of state schools. In 1810, state certifications of teachers were instituted and in 1812 children were prohibited from leaving school until they had passed a compulsory examination.

Regarded as a successful way of making every citizen useful to the state, the Prussian schooling system soon spread to most Western countries in the nineteenth century, including the USA and the UK.

Notes

1. **LEA =Local Education Authority(英国地方教育局)**: is a local authority in England and Wales that has responsibility for education within its jurisdiction. Since the Children Act 2004 each local education authority is also a children's services authority and the responsibility for both functions is held by the director of children's services.

2. **Luther—Martin Luther(马丁·路德)**: was a German priest and professor of theology who initiated the Protestant Reformation. He strongly disputed the claim that freedom from God's punishment of sin could be purchased with money. He thought that salvation is not earned by good deeds but received only as a free gift of God's grace through faith in Jesus as

redeemer from sin. His theology challenged the authority of the pope of the Roman Catholic Church by teaching that the Bible is the only source of divinely revealed knowledge and opposed sacerdotalism(祭司制度,僧侣政治) by considering all baptized Christians to be a holy priesthood. Those who identify with Luther's teachings are called Lutherans.

3. **Psalm** [诗篇(《圣经·旧约》中的一卷)]: is a book of the Hebrew Bible and the Christian Bible. In its current, most commonly used form consists of 150 songs and prayers referred to individually as psalms and referenced by chapter and verse, which "express virtually the full range of Israel's religious faith".

4. **Deuteronomy** [申命记(《圣经·旧约》中的一卷)]: is the fifth book of the Hebrew Bible, and the fifth of five books of the Jewish Torah/Pentateuch. The book consists of three sermons or speeches delivered by Moses, a recounting of the law (thought to be the Book of the Covenant found in Josiah's time), and supplementary material, including an account of Moses' death.

5. **John Calvin**(约翰·加尔文): was an influential French theologian and pastor during the Protestant Reformation. He was a principal figure in the development of the system of Christian theology later called Calvinism. His writing and preaching provided the seeds for the branch of theology that bears his name. The Reformed and Presbyterian churches, which look to Calvin as a chief expositor of their beliefs, have spread throughout the world.

6. **Prussia**(普鲁士): was a German kingdom and historic state originating out of the Duchy of Prussia and the Margraviate of Brandenburg. For centuries, the House of Hohenzollern ruled Prussia, successfully expanding its size by way of an unusually well-organized and effective army. Prussia shaped the history of Germany, with its capital in Berlin after 1451. After 1871, Prussia was increasingly merged into Germany, losing its distinctive identity. It was effectively abolished in 1932, and officially abolished in 1947.

New Words and Expression

1. compulsory[kəmˈpʌlsəri]	adj.		强制的,势在必行的,义务的
2. truancy[ˈtruːənsi]	n.		逃学,旷课;玩忽职守
3. slam[slæm]	v.		砰地关上,猛放,猛烈攻击
	n.		砰然声,猛烈抨击
	n.		满贯

Unit 1 Origin & History of Education 教育的起源和历史

4. rampart [ˈræmpɑːt]	n.	垒,壁垒,城墙
	vt.	用壁垒围绕,防卫,守卫
5. principality [ˌprinsiˈpæliti]	n.	封邑,公国,主权
6. hallmark [ˈhɔːlmɑːk]	n.	纯度标记,标志,特征
	vt.	标纯度
7. monastery [ˈmɔnəstəri]	n.	修道院,寺院
8. cloister [ˈklɔistə]	n.	修道院,寺庙,隐居地
	vt.	远离尘世,隐居,用环廊环绕
9. clergy [ˈkləːdʒi]	n.	[总称]牧师,神职人员
10. reluctant [riˈlʌktənt]	adj.	不情愿的,勉强的
11. corporal [ˈkɔːpərəl]	adj.	肉体的,身体的
	n.	(陆军或空军)下士
12. preliminary [priˈliminəri]	adj.	初步的,预备的
	n.	初步行动,准备,初步措施

I Vocabulary.

Fill in the blanks with the most suitable words. Change the form when necessary.

reluctant	compulsory	preliminary	slam	principality
corporal	hallmark	rampart	truancy	monastery

1. A teacher should not give students _____ punishment.
2. The plan has all the _____ of being a total failure.
3. A _____ is a building or collection of buildings in which monks live.
4. He closed the door with a _____.
5. The schools were fighting endlessly to combat _____.
6. Ministers have shown extreme _____ to explain their position to the media.
7. Perhaps the tower is part of the _____ of the city.
8. A _____ talk on the future of the bases began yesterday.

9. Attendance at evening prayers is not _____.
10. I've been to the _____ of Monaco.

II Translate the following words or phrases into English.

义务教育   _____
说服,使信服   _____
物质享受   _____
精神需求   _____
监督,管理,指导   _____

III Comprehension of the text.

Decide whether the following statements are true (T) or false (F) according to the passage.

1. National and local press have generated adverse news and stories about the fining and jailing of truants, who are regarded as shamefully irresponsible.
2. A third group of parents placed their children's material comfort below their spiritual needs.
3. In the early sixteenth century, there was only one state education system and most education activities were conducted in monasteries, cloisters and other religious institutions run by the Roman Catholic Church.
4. As many parents were reluctant to send their children to the training institutions run by the Catholic Church, Luther wrote an open letter to them to convince the importance of spiritual well-being of their children.
5. The elaborate version of compulsory education as we see today emerged at the beginning of the nineteenth century when the Kings of Prussia established a system of state-controlled compulsory schooling.

Text B A History of American Higher Education

导读:高等教育(Higher Education)广义上是指一切建立在中等教育基础上的专业教育,是培养高级专门人才的社会活动。高等教育是大学、文理学院、理工学院和师范学院等机构所提供的各种类型的教育,包括专科教育、本科教育和研究生教育,其基本入学条件为完成中等教育,学完课程后授予学位、文凭或证书,作为完成高等学业的证明。高等

Unit 1 Origin & History of Education 教育的起源和历史

教育的发展历史可以追溯到中世纪的大学,后来历经发展,主要是英国、德国、美国的大学的不断转型,形成了高等教育的三项职能,即:培养专门人才;科学研究;服务社会。作为一种教育方式,高等教育是人生存方式的一个阶段。从时间上说,高等教育是人生存过程中的终生学习选择阶段;从空间上说,高等教育是人进入完全社会生活的最后一个准备场所。高等教育还是高深文化知识传播创新的社会组织机构;在传播高深文化的同时,还复制或者再制了社会的价值、行为模式和道德规范。

Higher education in the United States has been molded and influenced by a variety of historical forces. On one hand, there are the patterns and traditions of higher learning which have been brought over from Western Europe. On the other hand, we find the native American conditions which have affected and modified the development of these transplanted institutions. Out of the interaction of these two essential elements and, most importantly, out of the growth of democracy in every area of American life, America has developed a truly unique system of higher education.

English influences

Oxford and Cambridge furnished the original model that the colonial colleges sought to copy. The prototype for the first English-American college was Emmanuel College, Cambridge University. As we read the explicit statements left by Harvard's founders, we find that the earliest Harvard College statutes were taken directly from the Elizabethan statutes of the University of Cambridge; that the phrase *pro modo Academiarum in Anglia* ("according to the manner of universities in England") is to be found in the first Harvard degree formula; that early Harvard, like Elizabethan Cambridge, welcomed "fellow commoners" as well as serious degree students, "gentlemen" who paid double tuition for the privilege of residing in the college and dining with the Fellows; that even the names of the four college classes—freshman, sophomore, junior sophister, and senior sophister—were borrowed directly from England. In other points involving student discipline, curriculum, administrative regulations, and degree requirements, Harvard followed English college precedents as closely and faithfully as she could; and Harvard, in turn, became the great prototype for all the later colleges of English America.

As late as the middle of the eighteenth century, President Clap of Yale prepared himself for his administrative duties by borrowing histories of Oxford and Cambridge and seeking information from Americans who had secured English college degree. When Clap waged his campaign of 1745 to secure a new Yale charter, he based it on a careful and detailed study of administrative practices at Oxford and Cambridge.

Even at William and Mary, English influence soon challenged an earlier Scottish trend. From 1729 to 1757, eight of thirteen faculty members were Oxford men, and of these eight, from Queens College. After 1757, a battle raged almost continuously between this Oxford-bred faculty and the native Virginian Board of Visitors. By 1766 the Visitors "had rid the college of the last of that band of able Oxford graduates, ministers all of them, whose chief fault had been that their ties with English were too close, that they looked too blindly to their homeland".

In almost every case, however, the English colonists eventually found that the unique conditions of the American physical and social environment produced unexpected changes and modifications in their academic institutions. Some of these were destined to be of great importance for the later development of higher education in the United States.

It was soon discovered that it would be impossible to erect in English-America any great university collection of colleges such as existed at Oxford or Cambridge. For one thing, it was doubtful that the Crown would ever grant the required royal charter for such an American university. Besides, the land was too vast and the people too poor. The narrow fringe of British settlements which faced the broad Atlantic on one side and trackless forests on the other represented what for that time was far western frontier of English civilization. All that could be done under these circumstances was to establish a number of scattered, widely separated degree granting colleges, thus diffusing educational effort.

After a time, still another colonial divergence from the English norm made an appearance. Because of the heterogeneity of the American population, collegiate boards of control were established which were interdenominational in make-up and at least one of which was completely secular. Nothing like this had yet been seen in the home country, although the University of Leyden in the Netherlands already followed this pattern.

Scottish influence

Other modifications were due mainly to Scottish influence. The post-reformation Scottish university, unlike Oxford or Cambridge, was nonresidential, professionally oriented, and under the control, not of the faculty, but of prominent lay representatives of the community. At the college of William and Mary some of these Scottish ideas seem to have been influential from the very founding. Commissary James Blair, founder and first president, was a graduate of Marischal College, Aberdeen, and the University of Edinburgh. Reverend William Smith, graduate of Aberdeen, exercised a great influence, as we shall see, over the curricular planning of both King's College in New York, later Columbia, and the College of Philadelphia. John Witherspoon, Scotch theologian who came to the New World in 1768 to become president of the College of New Jersey, later Princeton, exerted an important influence over American higher education.

Although Harvard was not immune to Scottish university influence, it was at William and Mary that it was felt most directly. The charter Blair obtained for the Virginia school resembled that of a Scottish "unicollege" institution. Like Aberdeen, Glasgow, King's, and Marischal, it incorporated both a university and a degree-granting college by a single letter-parent. At the same time, a governing board was created, made up of members of the nonacademic community; this was, in characteristic Scottish fashion, to have real administrative authority over the college. Even William and Mary's architecture reflected Scottish influence, as did Blair's early plans for a course of study.

Spanish and French influence

As an afterthought on how different the development of higher education in the United States might have been if Continental rather than English precedents had been dominant, we might look for a moment at the institutions of higher learning founders by the Spanish and French in America. Originally, the English and Continental European universities had a somewhat similar type of organization. Nevertheless, Oxford and Cambridge very early began to follow a largely independent line of development. By the time of the Renaissance, these English universities were changing into loosely federated associations of residential colleges. The Continental universities, on the other hand, were becoming nonresident graduate school providing specific types of post-baccalaureate training.

The French and Spanish universities in America represented the later Continental type of university. When Charles V of Spain in 1551 founded "the Royal and Pontifical University" of Mexico and the University of San Marcos in Lima, Peru, he accorded them all "the privileges, exemptions, and limitations of the University of Salamanca." This meant that they were definitely to follow the Continental model, because Salamanca was essentially a collection of graduate faculties in arts, theology, law, and medicine. Besides Mexico and Lima, eight other universities were chartered and opened for instruction before a single college appeared in English America. In all, the Spanish-Americans established twenty-three such institutions.

In contrast, higher education in New France developed more slowly. It was not until the 1660s that Bishop Laval developed at Quebec a "great seminary" for advanced theological training. Although modern Laval University developed from this nucleus, in colonial times the Quebec institution never covered as broad a filed as had the Spanish-American universities.

1. **Oxford(牛津大学)**: (informally Oxford University) is a public university in Oxford, United Kingdom. It is the second oldest surviving university in the world and the oldest in the English-speaking world. Although the exact date of foundation remains unclear, there is evidence of teaching there as far back as the 11th century. The University grew rapidly from 1167 when Henry II banned English students from attending the University of Paris. In post-nominals, the University of Oxford was historically abbreviated as Oxon (from the Latin *Oxoniensis*), although Oxf is nowadays used in official University publications.

2. **Cambridge(剑桥大学)**: (informally Cambridge University) is a public, research university located in Cambridge, United Kingdom. It is the second-oldest university in both England and the English-speaking world and the seventh-oldest globally. In post-nominals the university's name is abbreviated as *Cantab*, a shortened form of *Cantabrigiensis* (an adjective derived from *Cantabrigia*, the Latinised form of *Cambridge*).

3. **Harvard(哈佛大学)**: is a private Ivy League university located in Cambridge, Massachusetts, United States, established in 1636 by the Massachusetts legislature. Harvard is the oldest institution of higher learning in the United States and the first corporation (officially *The President and Fellows of Harvard College*) chartered in the country. Harvard's history, influence, and wealth have made it one of the most prestigious universities in the world.

4. **Yale(耶鲁大学)**: is a private Ivy League university located in New Haven, Connecticut, United States of America. Founded in 1701 in the Colony of Connecticut, the university is the third-oldest institution of higher education in the United States. Yale is widely considered one of the most prestigious and selective universities in the world.

5. **Renaissance(文艺复兴)**: was a cultural movement that profoundly affected European intellectual life in the early modern period. Beginning in Italy, and spreading to the rest of Europe by the 16th century, its influence affected literature, philosophy, art, politics, science, religion, and other aspects of intellectual inquiry. Renaissance scholars employed the humanist method in study, and searched for realism and human emotion in art.

Unit 1 Origin & History of Education 教育的起源和历史

6.**Quebec**(魁北克): is a province in east-central Canada. It is the only Canadian province with a predominantly French-speaking population and the only one whose sole official language is French at the provincial level. Quebec is Canada's largest province by area and its second-largest administrative division.

New Words and Expression

1. prototype[ˈprəutətaip]	n.	原型,范例,雏形
2. explicit[ikˈsplisit]	adj.	明确的,清晰的,清楚的,露骨的
3. formula[ˈfɔːmjulə]	n.	配方,公式,规则,代乳品
	adj.	方程式的,(赛车)级的
4. commoner[ˈkɔmənə]	n.	平民,自费学生,有共用权的人
5. erect[iˈrekt]	vt.	使竖立,建立,建造
	adj.	直立的,竖立的,笔直的
6. fringe[frindʒ]	n.	流苏,边缘,次要,额外补贴
	vt.	用流苏修饰,镶边
7. heterogeneity[ˌhetərədʒiˈniːəti]	n.	多相性,异质性
8. interdenominational[ˈintədiˌnɔmiˈneiʃənəl]	adj.	派系间的,宗派之间的
9. secular[ˈsekjulə]	adj.	世俗的,现世的,不朽的,非宗教的
	n.	牧师,凡人
10. commissary[ˈkɔmisəri]	n.	代表;委员;(部队,学校,矿场等的)杂货商店
11. baccalaureate[ˌbækəˈlɔːriət]	n.	学士学位,告别训辞
12. exemption[igˈzempʃən]	n.	免除(税)

I Vocabulary.

Match the word in Column A to the correct definition in Column B.

Column A

1. commissary
2. erect
3. exemption
4. secular
5. explicit
6. commoner
7. formula
8. prototype
9. interdenominational
10. baccalaureate

Column B

A. standing/sitting straight up
B. an original model on which something is patterned
C. of or relating to the worldly or temporal
D. a particular method of doing or achieving sth.
E. a shop that provides food and equipment
F. clear and easy to understand
G. shared by different religious groups
H. official permission not to pay sth.
I. a person without noble rank or title
J. the degree of bachelor conferred by universities and colleges

II Translate the following words or phrases into English.

（大学）新生,一年级学生　　　　　　　＿＿＿＿＿＿＿＿＿＿
（大学）二年级学生　　　　　　　　　　＿＿＿＿＿＿＿＿＿＿
（大学）三年级学生　　　　　　　　　　＿＿＿＿＿＿＿＿＿＿
（大学）四年级学生　　　　　　　　　　＿＿＿＿＿＿＿＿＿＿
学术机构,学院,研究所　　　　　　　　　＿＿＿＿＿＿＿＿＿＿
行政规章　　　　　　　　　　　　　　　＿＿＿＿＿＿＿＿＿＿
未预料到的变化　　　　　　　　　　　　＿＿＿＿＿＿＿＿＿＿
注定的,注定要　　　　　　　　　　　　＿＿＿＿＿＿＿＿＿＿
不受……影响的,对……有免疫力的　　　＿＿＿＿＿＿＿＿＿＿
寄宿制大学,寄宿学院　　　　　　　　　＿＿＿＿＿＿＿＿＿＿

III Comprehension of the text.

Decide whether the following statements are true (T) or false (F) according to the

Unit 1 Origin & History of Education 教育的起源和历史

passage.

1. The earliest Harvard College statutes were taken indirectly from the Elizabethan statutes of the University of Cambridge.
2. Harvard followed English college precedents closely and faithfully in terms of student discipline, curriculum, administrative regulations, and degree requirements, and in turn it became the great prototype for all the later colleges of English America.
3. From 1729 to 1757, eight of thirteen faculty members were Oxford men, from Queens College.
4. Only in some cases, the English colonists found that the unique conditions of the American physical and social environment produced unexpected changes and modifications in their academic institutions.
5. It is impossible to erect in English-America any great university collection of colleges such as existed at Oxford or Cambridge and there are two reasons mentioned in the article.
6. The post-reformation Scottish university, was professionally oriented, and under the control, of prominent lay representatives of the community, which was as like as the system of Oxford or Cambridge.
7. In characteristic Scottish fashion, it was possible to have real administrative authority over the college.
8. Originally speaking, there were somewhat slightly different types of organization in the English and Continental European universities.
9. The Spanish-Americans established twenty-three such institutions which were chartered and opened for instruction before a single college appeared in English America.
10. It was not until 1660 that Bishop Laval developed at Quebec a "great seminary" for advanced theological training.

▶▶ Supplementary Reading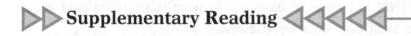

The Origins of Distance Education

Information technology and distance education are exciting developments in higher education. They provide extraordinary opportunities to transform the when, where and how of what we learn. Distance education built around new technology offers one way of meeting the need for a more flexible system, allowing people to dip in and out of education and periodically update their knowledge. The awareness of the possibilities of open and distance learning in education is increasing, and the use of new technologies to foster lifelong learning becomes increasingly attractive and appropriate. For this reason, the virtual campus will be added by conventional universities as one more way of delivering education.

Origins

In 1840, Sir Issac Pitman, the English inventor of shorthand, came up with an ingenious idea for delivering instruction to a potentially limitless audience: correspondence courses by mail. Pitman's concept was so hot that within a few years he was corresponding with a legion of far-flung learners. Within a few decades, regular, in some cases, extensive programs were available in the United Kingdom, Germany, the United States and Japan. By the 1900s, the first department of correspondence teaching was established at the University of Chicago. In Australia, the University of Queensland established a Department of External Studies in 1911. Before 1969, distance teaching had developed into an important sector of higher education in quite a few countries.

The founding of United Kingdom's Open University (OU) in 1969 marked a significant development of the second phase of distance learning, with its mixed-media approach to teaching. The OU sent learning materials to students by mail. Materials included carefully constructed texts and audio and video materials. These were supplemented with conventional broadcast radio and television. Each student was assigned a tutor who tutored over the telephone and in group sessions in the evenings or on weekends. The British Open University pioneered distance education on a massive scale. The OU and other open universities were important in raising the profile of distance education, effectively bringing distance teaching from the margins closer to the center stage of higher education.

At roughly the same time as the founding of the OU, satellites were moving into commercial use. PEACENET in the Pacific Basin was founded in 1971 and used in the first ever application of satellites in distance education.

Distance education is first and foremost a movement that sought not so much to challenge or change the structure of higher learning, but to extend the traditional universities and to overcome its inherent problems of scarcity and exclusivity. Second, distance education developed as a creative political response to the increasing inability of the traditional university structure to grow larger. Distance education dealt with the problem of too many students in a single physical space. The university could, in effect, reach out, offering not seats, but the opportunity to learn.

Growth

In the two decades following the opening of the British Open University in 1969, four open universities were established in Europe, and more than 20 were established in countries around the world.

There was considerable growth over the ensuing decades. In the United States, by the mid-1980s, more than 300,000 students were enrolled in university-taught distance education courses. In Canada, some 19 conventional universities were active in distance teaching. In Australia, the University of Queensland initiative had grown to some 3,000 students by the late 1960s. By the mid-1980s, some 40 institutions had an enrollment of external students equivalent to approximately 12% of higher education students. In the Soviet Union, where distance teaching was adopted in the late 1920s, all 61 universities eventually offered education by correspondence, and it is reported in the former German Democratic Republic that approximately one quarter of the university and technical college graduates attained their qualification by means of distance education. It is clear that distance education had developed into a substantive sector of higher education in quite a few countries.

In 1994 the OU was teaching more than 200,000 students, including young men and women in Russia, Hungary, the Czech and Slovak republics, Bulgaria and Romania. There are now OU offices located in Austria, Belgium, France, Germany, Greece, Italy, Luxembourg, the Netherlands, Portugal, Ireland, Spain and Switzerland.

In a number of cases, particular open universities have a student population that is bigger than that of the median-size university in the same country, and in a few cases bigger than the largest traditional university. Nonetheless, in many countries the substantive student population is made up of enrollment in distance teaching programs provided by many individual universities and colleges. The widening over time of the range of programs provided and the kinds of student populations served have in both cases, reinforced the trend toward further growth.

The majority of higher education institutions in the United States have distance learning programs. According to the United States Department of Education, about a quarter of the U.S. institutions that offered distance education courses in the fall of 1995 offered degrees that students could complete by taking distance education courses exclusively, and 7% offered certificates that could be completed that way. There were an estimated 690 degrees and 170 certificates.

As of 1997, enrollment had grown to become a substantive part of the university student population in many countries. In a number of countries distance education students compose some 10%–14% of the total undergraduate student population, and in a few cases the proportion is as high as 39%–40%.

Unit 2 Educational & Social Development
教育与社会发展

Text A Open and Distance Education: a Better Way of Competence Building and Sustainable Development

导读：远程开放教育是当今信息时代的发展趋势，它以一种新型的、多元化的、互动的方式传播教育。远程开放教育包括两层含义：一是远程教育（也叫远距离教育），二是开放教育。远程教育是一种现代化教育形式，它包括函授教育、广播电视教育、多媒体远程教育等，是利用媒体技术进行教学的一类教育。开放教育是实行不同程度开放入学政策，放宽或取消各种入学条件限制，教育技术上采用多媒体技术的教学方法，教学场所上突破了以课堂教学为主的传统教育限制，学生可以自学，可以利用计算机网络、电视、电话等多种媒体接受或反馈教学信息。两者关系密切，互不可分。远程开放教育是以学生为主体，在教师的指导下利用多媒体进行自学的教学模式。这种模式体现了以学生为中心的现代教育思想，适应了学习社会化的需要。

Globalization as a phenomenon influences all the discipline of life, also education. Still increasing demand for higher educated people is the cause for permanent education. It also forces newer, better, faster and more convenient ways of learning. There is fast progress in information technology, fulfilling this demand is possible by open and distance education. Distance education is a system where teacher and students are separated by physical distance and where they use technology like print, voice, data and video to convey the learning material through postal services, countries, internet, and CDs etc. Open and Distance Learning (ODL) system comes into existence where a student cannot go to the traditional institution due to distance, resource limitation, time constraint, physical disability, age, etc.

Competence building

Competence building considers the aspects such as strengthening the identity and foundation of emotional stability and self-esteem. It is necessary to improve the human capital. Competence includes the education and skills acquired through technique related to social behavior, an aptitude for team work and of initiative and a readiness to take risk. Competence building is important for the physical, mental, financial and legal power for the best performance. So competence building should be viewed in a more comprehensive and deeper way.

In the present era of globalization, there is much need of sustainable development and competence building process. Sustainable development is a pattern of resource use that aims to meet human needs while preserving the environment, so that these needs can be met not only in the present, but also for future generation. Sustainable development was formally defined for the first time in the "Brundtland Commission report" published in 1987 as "development that meets the needs of the present without compromising the ability of future generations to their own needs". This definition encompasses the ideas of limitations imposed by the state of technology and social organization on the ability of the environment to meet present and future needs. Sustainable development suggests that the needs of the future depend on how well we balance social, economic and environmental objectives or needs when making decisions today. Sustainable development ties concern together for the carrying capacity of natural system with the social challenges facing humanity.

Education for sustainable development

Important prerequisite to sustainable development is the issue of equity—equity for future generation and equity for those of the present generation, who have little or no access to natural resources and economic goods. Education plays an important role for human sustainable development. Education and training appear determinant factors for increasing creativity and rational thinking, problem solving capacities and competitiveness needed to foster the increasing complex cultural, social and technological decision involved in sustainable development. Education and training for sustainable development is not only a social issue but also a matter of economic policy. Decision makers today face two major challenges in reshaping education for sustainable development. One is devising institutional educational strategies and programs, taking into account all the educational actors and communication channels available. The other is increasing the quality and usefulness of the various educational and training processes, aimed primarily at citizens, economic partners and young people.

Strengthening worldwide co-operation in education should help each country devise the most effective ways and means of enabling its people to contribute for improving the material and spiritual living conditions of the present generation without denying life for future generation. Education for sustainable development stresses the achievement of continuous well-being by searching for an optimal balance in the formation and use of different resources and capital types—human capital, physical infrastructure and tools, natural resources, financial means, technology and decision system, the world of work and that of the media. Open and distance leaning (ODL) system plays a very important role in achieving these goals regarding sustainable development and competence building.

The role of ODL in sustainable development and competence building

The role of ODL in sustainable development and competence building is mainly to develop human capital and encourage technical progress, as well as foster the cultural conditions favoring social and economic changes. This is the key to creative and effective utilization of human potential and all forms of capital ensuring rapid and more equitable growth. Empirical evidences demonstrate that education is positively correlated with productivity and technological progress, because it enables companies to obtain and evaluate information on new technologies and economic opportunities.

ODL is especially well suited to deliver learning outcomes consistent with sustainability goals. Its emphasis on access, the service of personal needs and the supporting life long learning mirrors the way in which environmental values are best inculcated into personal and professional life. ODL plays a very important role in environmental sustainability. Technologies in e-learning distance education are helping the environment. On-line courses showed a 20% reduction in energy and 12% reduction in CO_2 emission compared to print-based courses. There is less carbon pollution in on-line delivery in ODL system, so it truly results in "dematerialization". In ODL system, students have to travel less for going to their study centers because study centers are mostly near to their residences, so consumption of petroleum oil becomes less. Built structure is also very economic in ODL system. These factors help in environmental sustainability and encourages for sustainable management. Thus it can be called as "Green Distance Education".

ODL is very helpful in "inclusive education" which is based on the aspects of human rights, equal opportunities, social justice and participation. It has multiple interpretations. Poverty, ethnicity, disability, gender or membership of a minority group may limit access or marginalize. Within education, inclusive education appreciates every learner's fundamental rights to learn and know that each child has unique abilities and needs. If given the right opportunity, all children can develop their potential. Inclusive education considers difference in the learning and physical abilities of children. ODL is very helpful in achieving these goals of inclusive education.

Authorities of the universities running distance education courses should sharply ensure that distance education centers do not get reduced to degree distribution institutions. So higher authorities of universities and distance institutions should ensure that only quality education should be provided through ODL. Proper library, laboratory and required study materials, essential equipment and materials for students should be in coordination with other related universities running similar courses located in the same area. Open and distance learning has been improvised upon by integrating various other methods which are successfully followed in other countries such as Virtual Education, Alternative Education and E-learning.

The need of the hour is to pool such innovative experience and disseminate the same effectively. The exchange of experiences within and between the countries would surely help to promote and transfer knowledge to the masses and benefit the society in the long run.

1. **Open and Distance Learning**(远程开放教育): is a field of education that focuses on teaching methods and technology with the aim of delivering knowledge, often on an individual basis, to students who are not physically present in a traditional educational setting such as a classroom. It has been described as "a process to create and provide access to learning when the source of information and the learners are separated by time or distance, or both". Its courses that require a physical on-site presence for any reason (including taking examinations) have been referred to as hybrid or blended courses of study.

2. **Brundtland Commission**(布伦特兰委员会): formally the World Commission on Environment and Development (WCED), known by the name of its Chair Gro Harlem Brundtland, was convened by the United Nations in 1983. The commission was created to address growing concern about "the accelerating deterioration of the human environment and natural resources and the consequences of that deterioration for economic and social

Unit 2　Educational & Social Development　教育与社会发展

development". In establishing the commission, the UN General Assembly recognized that environmental problems were global in nature and therefore it was in the common interest of all nations to establish policies for sustainable development.

3. **Inclusive Education（全纳教育）**: is an approach to educating students with special educational needs. Under the inclusion model, students with special needs spend most or all of their time with non-disabled students. It is about the child's right to participate and the school's duty to accept the child. A premium is placed upon full participation by students with disabilities and upon respect for their social, civil, and educational rights.

4. **Virtual Education（虚拟教育）**: refers to instruction in a learning environment where teacher and student are separated by time or space, or both, and the teacher provides course content through course management applications, multimedia resources, the Internet, videoconferencing, etc. Students receive the content and communicate with the teacher via the same technologies. This term is primarily used in higher education where so-called Virtual Universities have been established.

5. **Alternative Education（选择性教育）**: also known as non-traditional education or educational alternative, includes a number of approaches to teaching and learning other than mainstream or traditional education. It is often rooted in various philosophies that are fundamentally different from those of mainstream or traditional education. While some have strong political, scholarly, or philosophical orientations, others are more informal associations of teachers and students dissatisfied with some aspect of mainstream or traditional education. Alternative Education, which includes charter schools, alternative schools, independent schools, and home-based learning, varies widely, but often emphasizes the value of small class size, close relationships between students and teachers, and a sense of community.

6. **E-learning（在线学习，电子化学习或网络学习）**: comprises all forms of electronically supported learning and teaching. The information and communication systems, whether networked or not, serve as specific media to implement the learning process. The term will still most likely be utilized to refer to out-of-classroom and in-classroom educational experiences via technology, even as advances continue in regard to devices and curriculum. E-learning is essentially the computer and network-enabled transfer of skills and knowledge. E-learning applications and processes include Web-based learning, computer-based learning, virtual classroom opportunities and digital collaboration. Content is delivered via the Internet, intranet/extranet, audio or video tape, satellite TV, and CD-ROM. It can be self-paced or instructor-led and includes media in the form of text, image, animation,

streaming video and audio.

New Words and Expression

1. aptitude [ˈæptitjuːd]　　　　　　　n.　　天资；自然倾向；适宜
2. initiative [iˈniʃiətiv]　　　　　　　n.　　主动权；首创精神
　　　　　　　　　　　　　　　　adj.　　主动的；起始的
3. comprehensive [ˌkɔmpriˈhensiv]　adj.　综合广泛的；有理解力的
　　　　　　　　　　　　　　　　n.　　　综合学校
4. compromise [ˈkɔmprəmaiz]　　　vt.　　妥协；危害
　　　　　　　　　　　　　　　　vi.　　妥协；让步
　　　　　　　　　　　　　　　　n.　　　妥协；折中
5. encompass [inˈkʌmpəs]　　　　　vt.　　包含；包围，环绕；完成
6. optimal [ˈɔptiməl]　　　　　　　　adj.　最佳的；最理想的
7. empirical [emˈpirikəl]　　　　　　adj.　经验主义的，完全根据经验的
8. inculcate [ˈinkʌlkeit]　　　　　　vt.　　教育；谆谆教诲；教授；反复灌输
9. interpretation [inˌtəːpriˈteiʃən]　n.　　解释；翻译；演出
10. marginalize [ˈmɑːdʒinəlaiz]　　vt.　　排斥；忽视；使处于社会边缘
11. integrate [ˈintigreit]　　　　　　vt.　　使……完整；使……成整体；求……的积分；表示……的总和
　　　　　　　　　　　　　　　　vi.　　求积分；取消隔离；成为一体
　　　　　　　　　　　　　　　　adj.　整合的；完全的
　　　　　　　　　　　　　　　　n.　　　一体化
12. disseminate [diˈsemineit]　　　vt.　　宣传，传播；散布
　　　　　　　　　　　　　　　　vi.　　散布；广为传播

I　Vocabulary.

Fill in the blanks with the most suitable words. Change the form when necessary.

| aptitude | comprehensive | encompass | integrate | interpretation |
| initiative | compromise | optimal | inculcate | disseminate |

Unit 2 Educational & Social Development 教育与社会发展

1. He was educated at the local _____ school.
2. How can local communities work with planners and decision-makers to find some _____ solutions for the future?
3. If a child shows any musical _____ or interest, get an instrument into her hand early.
4. These so-called solar-energy zones _____ about 680,000 acres of land owned by the federal government.
5. It's hard for a state-run program to _____ ideals like thinking out of the box.
6. I wanted to go to Greece, however, my wife wanted to go to Spain. After a little talk, we _____ on Italy.
7. Can we _____ his silence as a refusal.
8. It has been very difficult to _____ all of the local agencies into the national organization.
9. This publication has been prepared to _____ the lessons learned to a wider audience.
10. Charles is shy and does not take the _____ in making acquaintances.

II Translate the following phrases into English.

人力资源   _____
可持续发展   _____
自然资源   _____
理性思维   _____
考虑;重视;体谅   _____
生活条件;居住环境   _____
基础设施建设   _____
符合;与……一致   _____
终身学习   _____
社会公正   _____

III Comprehension of the text.

Decide whether the following statements are true (T) or false (F) according to the passage.

1. Distance education is a system where teacher and students are integrated by physical distance and where they use technology like print, voice, data and video to convey the

learning material through postal services, internet, and CDs, etc.
2. Sustainable development was formally defined for the first time in the "Brundtland Commission report" published in 1978 as "development that meets the needs of the present without compromising the ability of future generations to their own needs".
3. Education and training for sustainable development are not only a social issue but also a matter of economic policy.
4. On-line courses showed a 12% reduction in energy and 20% reduction in CO_2 emission compared to print-based courses.
5. Proper library, laboratory and required study materials, essential equipment and materials for students should be in coordination with other related universities running similar courses located in the same area.

Text B Higher Education within a Knowledge-based Society

导读：知识社会是一个以创新为社会主要驱动力的社会，知识社会环境下的创新推动了创新民主化。知识社会也是一个大众创新、共同创新、开放创新成为常态的社会，知识、创新是知识社会的核心。在知识社会里，每个人都要学会在信息海洋里来去自如，培养认知能力和批评精神，以便区分有用信息和无用信息，拥有新知识；它也使得创新不再是少数科技精英的专利，而成为更为广泛的大众参与，推动了创新的民主化进程。知识社会更加关注全球问题；通过国际合作和科学协作，环境破坏、技术风险、经济危机和贫困等问题有望得到更好的解决；知识共享是知识社会的拱顶石，以大众创新、共同创新、开放创新为特点的创新是知识社会的实质，而知识社会是人类可持续发展的源泉。

Research in higher education is a quite new field of interest and can be seen as a multidisciplinary subject. Researchers from different fields of study are interested in learning about the complexity of higher education. They are looking on higher education from different angles as for instance, educational or political sciences, psychology, sociology, history, economy or law—different fields of research are interested in bringing light into the complex system of higher education (educational management and social science approach). Nevertheless the term higher education is relatively new and became popular in the 1970s because universities lost their exclusive right to provide higher education. From the middle age to the 1960s the main and often the only post secondary institution has been the university. After that time other forms of tertiary education emerged and higher education came up to include universities as well as vocational and professional institutions.

Until World War II, university education was a domain of the elite, but this changed dramatically. The following figure illustrates phases of higher education developments with a clear tendency towards more diversification and mercerization of higher education in a knowledge-driven economy. In the last phase especially research in higher education is emphasized "as primary differentiator of higher education institutions" in the 21st century.

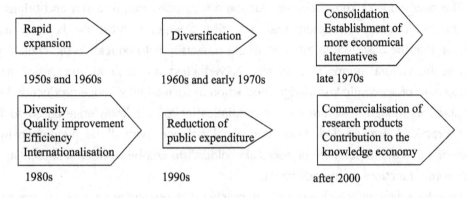

Figure 1 Phases of higher education developments

Today's university is facing great strain and tension because of ongoing societal developments. Knowledge changed to a factor of production and theoretical knowledge gains more importance as source of innovation and basis for political decisions in highly industrialized societies. The Nobel Prize winner Joseph Stiglitz stated that knowledge is a global public good though the source of brainpower is limited by genetic distributions of talent and cultural disadvantages. The nature of education is bound to change and will become a continuing life-time affair for the professional and technical person. In this context Daniel Bell articulated that we need especially postdoctoral universities where new knowledge and new techniques can be passed along.

The arrival of knowledge-based societies, of course, has a great importance according to the development of universities. One could say that they are the first institutions to benefit from this increasing usage of information. These days' universities compete with other institutions as, for instance, vocational colleges, research institutions and high-tech companies in popularity to cope with the increasing importance of knowledge. Universities cannot handle all these new forces and demands of the knowledge society, which means that they are in an unstable situation and lose their high status and power. They have to be powerful and successful but lose at the same time their clear position (success vs uncertainty). There is an intrinsic relationship between universities and knowledge societies but the future consequences are not foreseeable. One sees a future of knowledge as strategic resource for universities. Others see a world of academic capitalism. Thus, academia goes together with the knowledge society where "competition with other institutions and a loss of the monopoly of universities" prevail (virtual universities, corporate universities, media organizations, consortia, strategic alliances, private and public institutions).

The new mode of knowledge production affects academic research and brings new opportunities because entrepreneurial activities emerge. It must be kept in mind, however, that the basic stable function of the university is to educate researchers and to generate the cultural norms of a society. Nevertheless, an epistemic dimension in this development of academic knowledge production to societal knowledge production brings new practices though there are also uncertainties for today's knowledge-based society. Good practices are needed from traditional science with "the heterogeneity of knowledge and the importance of new stakeholders" to combine either academic as well as economic functions of the academia.

Therefore different mechanisms and practices of quality assurance are needed. A (internationally and nationally recognized) quality assurance system should be able to guarantee transparency and control of higher education programs and that diplomas and degrees of students are approved. Although nearly all over the world international and national quality assurance agencies have been developed there are different approaches to ensure quality (internal or external procedures, accreditation vs evaluations, quality audits etc.). While some countries established only one national agency (e.g. Finland) others have separate agencies with different responsibilities (e.g. Germany), which shows the political and cultural diversity of the countries all over the world. Furthermore, the initiative to establish international qualification frameworks helps small countries to set up a regional quality assurance system or assist different global quality assurance initiatives.

Tertiary education not only has to cope with lots of new challenges due to enormous changes (globalization, ICT, socio-political transformations, lifelong learning and knowledge-based society), but also faces new opportunities as playing the key role in today's society. Santiago et al. recommend some practical arrangements for a functioning quality assurance system:

· Avoid fragmentation of the quality assurance organizational structure;

· Avoid excessive costs and burdens;
· Improve quality information base;
· Improve information dissemination.

With these suggestions, current quality assurance systems, which vary among countries in their scope and emphasis, could be improved. Quality assurance schemes have to be developed as necessary instruments to adjust higher education institutions to the ongoing transformation processes. As the different systems are most of the time newly developed they should be able to adapt to changes and try to act quickly to the needs of our knowledge-based society. Quality assurance in higher education is not fully developed but still under construction.

1. **World War II(第二次世界大战)**: or the Second World War, was a global military conflict lasting from 1939 to 1945, which involved most of the world's nations, including all of the great powers; eventually forming two opposing military alliances, the Allies (同盟国) and the Axis(轴心国). It was the most widespread war in history, with more than 100 million military personnel mobilized. In a state of "total war", the major participants placed their entire economic, industrial, and scientific capabilities at the service of the war effort, erasing the distinction between civilian and military resources. Marked by significant events involving the mass death of civilians, including the Holocaust(大屠杀) and the only use of nuclear weapons in warfare, it was the deadliest conflict in human history, resulting in 40 million to over 70 million fatalities. The war ended with the total victory of the Allies over Germany and Japan in 1945. World War II altered the political alignment and social structure of the world. The United Nations was established to foster international cooperation and prevent future conflicts. The Soviet Union and the United States emerged as rival superpowers, setting the stage for the Cold War, which lasted for the next 46 years. Meanwhile, the influence of European great powers started to decline, while the decolonization of Asia and Africa began. Most countries whose industries had been damaged moved towards economic recovery. Political integration, especially in Europe emerged as an effort to stabilize postwar relations.

2. **Joseph Stiglitz(约瑟夫·斯蒂格利茨)**: born February 9th, 1943, is an American economist and a professor at Columbia University. He is a recipient of the Nobel Memorial Prize in

Economic Sciences(2001) and the John Bates Clark Medal(1979). He is also the former Senior Vice President and Chief Economist of the World Bank. He is known for his critical view of the management of globalization, free-market economists (whom he calls " free market fundamentalists") and some international institutions like the International Monetary Fund and the World Bank.

3. **Quality Assurance (质量保证)**: or QA for short, is the systematic monitoring and evaluation of the various aspects of a project, service or facility to maximize the probability that minimum standards of quality are being attained by the production process. QA cannot absolutely guarantee the production of quality products. Here QA refers to the guarantee of the higher education.

4. **Tertiary Education (高等教育或第三级教育)**: also referred to as third stage, third level, and post-secondary education, is the educational level following the completion of a school providing a secondary education, such as a high school, secondary school, university-preparatory school. Higher education is taken to include undergraduate and postgraduate education, while vocational education and training beyond secondary education is known as further education in the United Kingdom, or continuing education in the United States. Colleges, universities, institutes of technology and polytechnics are the main institutions that provide tertiary education (sometimes known collectively as tertiary institutions). Tertiary education generally culminates in the receipt of certificates, diplomas, or academic degrees.

5. **ICT (信息通信技术)**: also known as Information and Communication Technology is often used as an extended synonym for information technology (IT) but is usually a more general term that stresses the role of unified communications and the integration of telecommunications (telephone lines and wireless signals), intelligent building management systems and audio-visual systems in modern information technology. ICT consists of all technical means used to handle information and aid communication, including computer and network hardware, communication middleware as well as necessary software. In other words, ICT consists of IT as well as telephony, broadcast media, all types of audio and video processing and transmission and network-based control and monitoring functions.

Unit 2 Educational & Social Development 教育与社会发展

New Words and Expression

1. exclusive [ikˈsklu:siv]   adj. 独有的;排外的;专一的
                                n.   独家新闻;排外者
2. tertiary [ˈtə:ʃəri]   n.   第三纪;第三修道会会员;第三级教士
                                adj. 第三的;第三位的;三代的
3. elite [eiˈli:t]   n.   精英;精华;中坚分子
4. mercerization [ˌmə:səraiˈzeiʃən] n. [纺]丝光作用;碱化
5. differentiator [ˌdifəˈrenʃieitə] n. [自]微分器;微分电路;区分者
6. articulate [ɑ:ˈtikjulət]   vt. 清晰地发(音);明确有力地表达;用关节连接
                                vi. 发音;清楚地讲话;用关节连接起来
                                adj. 发音清晰的;口才好的;有关节的
7. postdoctoral [pəustˈdɔktərəl] adj. 博士后的;博士学位取得后的
8. capitalism [ˈkæpitəlizəm]   n.   资本主义
9. monopoly [məˈnɔpəli]   n.   垄断;垄断者;专卖权
10. epistemic [ˌepiˈsti:mik]   adj. 知识的;认识的,与认识有关的
11. transparency [trænsˈpærənsi] n. 透明,透明度;幻灯片;有图案的玻璃
12. accreditation [əˌkrediˈteiʃən] n. 达到标准;鉴定合格

Exercises

I Vocabulary.

Match the word in Column A to the correct definition in Column B.

Column A	
1. exclusive	2. elite
3. articulate	4. capitalism
5. accreditation	6. epistemic
7. postdoctoral	8. monopoly
9. transparency	10. tertiary

> Column B
> A. of or relating to knowledge or knowing
> B. belonging to or used by only one person or a group
> C. officially approval given by an organization stating that sb./sth. has achieved a required standard
> D. control by one company
> E. the most powerful, rich, or talented people within a particular group, place, or society
> F. an economic and political system in which property, business, and industry are owned by private individuals and not by the state
> G. third in order, third in importance, or at a third stage of development
> H. expressing oneself readily, clearly, or effectively
> I. being beyond the doctoral level
> J. something transparent especially

II Translate the following phrases into English.

知识社会	_____
阐明	_____
专有权	_____
第三级教育	_____
必然,必定	_____
高职院校,职业学院	_____
文化规范,文化准则	_____
质量保证,品质保证	_____
品质监察	_____
文化多样性	_____
适应	_____

III Comprehension of the text.

Decide whether the following statements are true (T) or false (F) according to the passage.

1. In the 1970s, universities lost their exclusive right to provide higher education; therefore the term higher education is relatively new and became popular.
2. Before World War II, university education was a domain of the elite, but after that,

this situation changed dramatically.
3. Although as source of innovation and basis for political decisions in highly industrialized societies, knowledge changed to a factor of production and theoretical knowledge gains less importance.
4. As Daniel Bell articulated that we needed especially postdoctoral universities, so new knowledge and new techniques could be passed along.
5. All these new forces and demands of the knowledge society can be handled by universities. In other words, universities are in a stable situation and tighten their high status and power.
6. The only basic stable function of the university is to generate the cultural norms of a society.
7. Two dimensions should be guaranteed in a quality assurance system: one is the transparency and control of higher education programs, the other is that the diplomas and degrees of students are approved.
8. In terms of the quality assurance agency, all the countries have separate agencies with different responsibilities, which show the political and cultural diversity of the countries all over the world.
9. Due to enormous changes, tertiary education not only has to cope with lots of new challenges, but also faces new opportunities as playing the key role in today's society.
10. In some countries, quality assurance in higher education is fully developed but in others it is still under construction.

 Supplementary Reading

The Global "Imagined Community"—
Global Civil Society and International Education

What is global civil society?

The idea of a "global civil society" grew out of the social movements and activism of those who challenged the communist states of Central and Eastern Europe in the late 1970s and 1980s. The distinction between civil society and the state was used to support the right of people to freely associate, which in their state-centric societies was not allowed. Although the term "civil society" can be traced in political philosophy back to the Greeks and Romans, this particular conception of civil society can be found in the late seventeenth and early eighteenth century work of Jeremy Bentham, who argued that the state and civil society were distinct entities.

Mary Kaldor has noted, therefore, that what she calls "The Ideas of 1989" provided the conceptual basis for current discussions about the creation of a "global civil society". At the same time, however, that the state in Central and Eastern Europe was being challenged with the idea that there should be a civil society where people were free to associate, many in the United States were making a complementary argument that a "good society" informed by social equality and justice was needed.

In addition to free associational life and the good society, Michael Edwards, former director of the Ford Foundation program on governance and civil society, claims that there is a necessary third component to a global civil society: the "public sphere", which provides the basis for the "revival of interest in direct, deliberative, or participatory democracy". It is the synthesis of these three perspectives that leads to a vibrant global civil society in which the global public sphere will "foster debates about international norms", states "will remain the duty bearers of international treaties", and the enforcement of "public compliance" will fall to transnational networks and international non-governmental organizations like Oxfam, Save the Children, and of course, NAFSA.

The role of international education

In the 2002 yearbook, *Global Civil Society*, produced by the Centre for the Study of Global Governance at the London School of Economics, researchers argued that the growing practice of studying abroad may be one of the catalysts "of the emergence and spread of global civil society" because "students are major transmitters of knowledge and ideas, and interlocutors across cultures." According to the UNESCO Institute for Statistics, in 2007, more than 2.8 million university-level students were enrolled in educational institutions outside of their country of origin, nearly 1 million more than in 1999. By 2020, estimates are that there is likely to be a further 150 percent increase to 7 million students studying abroad. In other words, with the support of various institutions, increasing numbers of students across the globe are, through their personal actions, creating one of the pillars of a global civil society.

Although there is some debate about the statistics, unfortunately, as many of us know, the United States is lagging far behind and currently sends just 1.8 percent of the global average of students studying abroad for a semester or more abroad using UNESCO's criteria, while the number increases to about 4 percent using Open Doors criteria. NAFSA and other international education organizations, through their support for the Simon Study Abroad Bill, as well as other initiatives, are attempting to change that. But technical solutions will not be enough. As a colleague, I argued in International Educator six years ago, "a more intentional approach" to study abroad programs is needed in which we educate students "to find solutions to problems that affect their communities, their nation, and the world".

This implies that our programs should concretely provide students with the insights necessary to overcome ethnocentrism, to be reflective about the limits of national identity, and to provide critical perspectives on the activities of corporations and states. For example, at BCA Abroad, we have taken several initiatives that are meant to enhance what Kaldor calls "a common consciousness of human society on a world scale". Thus, we have created a course, The Global Conversation, which links our students and others throughout the world in academic discussions and online learning circles while taking a contextual approach that "connects the dots" between the myriad problems the human species currently faces around the globe.

We also organize two international student conferences each academic year that allow U.S., European, and other students to come together to discuss important global issues with noted experts. In the spring, we hold a conference in Strasbourg, France, focused on European-U.S. relations, which we initiated because we realized that when our students went to study sites in Europe, they were often shocked by the different perspectives held by European students on many of today's most important issues.

In the fall, we focus on divided societies in Derry/Londonderry, Northern Ireland, because helping students to understand the problematic nature of identity is essential to create a more peaceful world. And finally, there's the annual Ron Moffatt Seminar for international education faculty and staff who are interested in the themes being discussed in this article.

When a student decides to study abroad, it suggests that to some extent he or she is prepared to experience social realities that may diverge from those home realities that too many never travel away from. One of our tasks as international educators is to enhance a student's experience of those other realities through program design. As I have argued in the volume edited by Ross Lewin, "Regardless of the type of program, we should be building in reflexivity—reflexivity about the culturally constructed nature of one's self, one's home society, and our understanding of the larger world." Central to that reflexive understanding of today's world is to understand how each of us is implicated in the maintenance of the nation-state system through our acceptance of the "imagined community" of a specific nation.

As Benedict Anderson points out in the book of that name, the idea of "imagined communities" provided a key cultural and political element in the development of modern nations. "Imagined communities" have also been central to the reified identities that many people hold too dearly, and which are so often implicated in war and genocide. In contrast, what we increasingly need today is an imagined community at the global level in which our identities are, as Maalouf says, "the sum of all our allegiances" and within which "allegiance to the human community itself would become increasingly important"; in other words, a global civil society. Although one rarely, if ever, hears NAFSA described as the largest and most vibrant global civil society organization in the field of international education, it seems clear that we should become conscious of this, and in the process knowingly help to create that global "imagined community".

Unit 3 Education & People's Overall Development

教育与人的全面发展

Text A Role of Education in the Developmental Process

导读：人的全面发展首先是指人的"完整发展"，即人的各种最基本或最基础的素质必须得到完整的发展。人的全面发展从根本上说是指人的劳动能力的全面发展，即人的智力和体力的充分、统一的发展；同时，也包括人的才能、志趣和道德品质的多方面发展，即培养受教育者在德、智、体、美等方面获得完整发展。人的全面发展是全面发展教育的目的，全面发展教育又是实现人的全面发展的教育保障和教育内涵。

With a deep interest in the application of developmental research to educational practice, we are excited by the implications of this work for understanding individual differences in development, as well as the role of the educational environment as a "specialist change agent". We outline an important direction toward which we believe the findings of Kovas et al. point research on development and education: analyzing the role of education in the developmental process.

Dynamic growth modeling allows us to consider the environment as another cluster of variables that affect a child's overall developmental outcomes. Education provides a crucial environment for children's academic development, without which hardly anyone would learn literacy, mathematics, science, or many other skills of modern societies. Considering education as a set of variables within growth equations makes clear that education will not be a distinct and independently acting entity, but rather a set of dynamic influence—both affecting as well as being affected by other environmental and within-child states. Measures of many factors will ultimately need to be combined in dynamic models of school learning, just as they are combined for predicting weather or analyzing the processes in a cell.

Kovas et al. highlight some relevant and intriguing findings such as that the non-shared environment of twins plays a major role in making genetically identical twins achieve to different academic levels. Although non-shared environment remains inadequately understood, we do know that it includes factors such as idiosyncratic experiences affecting one twin only, as well as differential treatment by parents or teachers. These provide an excellent opportunity for building growth models to facilitate analyzing processes of development and learning.

This latter point is vitally important to educators. Educators, by their very role, are an automatic part of a child's developmental "equation", and the extensively documented enormous effects of schools on skills and abilities demonstrate their importance. This means that it is not possible to maintain an extreme view that a child's academic potential is genetically predetermined. Genetics contribute significantly to a child's academic progress, but always as a function of other factors. These may include the "fit" of teaching to a child's individual needs or the presence of an environment that encourages academic engagement. The teaching environment makes possible the realization of a child's genetic propensities.

Teachers should also be aware that those same genetic propensities influence their own "state"; for example, certain personalities or learning profiles within a student can interact both positively and negatively with those of the teacher. Kovas et al. mention the work of Walker and Plomin, which aims to analyze the role of nature versus nurture within a school environment in greater depth. For example, using children from the study, these authors found that perceptions of the classroom environment are driven primarily by child-specific experiences, though such perceptions did not have a strong relationship with school achievement in their study. The perceptions questionnaire probed areas such as teacher helpfulness and peer integration, but this area is ripe for further research. Work exploring more specific experimental factors such as achievement-related motivation and engagement does suggest links to achievement. More focused work in this area will help elucidate these relationships.

In conclusion, the synthesis of Kovas, Haworth, Dale, and Plomin is a landmark in our understanding of the role of genetics and environment in the development of abilities and skills in children who go to school. The finding shows that genes have a significant influence on developmental continuity, while the environment primarily affects change and variation has profound implications. The study lays out this major step in a new kind of developmental analysis that analyzes the dynamics of development of skills and abilities in educational settings. The responsibility is now upon researchers of this

Unit 3 Education & People's Overall Development 教育与人的全面发展

generation and the next to take up the challenge to build on these ideas. We have suggested some ways to begin this scientific and educational journey. Returning to our initial questions: How exactly do skills develop and interact? What educational factors cause the most change? What combinations of genes mediate development and change, and how? With a combination of careful research like that of this study with explicit growth modeling of the intertwining processes, researchers can illuminate how students learn and develop the skills they need to thrive in the world of the 21st century.

Notes

Genetics(遗传学): a discipline of biology, is the science of genes, heredity, and variation in living organisms. It deals with the molecular structure and function of genes, with gene behavior in the context of a cell or organism, with patterns of inheritance from parent to offspring, and with gene distribution, variation and change in populations. Given that genes are universal to living organisms, genetics can be applied to the study of all living systems, from viruses and bacteria, through plants (especially crops) and domestic animals to humans (as in medical genetics).

New Words and Expression

1. cluster [ˈklʌstə]   n.   群;簇;丛;串
                              vi. 群聚;丛生
                              vt. 使聚集
2. crucial [ˈkruːʃəl]   adj. 重要的;决定性的;定局的;决断的
3. equation [iˈkweiʒən]   n.   方程式,等式;相等;[化学]反应式
4. intriguing [inˈtriːgiŋ]   adj. 有趣的;迷人的
5. idiosyncratic [ˌidiəsiŋˈkrætik] adj. 特质的;特殊的;异质的
6. propensity [prəuˈpensiti] n.   倾向,习性;癖好,偏爱
7. profile [ˈprəufail]   n.   侧面;轮廓;外形;剖面
8. perception [pəˈsepʃən]   n.   知觉;[生理]感觉;看法;洞察力;获取
9. probe [prəub]   n.   探针;调查
                              vi. 调查;探测
                              vt. 探查;用探针探测

10. elucidate [i'luːsiˌdeit]　　vt.　阐明；说明
11. intertwine [ˌintə'twain]　　vi.　纠缠；编结
　　　　　　　　　　　　　　　vt.　缠绕；纠缠
12. thrive [θraiv]　　　　　　　vi.　繁荣，兴旺；茁壮成长

I　Vocabulary.

Fill in the blanks with the most suitable words. Change the form when necessary.

| cluster | perception | elucidate | thrive | crucial |
| intriguing | probe | intertwine | idiosyncratic | propensity |

1. A _____ of stars is smaller than a constellation.
2. The governor appointed a committee to _____ the causes of the strike.
3. We have succeeded in one _____ regard: making this scandal public.
4. The note helps to _____ the most difficult parts of the text.
5. They _____ their fingers.
6. She is a woman of keen _____.
7. A business cannot _____ without good management.
8. He showed a _____ for violence.
9. Some of the members had been _____ to get the secretary dismissed.
10. Her blackboard technique was also extremely _____.

II　Translate the following phrases into English.

个体差异　　　　　　　_____
教育环境　　　　　　　_____
成长过程　　　　　　　_____
学术潜力　　　　　　　_____
遗传基因完全相同的　　_____
意识到　　　　　　　　_____

Unit 3 Education & People's Overall Development 教育与人的全面发展

学习档案,学习历程　　　　　　_____
展示,摆出,安排,筹划　　　　　_____
应战,接受挑战　　　　　　　　_____
把……建立于,以……为基础　　_____

III Comprehension of the text.

Decide whether the following statements are true (T) or false (F) according to the passage.

1. Education provides a crucial environment for children's academic development, with which anyone would learn literacy, mathematics, science, or many other skills of modern societies.
2. Measures of many factors will ultimately need to be combined in dynamic models of school learning, just as they are combined for predicting weather or analyzing the processes in a cell.
3. Although non-shared environment remains inadequately understood, we do know that it includes factors such as idiosyncratic experiences affecting one twin both, as well as differential treatment by parents or teachers.
4. Educators are an automatic part of a child's developmental "equation", and the extensively documented enormous effects of schools on skills and abilities demonstrate their importance.
5. The teaching environment makes impossible the realization of a child's genetic propensities.
6. Teachers should also be aware that those different genetic propensities influence their own "state".
7. Perceptions of the classroom environment are driven primarily by teacher-specific experiences, though such perceptions did not have a strong relationship with school achievement in their study.
8. Work exploring more specific experimental factors such as achievement-related motivation and engagement does suggest links to achievement.
9. Genes have a significant influence on developmental continuity, while the environment primarily affects change and variation has profound implications.
10. Although with the combination of careful research like that of this study with explicit growth modeling of the intertwining processes, researchers cannot illuminate how students learn and develop the skills they need to thrive in the world of the 21st century.

Text B Social Skills Development in Primary Education

导读：初等教育即小学教育，或称基础教育，是使受教育者打下文化知识基础和做好初步生活准备的教育。通常指一个国家学制中第一个阶段的教育，对象一般为6~12岁儿童。初等教育的学制为六年，一般为全日制普通小学。这种教育对提高国家民族文化水平极为重要，因此各国在其经济文化发展的一定历史阶段都把它定为实施义务教育或普及教育的目标。

The aim of the present research is to survey the views of teachers regarding social skills development in primary school students. The research was carried out using the qualitative research technique. A questionnaire prepared by the researcher was used to collect data. The results show that there are four main factors that play an important role in the development of primary school students' social skills: family, school, environment and the personal characteristics of individual students.

Family

The effect of family, which starts in the prenatal period and continues its influence until the end of an individual's life, is of great importance in a child's development. That a child is supported in the primary school period by his parents and spends sufficient and quality time with them is one of the important factors that substantially determine how a person will adapt during the lifelong socialization process.

Unconditional love exhibited by parents, regular care and support develop a child's basic sense of confidence. Positive communication between children and their parents in the primary school period is reflected on the children's social behaviors. Positive social relations and model parental behaviors may set patterns that children can repeat. As stated by the teachers, the children who are accepted by their families as they are can express themselves more easily in social environments and develop their social skills. Families should not only focus on the academic successes of their children but also support their social and emotional development. Parents should cooperate with schools and teachers in this area.

School

Primary schools are of great importance in a child's socialization process. Elementary school years constitute the most important period in which children develop attitudes and behaviors. In this period, children learn how to live with others in the same environment, how to share, how to communicate and how to express themselves. In the present research, teacher views support the idea that primary school has an important role in the development of young children.

Attaching importance to social activities at schools is one of the sub-themes that educators focus on most. Teachers emphasize that one of the most important aims of primary schools is to prepare children for a healthy social life.

It is also important that activities directed to enable students to gain social skills are shown in primary school curricula. Educators emphasize that lessons should be prepared in a way that enables an individual to develop his social skills, to realize himself and to actively participate in social activities. Again, the results of the present study show that the preference of student-centered teaching methods and techniques by the teachers is very important for developing children's social skills.

Primary school is the place where students' tendency to see their teachers role models reaches its highest level. It is known that at these ages the attitudes and behaviors of teachers significantly influence the social development of the child. Teachers also understand that their positive attitudes and behavior in school and the classroom environment will further encourage students to take part in social activities.

The democratic attitudes of teachers in classroom management and positive communication with students can enable students to have more self-confidence and to take part in social activities more voluntarily. According to Kücükahmet, the relationship between teacher and student in the classroom forms the basis of learning and education. Teachers who are conscious of their profession try to furnish their students with the necessary knowledge and skills on one hand; they can be a good model for children with their exemplary characters on the other hand.

It is understood from the teacher's views that the exams for passing from primary school to secondary school cause stress on primary school students and therefore, students cannot spare time for and be directed to social activities. As the educators, even if it is obligatory to test students for admission to secondary education, the necessary precautions should be taken in order to prevent this situation from negatively affecting the social development of students by way of causing pressure and stress on them.

Environment

According to the teachers, the environment is one of the factors which play an important role in the development of elementary school children's social skills. The environment may be much more dominant than the family and the school in some cases; for example, children may acquire a great deal of information and skills from their close groups of friends. According to Hartup, a child needs to make friends and participate in groups of friends in order to be able to adapt to her social environment. Friendship provides children with the necessary environments and conditions for learning and development, supports children in emotional and cognitive terms and helps them to learn how to take responsibility, how to protect their own rights and how to respect the rights and responsibilities of others. Therefore, children adopt the methods and the rules of social life. Children can develop the skills of working together in a group, struggling for the common goal and group success, obeying rules, leadership and communication thanks to the social and sporting activities in which they participated together with their peers.

One of the most important environmental factors for the social development of primary school students is children's playing games with their peers. Children recognize their own bodies, realize their abilities, get in the habit of taking responsibility and study regularly by way of learning how to share with their peers and help each other.

According to the teachers who participated in this project, some problems may occur in the social development of the children who spend a long time in front of television, computers and the Internet rather than spending time together with their peer groups in their close environments. Moreover, studies show that the children who watch television for a long time, addict to computer games and surf on the Internet for a long time cutting off communication with their close environments, exhibit anti-social behaviors and become passive individuals. However, it should be known that the use of these technologies in a controlled manner would contribute to the child's social development, knowledge and skill development. For example, some studies emphasize that using a computer plays a quite significant role in the cooperation training, problem solving, accessing information and the development of primary school students.

Children's personal characteristics

Teachers declare that children's personal characteristics play an important role in the development of their social skills as well as other factors in primary school. The characteristics such as developing language and communication skills in children, building personal characteristics such as self-confidence, self-discipline and expression of personal abilities are actually among the most important aims of primary education.

Language and expression skills play a key role in the development of the social skills such as starting relations between individuals, expressing oneself, giving information and joining a group. The children who have communication skills can easily join groups of friends and improve their self-confidence. According to Cartledge and Milbum, the most important aim of social skill education is to enable individuals to be aware of their feelings and thoughts, express their feelings, deal with undesired behaviors and develop behaviors which allow for positive social interaction.

Consequently, based on the teachers' views, the present research shows that family, school, environment and children's personal characteristics play an important role in the development of the social skills of primary school students.

1. **Social skills (社交技能)**: are any skills facilitating interaction and communication with others. Social rules and relations are created, communicated, and changed in verbal and nonverbal ways. The process of learning such skills is called socialization. The rationale for this type of approach to treatment is that people meet a variety of social problems and can reduce the stress and punishment from the experiences as well as increase their reinforcement by having the correct skills.

2. **Primary education (初等教育)**: is the first stage of compulsory education. It is preceded by pre-school or nursery education and is followed by secondary education. In most countries, it is compulsory for children to receive primary education, though in many jurisdictions it is permissible for parents to provide it. The transition to secondary school or high school is somewhat arbitrary, but it generally occurs at about eleven or twelve years of age. Some educational systems have separate middle schools with the transition to the final stage of education taking place at around the age of fourteen. The major goals of primary education are achieving basic literacy and numeracy amongst all pupils, as well as establishing foundations in science, mathematics, geography, history and other social sciences. The relative priority of various areas, and the methods used to teach them, are an area of considerable political debate.

3. **Socialization (社会化)**: is a term used by sociologists, social psychologists, anthropologists, politicians and educationalists to refer to the process of inheriting norms, customs and ideologies. It may provide the individual with the skills and habits necessary for participating within their own society; a society develops a culture through a plurality of shared norms, customs, values, traditions, social roles, symbols and languages. Socialization

is thus "the means by which social and cultural continuity are attained".

4.**Secondary education**(中等教育): is the stage of education following primary school. Secondary education is generally the final stage of compulsory education. However, secondary education in some countries includes a period of compulsory and a period of non-compulsory education. The next stage of education is usually college or university. Secondary education is characterized by transition from the typically compulsory, comprehensive primary education for minors to the optional, selective tertiary, "post-secondary", or "higher" education for adults.

New Words and Expression

1. prenatal [ˌpriːˈneitəl]	adj.	产前的;胎儿期的;[医]出生以前的
2. socialization [ˌsəuʃəlaiˈzeiʃən]	n.	社会化,社会主义化
3. elementary [ˌeliˈmentəri]	adj.	基本的;初级的;[化学]元素的
4. preference [ˈprefərəns]	n.	偏爱,倾向;优先权
5. exemplary [igˈzempləri]	adj.	典范的;惩戒性的;可仿效的
6. obligatory [ˈɔbligətəri]	adj.	义务的;必须的;义不容辞的
7. precaution [priˈkɔːʃən]	n.	预防,警惕;预防措施
	vt.	警惕;预先警告
8. cognitive [ˈkɔgnitiv]	adj.	认知的,认识的
9. peer [piə]	vi.	凝视,盯着看;窥视
	vt.	封为贵族;与……同等
	n.	贵族;同等的人
10. addict [əˈdikt]	n.	有瘾的人;入迷的人
	vt.	使上瘾;使沉溺
11. access [ˈækses]	vt.	使用;存取;接近
	n.	进入;使用权;通路
12. interaction [ˌintərˈækʃən]	n.	相互作用;[数]交互作用

Unit 3 Education & People's Overall Development 教育与人的全面发展

I Vocabulary.

Match the word in Column A to the correct definition in Column B.

Column A	
1. elementary	2. preference
3. obligatory	4. cognitive
5. precaution	6. peer
7. access	8. interaction
9. addict	10. prenatal

Column B

A. the people who are the same age as you or who have the same status as you

B. the mental process involved in knowing, learning, and understanding things

C. occurring, existing, or performed before birth

D. very simple and basic

E. a way of entering or reaching a place

F. binding in law or conscience

G. mutual or reciprocal action or influence

H. a greater interest in or desire for sb. or sth. than else

I. an action that is intended to prevent something dangerous or unpleasant from happening

J. To cause to become physiologically or psychologically dependent on a habit-forming substance

II Translate the following phrases into English.

社交技能　　　　　　　　　　_____

实行,执行;完成,实现　　　　_____

无条件的爱　　　　　　　　　_____

沉溺于,醉心于　　　　　　　　_____
以学生为中心的教学模式　　　_____
觉察,意识到　　　　　　　　_____
中等教育　　　　　　　　　　_____
为……努力　　　　　　　　　_____
遵守规则　　　　　　　　　　_____
自律,自我约束　　　　　　　_____

III　Comprehension of the text.

Decide whether the following statements are true (T) or false (F) according to the passage.

1. There are four main factors that play an important role in the development of primary school students' social skills: family, school, environment and the personal characteristics of individual students.
2. The effect of family starts in the postnatal period and continues its influence until the end of an individual's life and it is of great importance in a child's development.
3. Families play an important role in children's development in social skills. Parents should not only focus on the academic successes of their children but also support their social and emotional development.
4. Elementary school years constitute the most important period in which children develop attitudes and behaviors and in which children learn how to live with others in the same environment, how to share, how to communicate and how to express themselves.
5. Preparing children for a healthy social life is the most important aims of primary schools, according to the teachers.
6. Teachers who are conscious of their profession try to furnish their students with the necessary knowledge and skills on one hand; they may not be a good model for children with their exemplary characters on the other hand.
7. According to the teachers, the stress on primary school students caused by the exams for passing from primary school to secondary school makes those children have no spare time for social activities.
8. The environment is one of the factors which play an important role in the development of elementary school children's social skills, which may be much more dominant than the family and the school in some cases.

9. Although some problems may occur in the social development of the children who spend a long time in front of television, computers and the Internet rather than spending time together with their peer groups in their close environments, it should be known that the use of these technologies in a controlled manner and relevantly would contribute to the child's social development, knowledge and skill development.

10. The characteristics such as developing language and communication skills in children, building personal characteristics such as self-confidence, self-discipline and expression of personal abilities are actually the most important aims of primary education.

 Supplementary Reading

Social Emotional Development: a New Model of Student Learning in Higher Education

Aristotle once wrote that those who are "angry with the right person, to the right degree, at the right time, for the right purpose, and the right way are at an advantage in any domain of life" (*Nicomachean Ethics*). Although science has generally focused on a rational explanation of human behavior and performance, it is often the emotional side of our nature that influences our thoughts, actions, and results.

Similarly, although higher education is generally lauded for developing academic knowledge in their students, its leaders are routinely criticized for not adequately preparing students for the types of roles and leaders that organizations need. That is, students are often not equipped with the social and emotional competence to fully capitalize on their academic knowledge. It is not enough to produce the best and the brightest technical experts.

Universities must also address the whole student (intellectual, emotional and social) to better prepare graduates for future success. This requires educators to approach learning as a process that engages students in a teaching and learning relationship that at the very least includes faculty and peers. Students who are able to develop their capacity to understand themselves, the world around them, build meaningful relationships, and foster positive changes have an advantage in school, work, and life. A promising field of recent research that may help guide educators in whole student education is in the maturity of social and emotional proficiency. The concept of social and emotional development (SED) is introduced as the desirable, sustainable enhancement of personal capacity to utilize emotional information, behaviors, and traits to facilitate desired social outcomes. A model of SED is proposed that includes four distinct, but inter-related factors: (1) self awareness—the knowledge and understanding of your emotional state, assessing your strengths and limitations, and recognizing your preferences; (2) consideration of others—the thoughtful regard for the person and situation in anticipating the likely consequences before thinking and acting; (3) connection to others—the ease and effort in developing meaningful, quality relationships with others; and (4) impacting change—the propensity to influence others by seeking leadership opportunities and motivating others to change. The purpose of SED is to provide a theoretical and practical framework to understand and facilitate increasing student social and emotional capacity to recognize emotional cues, process emotional information, and utilize emotional knowledge to adapt to social challenges.

Philosophers and social scientists have long wrestled with the phenomenon of emotion and its impact on human relationships, debating the nature and extent to which emotion influences the human decision-making processes and the subsequent relational outcomes of those decisions. The present paper makes a unique contribution to the growing literature on social and emotional competence. It has long been maintained that social and emotional competencies are critical to success in the workplace. However, a large portion of the existing research on developing or training these competencies has focused on working adults, executive training programs, and MBA students.

Lindebaum suggested that workplace training programs might not be the best medium to develop emotional competencies due to barriers such as employer policies that shape employee behaviors. Attempting to develop on-the-job emotional competencies has been described as a short-term job-centered training method whereas a whole-person education approach calls for more extended efforts. A whole person approach to developing emotional competencies "may be better framed as a personal development undertaking, where individuals exercise responsibility and self-direction in their education".

A model of SED is presented for college students. This population is distinct from working adults in several key ways. College students tend to be younger with less work experience and are undergoing major developmental changes from adolescent to adult. The college campus presents unique opportunities for social interaction that are especially relevant to the proposed model, since being successful in college calls for students to be fully engaged emotionally and socially with their peers, teachers, and other members of campus. Thus, social and emotional development is a key quality of value to higher education institutions in addition to students' future co-workers and managers. This is particularly important in a world where so many social interactions are technology driven and limited in scope.

SED provides a potential model of understanding and intervention for educators to examine and enhance the capacity of students to interact in an emotional and social environment. Too often, educators focus on narrow discipline-based content delivery, ignoring the full growth potential of our students. This is particularly the case in higher education, where the maturation of our students, transitioning from teenagers to young adults with the future expectations of career, family, and friends (not to mention significant debt in many cases) is often ignored both inside and outside the classroom. By focusing attention on whole-student development, including social and emotional along with more traditional academic skills, higher education will be better positioned to prepare students for an increasingly dynamic world as well as provide greater value added benefit for the time and cost of education.

Unit 4 Educational System & Educational Law
教育制度与教育法

Text A　E-learning and Evaluation in Modern Educational System

导读：网络学习(E-learning)又称数字学习,也译电子化学习、在线学习,它强调的是数字技术,强调用技术来改造和引导教育。E-learning 主要通过互联网进行学习与教学活动,它充分利用现代信息技术所提供的、具有全新沟通机制与丰富资源的学习环境,实现一种全新的学习方式。学习的知识不再是一本书,也不再是几本参考书,而是将有关的专业知识建立成数据库。在数据库的支持下,知识体系将被重新划分,学习内容将发生重新组合,学习与研究方法也将发生新的变化。

Implementation of information and communication technologies as well as emersion of new user interfaces and Web 2.0 technologies changes the way of education system, the way of living and business transactions in general. The way we communicate, operate, produce and live is also changing. In accordance with it, the systems of education change from being traditional to being modern. With the development of certain software, students' class attendance no longer represents an important factor, as they can now learn from distance using the mentioned software, taking the learning process one step further.

Confucius, the famous Chinese thinker and philosopher, once said, "I hear and I forget, I see and I remember, I do and I understand." We all know this instinctively, but perhaps Edgar Dale, an U. S. educationist at Ohio State University, explained it the best. He made some study to explain. The results of his study showed a significant deviation between different learning methods. Dale could divide those methods into passive and active learning, and each of them into a nature of enrollment, as reading, looking at pictures, seeing a movie, giving a talk or doing a presentation. The results indicated that

Unit 4 Educational System & Educational Law 教育制度与教育法

the student group that learned from reading remembered only about 10% of what was written, while the student group that learned from watching a demonstration or an exhibit remembered 50%, and the group that actually did the real thing or simulated a real experience remembered an astonishing 90%. Moreover, students who remembered by reading or hearing were able to define or describe the things they remembered. Students who remembered by hearing and seeing were able to apply what they learned, but only those who learned by saying or saying and doing could analyze, evaluate and criticize what they knew.

Science, people and technology are changing too rapidly to follow them using the traditional teaching methods. Thus, only new and innovative learning methods can make a difference. By using E-learning, it is hoped to achieve changes in the way of thinking and learning and to shift from a vertical hierarchy to a horizontal one, where professors and students can call each other colleagues, thus, referring to one another as practically equals, emphasizing the idea of a common goal—innovative learning. Moreover, it is hoped to shift from defined course materials years or even decades ago to an adaptive learning system where students get to choose the topics they would like to explore further. By giving them this option, Dale's core of learning is being implemented, and doing research by themselves and presenting this research in front of the whole class will help them remember it much better than they would have if a professor just made them learn it. Those implementations would most likely lead to a change in the learning system. Students' knowledge will no longer have to be acquired merely from professors' lectures that will then be expected to reproduce, but by reproducing a knowledge based on experience. It is needless to say, not only this knowledge will be much better understood, but also the students will remember it much longer and much better.

Learning is a process of achieving certain competence that can be defined as a dynamical combination of cognitive and meta-cognitive skills, knowledge and understanding, as well as the development of social skills and growth in ethical values. The target of every educational program should be to enable its participants to have an optimal balance in developing all the above. E-learning enhances the quality of educational process by enabling the practice of new roles in the process of learning. In addition, during this process, lifelong learning technologies are used. There are different forms of E-learning: (1) ICT (information and communication technologies); (2) mixed learning as a combination of classroom teaching and teaching over the system; and (3) learning at distance. When choosing a form of e-learning, one should have in mind the type of the course it should be applied to as well as the needs and possibilities of students and professors. E-learning should not be seen as an alternative educational system but as an enhancement of the existing one.

Today, we are faced with a new generation of students, and the aberrational characteristics presenting among them in comparison with the older generations are only going to be more emphasized with the upcoming ones. The new generations of students are capable of fast information adoption and multitasking, and they call for a random access to information ("anytime, anywhere"), as they are accustomed to Google-like informational systems and multiple media operating. They expect to be rewarded at all time. Past educational systems were based on the idea of delivering the knowledge to students who accepted the given knowledge in a passive manner. Professors played the role as keepers of the knowledge. Through E-learning, a new educational environment can be set and an environment can be constructed in the direction of interaction, processing information, researching and problem-solving. The students are asked to actively get involved, and often work in teams. The role of the professor is to design the methods of learning and help the students develop their talents and capabilities.

1. **E-learning(网络学习)**: comprises all forms of electronically supported learning and teaching. The information and communication systems, whether networked or not, serve as specific media to implement the learning process. It is essentially the computer and network-enabled transfer of skills and knowledge. E-learning applications and processes include Web-based learning, computer-based learning, virtual classroom opportunities and digital collaboration. Content is delivered via the Internet, intranet/extranet, audio or video tape, satellite TV, and CD-ROM.

2. **Web 2.0(网络 2.0)**: is associated with web applications that facilitate participatory information sharing, interoperability, user-centered design, and collaboration on the World Wide Web. A Web 2.0 site allows users to interact and collaborate with each other in a

Unit 4 Educational System & Educational Law 教育制度与教育法

social media dialogue as creators of user-generated content in a virtual community, in contrast to websites where users are limited to the passive viewing of content that was created for them. Examples of Web 2.0 include social networking sites, blogs, wikis, video sharing sites, hosted services, web applications, mashups and folksonomies.

3. **Confucius(孔子)**: was a Chinese thinker and social philosopher of the Spring and Autumn Period. The philosophy of Confucius emphasized personal and governmental morality, correctness of social relationships, justice and sincerity. Confucius' thoughts have been developed into a system of philosophy known as Confucianism.

4. **Xunzi(荀子)**: was a Chinese Confucian philosopher who lived during the Warring States Period and contributed to one of the Hundred Schools of Thought. Xunzi believed man's inborn tendencies need to be curbed through education and ritual, counter to Mencius's view that man is innately good. He believed that ethical norms had been invented to rectify mankind. Educated in the state of Qi, Xunzi was associated with the Confucian school, but his philosophy has a pragmatic flavor compared to Confucian optimism. Some scholars attribute it to the divisive times. Xunzi was one of the most sophisticated thinkers of his time, and was the teacher of Li Si and Han Feizi.

New Words and Expression

1. implementation [ˌimplimən'teɪʃən] n. 实现；履行；安装启用
2. interface ['intəfeis] n. 界面；接口；接触面
3. emersion [i'mə:ʃən] n. 出现；脱出
4. abstraction [æb'strækʃən] n. 抽象；提取；抽象概念；空想；心不在焉
5. deviation [ˌdi:vi'eiʃən] n. 偏差；误差；背离
6. competence ['kɔmpitəns] n. 能力，胜任；权限；作证能力
7. dynamical [dai'næmikəl] adj. 动力学的；有生气的；有力的
8. aberrational [ˌæbə'reiʃənəl] adj. 背离真实的；偏离真理的；不正直的
9. in accordance with 依照，与……一致
10. be accustomed to 习惯于

I Read the text and answer the following questions.

1. What is the topic or subject discussed in the text?
2. In your own words, what is the writer's main idea about this topic?
3. What is the Chinese meaning of "I hear and I forget, I see and I remember, I do and I understand."?
4. What is the definition of "learning" in the passage?
5. What is the value of E-learning?

II Choose the correct letter A, B, C, or D.

1. Different learning methods used in Dale's study are the following except _____.
   A. reading a book   B. listening to music
   C. giving a talk   D. seeing a movie

2. In Dale's study, _____ is the most useful learning methods.
   A. looking at an exhibit   B. participating in a discussion
   C. reading books   D. doing a presentation

3. Which is the idea of Dale?
   A. I hear and I forget, I see and I remember.
   B. Despite the quicker adapting that is nowadays required, the majority of the learning institutions still rely on the old fashion way of information transmitting
   C. Doing research by students will be better for them to study than doing by professors.
   D. Students should learn from professors' lectures and produce knowledge based on them.

4. The writer mentioned _____ ways for E-learning.
   A. two   B. three   C. four   D. five

5. The new generations of students are good at _____.
   A. fast information adoption
   B. multitasking
   C. Google-like informational systems and multiple media operating
   D. all of above

Unit 4　Educational System & Educational Law　教育制度与教育法

III Comprehension of the text.

Decide whether the following statements are true (T) or false (F) according to the passage.

1. With the development of certain software, students' class attendance represents an important factor.
2. Learning from reading remembers more than learning from watching a demonstration.
3. New and innovative learning methods can be suitable for science, people and technology.
4. Lifelong learning technologies are used in the E-learning.
5. E-learning should be seen as an alternative educational system.

Text B　Legislation and Equality in Basic Education

导读：随着世界经济和社会的进步越来越依靠知识、技术、技能和能力，人力资源将成为国家在全球市场生存中的决定因素。在这种新的社会历史条件下，使所有儿童、青年和成人的基本学习需要真正得到满足，是世界各国旨在缩小差别、促进社会全面进步的一个必要手段，因此基础教育的意义和作用受到了高度的关注，它要满足全民的基本学习需求，要求世界各国在现行基础教育服务范围，保障每一个体的基本权利。同时，也强调世界各国必须注重基础教育的平等性。

Despite its different meanings and manifestations, the principle of equality has been used to confront social inequalities in a variety of stratified societies and cultures. While the United Nations is striving for universal primary education for children across the globe by 2015, educational inequality persists and has become a significant challenge for educational policy-makers, scholars, and practitioners worldwide. With reference to compulsory schooling legislation, in China, law is used in policy-making as a pragmatic instrument to address specific educational problems, and as a last resort, holds governments of various levels accountable for improving education. In doing so, law can be a device of social justice to promote equality in education by serving as an important mechanism to check and balance the state's power regarding its obligations toward providing basic education, redistributing public resources, reducing disparities, and promoting equality in compulsory schooling. However, using legislation to promote equity in basic education is constrained by economic conditions and other extra-legal factors. Effecting change requires favorable economic, social, and cultural conditions, as well as the cooperation of those who interpret and enforce the law.

Many sociological and educational studies have discussed the relation between equality and education. For example, Horton and Hunt argued that in modern society, people are given status or rewards according to their merits, which are often measured by results of schooling, and in turn can affect individuals' life chances. Dahrendorf considered education as an important vehicle of social mobility in stratified society and equal educational opportunity as a basic right of every person. Levin expanded the meaning of educational equality to include: equality of educational access, equality of educational participation, equality of educational results, and equality of educational effects on life chances. Equality of opportunity within education, as Bilton argued, needs to be ensured so that opportunities for success in school are the same for everyone with similar abilities, regardless of sex, ethnicity, and socio-economic background. Iannelli and Paterson concluded, however, that the social project of "using education to equalize life chances has been a failure". They even argued that education "cannot be used, on its own, to eradicate social inequalities, and is relatively powerless to counter the middle-class strengths of effective networks, self-confident aspirations and sheer wealth".

Despite the debate, the provision of basic education for all with a minimum period of schooling is still believed to be a vital means for reducing inequality within and between societies. Since World War II, the UN has advocated a rights-based approach to basic education. In the Universal Declaration of Human Rights, the UN declared that "everyone has the right to education" and that education shall be "free" and "compulsory", at least during the elementary and fundamental stages. This right can empower individuals to achieve "the goals of personal autonomy and efficacy" and enable them to determine the course of their lives.

In response to these global aspirations, many countries have adopted strategies to provide basic education for all. Of these strategies, compulsory schooling legislation is a particularly common one. Legislation can compel the state to provide eligible children with free basic education for a minimum period of, for example, six or nine years and compel parents to send their children to school. As a result, despite such problems as gender disparity, the number of children in the world enrolled in primary school

Unit 4　Educational System & Educational Law　教育制度与教育法

increased by 6% to 688 million from 1999 to 2005, and the number of children out of school dropped from 96 million in 1999 to 72 million in 2005. However, providing and legislating compulsory schooling does not necessarily mean the complete eradication of educational inequalities in compulsory schooling. Many studies have shown that inequality in school education continues to exist in many forms. As noted by Coleman, Jencks, Levin, and Ballantine, they include: inequalities in educational input and output, and educational opportunity and life chances for children of different social groups, for boys and girls, and for local and non-local students. Inequality of students' academic performance can be caused by many factors, such as cultural practices, social class, family background, ethnicity, gender, and sexuality. Using legislation as a means to institutionalize equality in basic education is part of an international trend of increasing reliance on legislation to bring about social change.

1. **Basic education (基础教育):** refers to the whole range of educational activities taking place in various settings (formal, non-formal and informal) that aim to meet basic learning needs. According to the International Standard Classification of Education (ISCED), basic education comprises primary education (first stage of basic education) and lower secondary education (second stage). In countries (developing countries in particular), basic education often includes also pre-primary education and/or adult literacy programs.

2. **The Universal Declaration of Human Rights (UDHR) (世界人权宣言):** is a declaration adopted by the United Nations General Assembly on 10 December 1948. The Declaration arose directly from the experience of the Second World War and represents the first global expression of rights to which all human beings are inherently entitled. It consists of 30 articles which have been elaborated in subsequent international treaties, regional human rights instruments, national constitutions and laws.

New Words and Expression

1. manifestation [ˌmænifeˈsteiʃən]   n.   表现;显示;示威运动
2. stratified [ˈstrætifaid]   adj.   分层的;形成阶层的;分为不同等级的
3. pragmatic [prægˈmætik]   adj.   实际的;实用主义的;国事的
4. mechanism [ˈmekənizəm]   n.   原理,途径;进程;机制;机械装置;技巧
5. disparity [disˈpærəti]   n.   不同;不一致;不等
6. provision [prəuˈviʒən]   n.   规定;条款;准备
7. efficacy [ˈefikəsi]   n.   功效,效力
8. autonomy [ɔːˈtɔnəmi]   n.   自主权,自主性
9. eligible [ˈelidʒəbl]   adj.   合格的,合适的;符合条件的;有资格当选的
10. accountable for   负责,对……负责任
11. with reference to   关于(等于 in reference to)
12. hold accountable for   对……负责任

Exercises

I Choose the meaning of the following words used in the text.

1. manifestation
    A. a very clear sign that a particular situation or feeling exists
    B. the act of appearing or becoming clear
    C. the appearance of a ghost or a sign of its presence
    D. evidence

2. stratified
    A. various   B. having several layers of earth, rock etc.
    C. having different social classes   D. useful or right

3. pragmatic
    A. concerned with the study of scientific ideas
    B. solving problems in a sensible way rather than by having fixed ideas or theories
    C. based on carefully organized methods
    D. related to the style of a piece of writing or art

4. disparity

Unit 4　Educational System & Educational Law　教育制度与教育法

  A. change   B. variation

  C. equal pay, rights, or power   D. a difference connected with unfair treatment

 5. eradicate

  A. to forget   B. to destroy or get rid of something

  C. to build   D. to understand

 6. autonomy

  A. freedom to govern a region, country without being controlled by anyone else

  B. the ability to make your own decisions without being influenced by anyone else

  C. a person who behaves like a machine, without thinking or feeling anything

  D. a machine that moves without human control

 7. efficacy

  A. the quality of being able to produce the result that was intended

  B. a figure made of wood, paper, stone that looks like a person

  C. the physical or mental energy that is needed to do something

  D. an attempt to do something

 8. aspiration

  A. the sound of air blowing out that happens when some consonants are pronounced

  B. someone who hopes to get a position of importance or honor

  C. a strong desire to have or achieve something

  D. a way of speaking or behaving

 9. eligible

  A. very beautiful and graceful

  B. clever and simple

  C. upset and unhappy

  D. qualified for or allowed or worthy of being chosen

 10. institutionalize

  A. to make something systematize

  B. cause to be admitted

  C. to officially tell somebody what to do

  D. to inform somebody about something

II Comprehension of the text.

Decide whether the following statements are true (T) or false (F) according to the passage.

 1. The United Nations has already solved the problem of primary education for children

across the globe.

2. Using legislation to promote equity in basic education is only constrained by economic conditions.
3. Levin considered education as an important vehicle of social mobility in stratified society and equal educational opportunity as a basic right of every person.
4. Iannelli and Paterson argued that education cannot be used, on its own, to eradicate social inequalities, and is relatively powerless to counter the middle-class strengths of effective networks, self-confident aspirations and sheer wealth.
5. Providing and legislating compulsory schooling means the complete eradication of educational inequalities in compulsory schooling.

III Translate the following sentences into Chinese.

1. While the United Nations is striving for universal primary education for children across the globe by 2015, educational inequality persists and has become a significant challenge for educational policy-makers, scholars, and practitioners worldwide.
2. With reference to compulsory schooling legislation, in China, law is used in policy-making as a pragmatic instrument to address specific educational problems, and as a last resort, holds governments of various levels accountable for improving education.
3. Equality of opportunity within education, as Bilton argued, needs to be ensured so that opportunities for success in school are the same for everyone with similar abilities, regardless of sex, ethnicity, and socio-economic background.
4. In the Universal Declaration of Human Rights, the UN declared that "everyone has the right to education" and that education shall be "free" and "compulsory", at least during the elementary and fundamental stages.
5. As a result, despite such problems as gender disparity, the number of children in the world enrolled in primary school increased by 6% to 688 million from 1999 to 2005, and the number of children out of school dropped from 96 million in 1999 to 72 million in 2005.

Supplementary Reading

Major Continuities and Changes in the Basic Education Law

Since national educational systems were first organized in the 18th century,

Unit 4 Educational System & Educational Law 教育制度与教育法

legislation has been used to initiate and enforce various educational policies. One of the earliest types of education law-making was compulsory schooling legislation. Today over 170 countries use legal means to protect children's rights to access compulsory schooling for a minimum period. Despite being a late-comer, in 1986 China enacted the Basic Education Law and began to provide 9 years of compulsory schooling. However, the law was significantly revised.

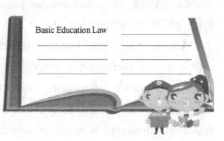

The Basic Education Law was expanded from 18 articles of about 1,800 words to 63 articles of over 7,000 words. Further, content analysis of the old and new versions of the Basic Education Law reveals continuities and changes. The law continues to defend the rights of children to access basic education. The changes reflect how the NPC used revision of the law to reveal how government at various levels had failed to provide basic education to their citizens' satisfaction. Through the revised law the NPC attempted to force the state administration to become more accountable for implementing and enforcing its basic education policies and measures.

Similar to the old version, the revised law continued to defend citizens' rights to access compulsory schooling by keeping five major policy principles of basic education for all. First, the revised law acknowledged the importance of the fundamental function of education in training for the socialists guide the constructors and successors in ideals, morality, knowledge and discipline. According to the NPC Law Committee (2006), in a second deliberation of a draft of the revised law in June 2006 it was agreed to de-ideologize the provision by deleting this clause.

However, the ideological tone was finally kept in a third deliberation and passed. Second, the revised law reiterated the principle of equal opportunity for eligible children over age 6 (or 7 in areas with less developed conditions) to receive 9 years of compulsory schooling. The revised law re-emphasized the nondiscriminatory nature of admission to basic education for all regardless of a student's physical condition, gender, ethnicity, religion and socio-economic status. The revised law also added a new provision to protect the right of juveniles to receive basic education. Third, to ensure such equal opportunity, the revised law continued to stipulate a policy of examination-free admission by catchment area in the place of their parents' or guardians' household registration. According to the former State Education Commission (1987) catchment area refers to schools within 3 km of the student's residence, rather than the nearest school.

Fourth, parents or guardians are legally obliged to send their eligible children to school. Fifth, child labor remains illegal.

Unlike the 1986 version, which was concerned primarily with the quantity and efficiency of compulsory schooling, the 2006 version dealt more with the quality and fairness of basic education. The clause on promoting the universalization of basic education by areas and stages in the old law was deleted. As shown below, the revised law also stipulated a series of legislative changes with a view to remedying the legal loopholes of the old version and addressing new concerns and problems arising from social and educational changes since the 1980s. These problems included: the effects of examinations on teaching and learning, widespread fee abuses, the lack of a mechanism to ensure investment in basic education and an increase in disparity. The first problem is related to the quality of education, whereas the other three are more related to issues of equality in compulsory schooling. A very pressing problem in compulsory schooling legislation that drew the NPC's law-makers' attention is the increasing concern about students' heavy workload and the quality of their education. After many state measures failed to address these concerns, law-makers were invited to decide on the interests of various stakeholders concerning student workload and to promote quality education.

Unit 5 Educational Justice
教育公平

Text A Educational Justice in Schools

导读：教育公平是要确保每个人不受性别、种族、出身、经济地位、居住环境等条件的影响，均享有平等的受教育的权利和义务，被提供相对平等的受教育的机会和条件。然而受教育者之间存在差异，每个人又是各不相同的，接受教育和掌握知识的水平不一致，仅仅保证教育权利和教育条件的公平，还不足以保证受教育者的公平。

What are the right normative grounds for evaluating education policy? I want to propose, briefly, four proper goals of education, and one distributive principle. The goals are as follows:

- Education should prepare children to become autonomous, self-governing individuals, capable of making good judgments about how to live their own lives, and to negotiate for themselves the complexity of modern life;
- Education should equip children with the skills and knowledge necessary for them to be effective participants in the economy, so that they can have a good range of options in the labor market, and have access to the income necessary to flourish in a market economy;
- Education should play a role in preparing children to be flourishing adults independently of their participation in the economy;
- Education should prepare children to be responsible and effective participants in political life—good citizens. It should do this both for their sake, because a flourishing life is more secure if one is capable of making use of the rights of citizenship; and for the sake of others, because a flourishing life is more secure if others are capable of abiding by the duties of good citizenship.

The distributive principle is the principle of educational equality: The simple version says that every child should have an equally good education. But what this means is obviously contested. When you compare children with similar talents, and similar levels of willingness to exert effort, it is pretty intuitive to say that educational equality is satisfied when they receive a similar level of educational resources. But consider Hattie, who is blind, and Sid, who is equally talented and hardworking, but sighted. In their case it seems intuitive that equality requires that more resources should be devoted to Hattie in particular, resources devoted to correcting fully for her disability. Consider an even more difficult case: Kenneth, who is highly talented, and Hugh, who has a serious cognitive disability. Again, it seems that Hugh should be granted more resources, but this time it is hard to see that they could correct for the disability, unless we were willing to disable Kenneth. I shall not resolve these difficulties here. The principle of educational equality has two straightforward implications. First, children with similar levels of ability and willingness to exert effort should face similar educational prospects, regardless of their social background, race, ethnicity, or sex. Second, that children with lower levels of ability should receive at least as many educational resources as those who are more able.

Since most of the ensuing discussion focuses on the principle of educational equality rather than the goals of education, I want to emphasize the importance of equality rather than improving the prospects of the least advantaged. The egalitarian theory within which my own view of educational justice is nested in fact emphasizes not equality, per se, but benefiting the least advantaged, and gives that principle priority over equality—so that when we have a choice between an equal distribution of a smaller pie and an unequal distribution of a larger pie in which all get more than under the equal distribution of the smaller pie, we choose inequality. If a tax proposal, for example, were to inhibit growth so that the worst off were even worse off, although more equally well off with others, that would be a bad thing for them, and for everyone else. But this general rule does not apply to all areas of life. The quality of someone's education has a real influence on their expected lifetime income, but its influence is dependent on the quality of her competitors' education.

Getting Sharon from only 2 up to 3 grade Cs does not do much good for her if we simultaneously get her nearest competitor Linda up from 3 to 4 grade Cs. The employer will still prefer Linda to Sharon. So merely raising the floor of achievement in education does not help the less advantaged in the pursuit of earnings in the labor market unless we simultaneously diminish the achievement gap. The size of the gap matters because of the particular connection education has to other, unequally distributed, goods. When I refer to "benefiting the least (or less) advantaged" in the context of education, then, I should be understood as being concerned with benefiting the least advantaged relative to others.

New Words and Expression

1. normative ['nɔːmətiv]	adj.		规范的,标准的
2. equip with			装配,配备,备有
3. flourish ['flʌriʃ]	vi.		繁荣,兴旺;茂盛;活跃
4. for the sake of			为了;为了……的利益
5. abide by			遵守……
6. intuitive [in'tjuːitiv]	adj.		直觉的;凭直觉获知的
7. egalitarian [iˌgæli'tɛəriən]	adj.		平等主义的
	n.		平等主义;平等主义者
8. per se			本身,自身
9. be worse off			处境较坏,情况恶化
10. be concerned with			涉及……;担心……

I Choose the correct letter A, B, C, or D.

1. What are the right normative grounds for evaluating education policy according to the writer?
   A. Four proper goals of education.
   B. One distributive principle.
   C. Four goals of education and one distributive.
   D. Two distributive principles.

2. The followings are the goals of education except _____.
   A. Education should play a role in preparing children to be flourishing adults independently of their participation in the economy
   B. Education should prepare children to be responsible and effective participants in political life—good citizens
   C. Education should equip children with the skills and knowledge necessary for them to be effective participants in the economy, so that they can have a good range of options in the labour market, and have access to the income necessary to flourish in a market economy
   D. Everyone should have an equal education

3. What is the distributive principle of education?
   A. Every child should have an equally good education.
   B. Children should become autonomous, self-governing individuals, capable of making good judgments about how to live their own lives, and negotiate for themselves the complexity of modern life.
   C. Children are full of the skills and knowledge necessary for them to be effective participants in the economy.
   D. Children can have a good range of options in the labour market, and have access to the income necessary to flourish in the market economy.

4. The writer mentioned the example of _____ to show some difficulties in the principle of educational equality.
   A. Considering Hattie   B. Considering Sid
   C. Considering Kenneth and Hugh D. all of above

5. Which is not the idea of the writer?
   A. To emphasize the importance of equality rather than improving the prospects of the least advantaged.
   B. Children with similar talents, and similar levels of willingness to exert effort will get the similar quality of education.
   C. The quality of someone's education has an influence which is dependent on the quality of her competitors' education on their expected lifetime income.
   D. Children with lower levels of ability should receive at least as many educational resources as those who are more able.

II Vocabulary.

Fill in the blanks with the most suitable words. Change the form when necessary.

| equip | flourish | abide | egalitarian | intuitive |
| priority | exert | talented | emphasize | normative |

1. He won both games without even seeming to _____ himself.
2. The plants _____ in the warm sun.
3. The boys _____ themselves with torches and rope, and set off.
4. He seemed to have a/an _____ awareness of how I felt.
5. Manufacturers are making safety a design _____.
6. You have to _____ by the referee's decision.
7. The social forces for service also exist some _____ issues.
8. The _____ artist carved an interesting decoration from this piece of tree root.
9. Our government tries to establish an _____ country.
10. It should be _____ that flying is a very safe way to travel.

III Translate the following sentences into Chinese.

1. Education should prepare children to become autonomous, self-governing individuals, capable of making good judgments about how to live their own lives, and to negotiate for themselves the complexity of modern life.
2. Education should equip children with the skills and knowledge necessary for them to be effective participants in the economy, so that they can have a good range of options in the labor market, and have access to the income necessary to flourish in a market economy.

3. Education should play a role in preparing children to be flourishing adults independently of their participation in the economy.
4. Education should prepare children to be responsible and effective participants in political life—good citizens.
5. When you compare children with similar talents, and similar levels of willingness to exert effort, it is pretty intuitive to say that educational equality is satisfied when they receive a similar level of educational resources.

Text B Efficiency and Equity of European Education and Training Policies

导读：教育与培训政策的平等是民主化的一个重要内容，是人们不受政治、经济、文化、民族、信仰、性别、地域等的限制，在法律上享有同等的受教育与受培训权利、在事实上具有同等的受教育和培训机会。而教育与培训政策的有效性是指教育与培训政策能完成活动和达到的结果的程度。二者的有效性与平等性时而互补互助，相辅相成，时而互不影响，各自发展，时而又给对方的发展造成不利影响。

Any society aims for economic prosperity coupled with equality of opportunity. Thus, it is not a surprise that European Union heads of state could agree on the so-called "Lisbon strategy" with its goal to become "the most competitive and dynamic knowledge-based economy in the world, capable of sustainable economic growth with more and better jobs and greater social cohesion". At the same time, it has been realized that education and training systems that create efficient and equitable outcomes are key to economic prosperity and social cohesion. This has been stressed by leading European economic advisors, and the European Union puts education and training at center stage in its agenda for jobs and growth. For example, the European Council concludes that "education and training are critical factors to develop the EU's long-term potential for competitiveness as well as for social cohesion". But how can an efficient and equitable education and training system be achieved in practice?

The strong upsurge of applied research in the economics of education over the past decade has produced ample evidence that the monetary and non-monetary prosperity of individuals and nations indeed hinges on education and training. Education produces substantial returns to the individual in terms of earnings and employability, significant effects on economic growth and noteworthy non-monetary benefits for the individual and for society as a whole, among others in terms of superior health, civic participation, and reduced crime. Given the effects of education on individual wellbeing, the distribution of education is also crucial for societal inequality.

So, efficient education and training systems can create economic growth, and equitable systems can create social cohesion. For some European politicians, education and training are, therefore, high on the policy agenda because they can boost efficiency, for others because they can boost equity. But what is the relationship between efficiency and equity? Many governments tend to think that there is a trade-off that forces them to choose between efficiency and equity in their prioritizing. But achieving more equity in the design of education systems may help to evade the need for intense redistributive policies at later ages, which are often viewed as obstacles to the creation of growth and jobs in Europe.

In reality, the relationship between efficiency and equity in education and training systems may take different forms. In some cases, efficiency and equity may be independent from one another. In other cases, there may be trade-offs in the extent to which the two goals can be achieved. And in still other cases, there may be complementarities in the achievement of the two goals. Thus, certain policies may bring education and training systems closer to efficiency without having any impact on equity. Other policies may be highly equitable without affecting efficiency. Other policies may advance both efficiency and equity in a complementary way. And still other policies may show a trade-off by advancing either efficiency at the detriment of equity or equity at the detriment of efficiency.

The reviewed evidence shows that efficient policies need not be inequitable, and equitable policies need not be inefficient. Countries do not necessarily have to choose between efficiency and equity. There are ways to evade trade-offs between them, whereas current attempts to reach one or the other sometimes turn out to be both inefficient and inequitable.

While a universally accepted definition of equity is elusive, it seems that most people could agree to some variant close to the concept of equality of opportunity proposed by Roemer. The central idea of this concept is that inequality should be tolerated only if it is due to differences in effort, but not if it is due to circumstances which are beyond a person's control. Thus, equity would demand that a person's expected educational outcome should be a function only of her effort, but not of her circumstances, such as race, gender, or family background. The concept of efficiency is much more straightforward, representing a situation where a maximum aggregate outcome of the educational production process is obtained with given input or a given aggregate outcome with minimum input. Under this concept, an efficient situation is one which would be preferred by any individual who is ignorant of her position in society. In the calculus of applied welfare economics, equity and efficiency goals can be combined by maximizing welfare functions.

Relative to the well established and extensive literature on the economic and social impacts of education and training, many parts of the literature on efficiency and equity in education and training are not as well developed. Ultimately, profound country specific empirical assessments would be required to evaluate the specific efficiency and equity consequences of different policies. Still, the available literature has produced evidence consistent enough to warrant a general unifying perspective and many specific features for a Europe-wide assessment. At the same time, it should be borne in mind that uncertainties remain for some parts of the assessment, which will be mentioned where necessary.

1. **European Union(EU)(欧洲联盟)**: is an economic and political union of 27 member states which are located primarily in Europe. The EU traces its origins from the European Coal and Steel Community (ECSC) and the European Economic Community (EEC) formed by six countries in the 1950s. In the intervening years the EU has grown in size by the accession of new member states, and in power by the addition of policy areas to its remit. The Maastricht Treaty established the European Union under its current name in 1993. The last amendment to the constitutional basis of the EU, the Treaty of Lisbon, came into force in 2009.

2. **Lisbon Strategy(里斯本策略)**: also known as the Lisbon Agenda or Lisbon Process, was an action and development plan for the economy of the European Union between 2000 and 2010. It was set out by the European Council in Lisbon in March 2000, and by 2010 most of its goals were alleged by some as not achieved.

3. **The European Council(欧洲理事会)**: refers to the regular meetings of the heads of state or

Unit 5   Educational Justice   教育公平

of government in the European Union. It comprises the heads of state or government of EU member states, along with its President and the President of the Commission. The High Representative takes part in its meetings, which are chaired by its President: currently Donald Tusk.

4. Roemer(Buddy Roemer): is an American politician who served as the 52nd Governor of Louisiana, from 1988 to 1992. He was elected as a Democrat but switched to the Republican Party on March 11, 1991. Prior to serving as Governor, he was a member of the United States House of Representatives from 1981 to 1988.

New Words and Expression

1. sustainable [sə'steinəbl]	adj.	可以忍受的;足可支撑的;养得起的
2. cohesion [kəu'hi:ʒən]	n.	凝聚;结合
3. upsurge ['ʌpsə:dʒ]	n.	高潮,高涨
	vi.	涌起,高涨
4. in terms of		依据;按照;在……方面;以……措词
5. wellbeing	n.	幸福;福利;安乐
6. trade-off ['treidɔf]	n.	交换,交易;权衡;协定
7. elusive [i'lju:siv]	adj.	难懂的;易忘的;逃避的;难捉摸的
8. variant ['vɛəriənt]	adj.	不同的;多样的
9. calculus ['kælkjuləs]	n.	微积分学
10. aggregate ['ægrigət]	adj.	聚合的;集合的;合计的
11. couple with		与……相结合,伴随
12. ample ['æmpl]	adj.	丰富的;足够的;宽敞的
13. monetary ['mʌnitəri]	adj.	货币的;财政的
14. hinge on		以……为转移,靠……转动
15. noteworthy ['nəut,wə:ði]	adj.	值得注意的;显著的
16. evade [i'veid]	vt.	逃避;规避;逃脱
17. complementary [,kɔmpli'mentəri]	adj.	补足的,补充的
18. detriment ['detrimənt]	n.	损害;伤害
19. straightforward [,streit'fɔ:wəd]	adj.	简单的;坦率的;明确的;径直的
20. warrant ['wɔrənt]	vt.	保证;担保;批准;辩解

I Choose the correct letter A, B, C, or D.

1. The goal of _____ is to become the most competitive and dynamic knowledge-based economy in the world, capable of sustainable economic growth with more and better jobs and greater social cohesion.
   A. European Union
   B. European Council
   C. Lisbon Strategy
   D. European economic advisors

2. Education and training systems that create efficient and equitable outcomes are important for _____.
   A. economic prosperity
   B. jobs
   C. social cohesion
   D. economic prosperity and social cohesion

3. The research in the economics of education shows that the monetary and non-monetary prosperity of individuals and nations hinges on _____.
   A. education
   B. training
   C. job
   D. education and training

4. According to the writer, efficient education and training systems can create _____, and equitable systems can create _____.
   A. economic growth; social cohesion
   B. social cohesion; economic growth
   C. economic growth; earnings
   D. earnings and employability; social cohesion

5. Achieving more equity in the design of education systems may help to _____ the need for intense redistributive policies at later ages.
   A. increase
   B. get out of
   C. admit
   D. face with

6. The following sentences can show that the relationship between efficiency and equity in education and training systems may take different forms except _____.
   A. Some policies may bring education and training systems closer to efficiency without having any impact on equity
   B. Some policies may be show that efficiency and equity may be dependent on each other
   C. Some policies may be equitable without influencing on efficiency

Unit 5 Educational Justice 教育公平

　　D. Some policies may advance both efficiency and equity in a complementary way
7. Which statement is not true according to Roemer?
　　A. Inequality should be tolerated only if it is due to differences in effort.
　　B. Inequality should not be tolerated if it is due to circumstances which are beyond a person's control.
　　C. Equity would demand that a person's expected educational outcome should be a function of her effort and circumstances.
　　D. The concept of efficiency is much simpler.
8. What is the central idea of Roemer's concept of equality of opportunity?
　　A. Inequality should be tolerated only if it is due to differences in effort, but not if it is due to circumstances which are beyond a person's control.
　　B. Equity would demand that a person's expected educational outcome should be a function only of her effort, but not of her circumstances, such as race, gender, or family background.
　　C. The concept of efficiency is much more straightforward, representing a situation where a maximum aggregate outcome of the educational production process is obtained with given input or a given aggregate outcome with minimum input.
　　D. An efficient situation is one which would be preferred by any individual who is ignorant of her position in society.
9. What is the meaning of "elusive" in the 6th paragraph?
　　A. difficult to find　　　　　　　B. difficult to achieve
　　C. difficult to see　　　　　　　D. difficult to describe
10. Which is not the meaning of "warrant" in the last paragraph?
　　A. guarantee　　　　　　　　　B. provide
　　C. assure　　　　　　　　　　　D. confirm

II Vocabulary.

Fill in the blanks with the most suitable words. Change the form when necessary.

| equitable | ample | evade | warrant | upsurge |
| variant | elusive | boost | assess | straightforward |

1. The meaning of the poem was somewhat _____.
2. You will have _____ opportunity to state your case later.
3. There has been an _____ in complaints about the police.

4. Gorky said, "Time is the most _____ judge."

5. There are wide regional _____ in house prices.

6. You cannot go on _____ your responsibilities forever.

7. The system itself is perfectly _____.

8. The advertising campaign is intended to _____ sales.

9. The Company shall use its best endeavors to provide accurate information but shall not _____ the accuracy thereof.

10. It is difficult to _____ the effects of the new legislation just yet.

III Comprehension of the text.

Decide whether the following statements are true (T) or false (F) according to the passage.

1. European Union heads of state could agree on the goal of the so-called "Lisbon Strategy".

2. Given the effects of education on social cohesion, the distribution of education is crucial for societal inequality.

3. For all the European politicians, education and training are high on the policy agenda.

4. There are many accepted definitions of equity so that most people could not agree to the concept proposed by Roemer.

5. In the calculus of applied welfare economics, equity and efficiency goals can be combined by maximizing welfare functions.

Supplementary Reading

Educational Policy, Housing Policy and Social Justice

I believe—applies to the way in which education, housing policy and systemic injustice are linked together in contemporary Britain. I follow this general preamble with a concrete example. A close friend was for many years a vicar within a tough housing estate in the north of England, and during that time I got to know the region quite well. Some twenty thousand people lived closely together, many of them in subsidized housing. Local crime was high, and the regional schools, especially at the secondary level, had major problems with respect to truancy, exclusion and educational standards. Many of the teachers, given the overall situation, did an amazingly good job, but it is pretty obvious that, by and large, the children were disadvantaged—in comparison with, say, the state schools that my own children went to (in the local village and a nearby comprehensive) within the part of Cambridge shire in which I live.

Perhaps a more telling comparison is between the housing estate referred to and the city of St John's, Newfoundland, where I lived for twenty nine years. Here the housing for those economically disadvantaged is not concentrated in one or two large estates, but is spread out in smaller concentrations in different parts of the city. The largest concentrations of public housing in St John's are in areas that each contains approximately 200 dwellings. The average number of occupants in these dwellings is 2.5, so that each of these areas houses roughly 500 persons, and of course, many fewer children.

The result of this system is that most schools have a share of children from economically and socially challenged backgrounds. Unlike the example from the north of England, this means that children from deprived backgrounds are much more likely to be in a school in which a good educational level is possible, and—at the same time—children from more privileged backgrounds are much more likely to rub shoulders with children who came from a very different background. There is a sharing of both pain and gain. Such mixing, in my view, is highly desirable for all concerned, children, teachers and parents. The situation is also helped by the fact that a far smaller proportion of economically well-off families in Newfoundland send their children to private schools than in Britain. As a result, the average state school is more socially balanced.

Perhaps I have somewhat idealized the situation in St John's, but my principal point can still be made, namely that, in practice, we cannot separate educational policy from housing policy, and that both of these are intimately related to social justice—by which I mean the attempt to give every child a reasonably fair chance of a good education. The reasons for this claim are easy to see. Unless children are to be bussed from one region to another, concentrations of people who are economically deprived are closely related to matters such as lack of motivation and lack of parental supervision.

In these circumstances I am amazed at how well some schools cope with the difficulties. Nevertheless, it is apparent that—looking at Britain as a whole—we live in a hugely unjust society in which, within the state sector, children in some areas have a fair chance of a good education and others very little. One can always find occasional exceptions—those who by heroic personal drive or heroic local teachers have survived against the odds—but such happy outcomes should not be used to avoid the issue of social inequality. One of the likely reactions to my claim, and the implication that we ought to do something about it—for example, by adopting a housing system that is closer to the example of St John's than to the northern estate referred to—is that a major change of this kind is impractical. Indeed, in the short run, it is. But surely with matters such as educational reform and housing reform we must take the long view, and resist political programs that only look to winning the next election—an outlook that is unlikely to go beyond about five years. Every year there are opportunities to rebuild some areas and most years there are new developments. I am pleading that in all such cases, there should be a deliberate policy of mixed housing, with relatively small concentrations of housing for the disadvantaged—perhaps—of a size that would not take up more than twenty per cent of places in the local primary school. There should be a balance between at least four kinds of property: three or four bedroom detached houses likely to be used by the so-called professional classes; three bedroom houses for the traditional "artisan" class; social housing; bungalows or apartments suitable for the elderly. Given such a policy, my claim is that the educational problems in many of the worst schools would gradually be eased. There would still be an element of injustice, because the state system can never adequately compensate for poor parenting, but at least there would be a realistic chance of every child attending a school in which they could discover the joys of learning.

Unit 6 Educator & Educational Thoughts
教育家与教育思想

Text A Disciples of Confucius

导读：孔子是我国古代伟大的思想家和教育家，儒家学派创始人，世界最著名的文化名人之一。孔子首次提出"有教无类"，认为世界上一切人都享有受教育的权利。他认为教师在教书育人的过程中应该"诲人不倦"，"循循善诱"，"因材施教"；认为学生应该有好的学习方法如"举一反三""温故而知新"；学习还要结合思考"学而不思则罔，思而不学则殆"；好学"三人行必有我师"；学习态度要端正。孔子的教育思想，至今仍然有重要的启发和教育意义。

Confucius' teachings were later turned into an elaborate set of rules and practices by his numerous disciples and followers who organized his teachings into the Analects. Confucius' disciples and his only grandson, Zisi, continued his philosophical school after his death. These efforts spread Confucian ideals to students who then became officials in many of the royal courts in China, thereby giving Confucianism the first wide-scale test of its dogma.

Two of Confucius' most famous later followers emphasized radically different aspects of his teachings. In the centuries after his death, Mencius and Xunzi (荀子) both composed important teachings elaborating in different ways on the fundamental ideas associated with Confucius. Mencius articulated the innate goodness in human beings as a source of the ethical intuitions that guide people towards rén, yì, and lǐ, while Xunzi underscored the realistic and materialistic aspects of Confucian thought, stressing that morality was inculcated in society through tradition and in individuals through training. In time, their writings, together with the

Analects and other core texts came to constitute the philosophical corpus of Confucianism.

This realignment in Confucian thought was parallel to the development of Legalism, which saw filial piety as self-interest and not a useful tool for a ruler to create an effective state. A disagreement between these two political philosophies came to a head in 223 BC when the Qin state conquered all of China. Li Ssu, Prime Minister of the Qin Dynasty convinced Qin Shi Huang to abandon the Confucius' recommendation of awarding fiefs akin to the Zhou Dynasty before them which he saw as counter to the Legalist idea of centralizing the state around the ruler. When the Confucian advisers pressed their point, Li Ssu had many Confucian scholars killed and their books burned—considered a huge blow to the philosophy and Chinese scholarship.

Under the succeeding Han Dynasty and Tang Dynasty, Confucian ideas gained even more widespread prominence. During the Song Dynasty, the scholar Zhu Xi (AD 1130-1200) added ideas from Daoism and Buddhism into Confucianism. In his life, Zhu Xi was largely ignored, but not long after his death his ideas became the new orthodox view of what Confucian texts actually meant. Modern historians view Zhu Xi as having created something rather different, and call his way of thinking Neo-Confucianism. Neo-Confucianism held sway in China, Korea, and Vietnam until the 19th century.

The works of Confucius were translated into European languages through the agency of Jesuit scholars stationed in China. Matteo Ricci started to report on the thoughts of Confucius, and father Prospero Intorcetta published the life and works of Confucius in Latin in 1687. It is thought that such works had considerable importance on European thinkers of the period, particularly among the Deists and other philosophical groups of the Enlightenment who were interested by the integration of the system of morality of Confucius into Western civilization.

In the modern era, Confucian movements, such as New Confucianism, still exist but during the Cultural Revolution, Confucianism was frequently attacked by leading figures in the Communist Party of China. This was partially a continuation of the condemnations of Confucianism by intellectuals and activists in the early 20th Century as a cause of the ethnocentric close-mindedness and refusal of the Qing Dynasty to modernize that led to the tragedies that befell China in the 19th Century. In modern times, Asteroid 7853, "Confucius", was named after the Chinese thinker.

Unit 6 Educator & Educational Thoughts 教育家与教育思想

1. **Mencius(孟子)**: also known by his birth name Meng Ke or Ko, was born in the State of Zou. He was a Chinese philosopher who was arguably the most famous Confucian after Confucius himself.

2. **Legalism(法家)**: is a Classical Chinese philosophy that emphasizes the need for order above all other human concerns.

3. **Matteo Ricci(利玛窦)**: was an Italian Jesuit priest, and one of the founding figures of the Jesuit China Mission, as it existed in the 17th-18th centuries. His current title was Servant of God.

4. **Li Ssu(李斯)**: was the influential Prime Minister of the feudal state and later of the dynasty of Qin, between 246 BC and 208 BC. A famous Legalist, he was also a notable calligrapher. Li Ssu served under two rulers: Qin Shi Huang, king of Qin and later First Emperor of China—and his son, Qin Er Shi. A powerful minister, he was central to the state's policies, including those on military conquest, draconian centralization of state control, standardization of weights, measures and the written script, and persecution of Confucianism and opponents of Legalism. His methods of administration of China are seen by some as being an early form of totalitarianism.

5. **Zhu Xi(朱熹)**: was a Song Dynasty(960-1279) Confucian scholar who became the leading figure of the School of Principle and the most influential rationalist Neo-Confucian in China. His contribution to Chinese philosophy included his assigning special significance to the Analects of Confucius, the Mencius, the Great Learning, and the Doctrine of the Mean, his emphasis on the investigation of things, and the synthesis of all fundamental Confucian.

6. **The Deists(自然神论者)**: are a partial list of people who have the belief in a God based on natural religion only, or belief in religious truths discovered by people through a process of reasoning, independent of any revelation through scripture or prophets. They have been selected for their influence on Deism, or for their fame in other areas.

New Words and Expression

1. dogma [ˈdɔgmə] n. 教条,教理;武断的意见
2. underscore [ˌʌndəˈskɔː] vt. 强调;划线于……下
3. inculcate [ˈinkʌlkeit] vt. 教育;谆谆教诲;教授;反复灌输
4. analects [ˈænəlekts] n. 文选;论集
5. filial [ˈfiljəl] adj. 孝顺的;子女的,当作子女的
6. orthodox [ˈɔːθədɔks] adj. 正统的;传统的;惯常的
7. deist [ˈdiːist] n. 自然神论者;自然神论信仰者
8. condemnation [ˌkɔndemˈneiʃən] n. 谴责;定罪;非难的理由;征用
9. ethnocentric [ˌeθnəuˈsentrik] adj. 种族优越感的;民族中心主义的
10. realignment [ˌriːəˈlainmənt] n. 重新排列;重新组合;改组

Exercises

I Choose the correct letter A, B, C, or D.

1. _____ continued his philosophical school after his death.
   A. Confucius' followers
   B. Confucius' followers and his only grandson
   C. Confucius' followers and his disciples
   D. Confucius' disciples and his only grandson

2. _____ who composed important teachings elaborating in different ways on the fundamental ideas associated with Confucius' were two of Confucius' most famous later followers.
   A. Xunzi and Zisi
   B. Xunzi and Mencius
   C. Mencius and Zisi
   D. Zisi and Zhu Xi

3. _____ convinced Qin Shi Huang to abandon the Confucians' recommendation of awarding fiefs akin.
   A. Li Ssu
   B. Zhu Xi
   C. Legalist
   D. Zisi

4. Which dynasty did not accept Confucian thought?
   A. Han Dynasty
   B. Tang Dynasty
   C. Qin Dynasty
   D. Song Dynasty

Unit 6 Educator & Educational Thoughts 教育家与教育思想

5. _____ started to report on the thoughts of Confucius, and _____ published the life and works of Confucius in Latin in 1687.

 A. Jesuit scholars; Matteo Ricci   B. Jesuit scholars; Prospero Intorcetta
 C. Prospero Intorcetta; Matteo Ricci   D. Matteo Ricci; Prospero Intorcetta

II   Vocabulary.

Fill in the blanks with the most suitable words. Change the form when necessary.

underscore	inculcate	constitute	conquer	orthodox
dogma	filial	ethnocentric	attack	articulate

1. This is an _____, arrogant attitude.
2. The numbers _____ a trend that has occurred in previous economic downturns.
3. Her staff find her bossy and _____.
4. The _____ Thanksgiving dinner includes turkey and pumpkin pie.
5. The village had been _____ by the French air force.
6. She tries very hard to _____ traditional values into her students.
7. Now I've tried to _____ exactly what I felt to be the truth.
8. The 50 states _____ the USA.
9. Ching Ming Festival is a way that Chinese show _____ piety.
10. The Normans _____ England in 1066.

III   Read the text and answer the following questions.

1. What did Xunzi stress according to Confucian thought?
2. What did Li Ssu do to abandon Confucian thought?
3. Whose thought called Neo-Confucianism was famous in China, Korea and Vietnam?
4. How was Confucian thought spread to Europe?
5. What is the main idea of this passage?

Text B   Educational Thought and Teaching

导读： 教育思想是指人们对人类特有的教育活动现象的一种理解和认识，这种理解和认识常常以某种方式加以组织并表达出来，其主旨是对教育实践产生影响。教育思想具有实践性、多样性、历史性、社会性、继承性、可借鉴性、预见性和前瞻性的特征。教育思想有助于人们理智地把握教育现实，使人们依据一定的教育思想从事教育实践；有助于人们认清教育工作中的成绩和弊端，使教育工作更有起色；有助于人们合理地预测未来，勾画教育发展的蓝图。

　　The oriental world contains the two oldest and if they could be juxtaposed the two basic theories of education. In Indian philosophies we find strong elements of other earthly concentration and contemplation of Heaven. In the teachings of Chinese philosophies there appears an equally strong theme of preparation for life of activity on Earth. Every subsequent theory embodies in some measure man's explorations in these two directions.

　　The teachings emanating from India were and are a majestic illustration of a whole range of oriental philosophies which regard education as a means through which men can prepare themselves for life, or for the life of the spirit. One of the central heaven-centered conceptions of this education is dharma or duty, the capacity to uphold and support the eternal laws within and without one. Human desires, the quest for satisfaction of material needs, the thirst for fulfillment of the senses, these are the obstacles with which men must contend in their search for eternity. In extreme forms of reflection only the relinquishment of mortal wants can ensure repose and happiness and ultimately salvation. Education thus is a process of inculcating self discipline, so that the mind and the body can be freed from concern for life. To this heavenward aim, other aims are subordinated. Inward-directedness, self-introspection, and contemplation are the ends of schooling.

　　The teaching coming from China stressed the opposite tradition in education. At its center lie the wholehearted dedication to life and the proprieties of daily living. Men like Confucius do not reject the heritage of divine revelation and the supernatural derivation of the moral order. On the contrary they have often busied themselves with the salvaging and re-edition of sacred Chinese scriptures. But for the Chinese, Heaven is a given quantity, a heritage to be accepted piously and without question. The more immediate concern of man is life. "While you don't know about life, what can you know about death." For Confucius and his future countless followers, the class of Chinese literati, who through his precepts became the class of officials in China, the virtuous life, decorum in mores and manners, service and responsibility toward others, were the canons of the system. Education was to be completely dedicated to these canons. It thus became a means to inculcate good precepts, and a way to pass on ancient wisdom. Teaching by example, by immersing oneself in the cultural heritage of the age became the model of good living and good pedagogy.

Both the heaven-centered and the earth-centered teachings resulted in practice in systems of formal education in which children were forced to memorize ancient writings by repetition by rote, while older students apprenticed or clustered informally around their teachers. Oriental education allowed much room for mystic or intellectualized approach to living. More practical preparation was less conspicuous or imparted on a family basis. This may be the reason why in the nineteenth and twentieth century the education of Asians was affected by the more practical Western theories, with British type of education in India, French and Dutch intellectual influences on Indonesia, former Soviet influences on China and UNESCO's fundamental education in all underdeveloped regions.

Western educational practices owe a great deal to Plato and Aristotle. The teachings of these two philosophers are best known parts of development of Greek thought and practice in education. The early Greek cosmologists were concerned with the nature of existence and with man's relationship to the universe. On the other hand, concern with the cosmos did not prevent the Greeks from developing a scientific philosophy which arose alongside with the rationalistic conception of man as the center of knowledge. The Greek philosophy recognized that the aim of education is to sensitize man both to the infinity, and to the business of social life on earth. The model to which all educational processes were destined to lead was "man beautiful and virtuous". Greek education remained for all times a model of activity of man as an idealistic and thinking, but also rational and political being adjusting himself through reason to social and spiritual levels of life. Plato and Aristotle left provocative social proposals in Republic and Politics respectively, but they also pointed the way to eternal verities, the logos.

Greek thought had a significant impact upon Rome. One of the several outstanding Roman thinkers, Quintilian concentrated on elaborating a system of education based on oratory as a means to restore the moral virtues. Quintilian emphasized both moral values and "actual practice and experience of life" a natural interest in a nation whose claim to fame lay not only in the powers of intellectual concentration but also in military prowess and administrative skill. Part of Quintilian's tragedy was that he advocated eloquence and republican virtue at the time when it could no longer serve public good, but it could only be used by careerists and sycophants around the imperial throne. His precise pedagogical devices were thus deprived of the vigorous goals, in the service of which they could have been used in an earlier age.

With Aquinas the dichotomy between earth-centered and heaven-centered education loses its overwhelming significance. Several later heaven-centered and mystic schools such as the pietists of Hermann Francke continued to flourish. Several educational theories retain a spiritual and idealistic dimension. But in the broadest sense man surrenders his curiosity and quest of the unknown to the overriding certainty that life on earth must be seriously cultivated.

1. **UNESCO(United Nations Educational, Scientific, and Cultural Organization)** (联合国教科文组织): is a specialized agency of the United Nations established on 16 November 1945. Its stated purpose is to contribute to peace and security by promoting international collaboration through education, science, and culture in order to further universal respect for justice, the rule of law, and the human rights along with fundamental freedoms proclaimed in the UN Charter. It is the heir of the League of Nations' International Commission on Intellectual Cooperation.

2. **Plato**(柏拉图): was a classical Greek philosopher, mathematician, student of Socrates, writer of philosophical dialogues, and founder of the Academy in Athens, the first institution of higher learning in the Western world. Along with his mentor, Socrates, and his student, Aristotle, Plato helped to lay the foundations of Western philosophy and science.

3. **Aristotle**(亚里士多德): was a Greek philosopher, a student of Plato and teacher of Alexander the Great. His writings cover many subjects, including physics, metaphysics, poetry, theater, music, logic, rhetoric, linguistics, politics, government, ethics, biology, and zoology. Together with Plato and Socrates, Aristotle is one of the most important founding figures in Western philosophy. Aristotle's writings were the first to create a comprehensive system of Western philosophy, encompassing morality and aesthetics, logic and science, politics and metaphysics.

4. **Thomas Aquinas**(托马斯·阿奎纳): was an Italian Dominican priest of the Catholic Church, and an immensely influential philosopher and theologian in the tradition of

Unit 6   Educator & Educational Thoughts   教育家与教育思想

scholasticism, known as Doctor Angelicus, Doctor Communis, or Doctor Universalis. He was the foremost classical proponent of natural theology, and the father of Thomism. His influence on Western thought is considerable, and much of modern philosophy was conceived as a reaction against, or as an agreement with his ideas, particularly in the areas of ethics, natural law and political theory.

New Words and Expression

1. juxtapose [ˌdʒʌkstəˈpəuz]	vt.	并列;并置
2. emanate from	v.	发源于;出自;放射
3. majestic [məˈdʒestik]	adj.	庄严的;宏伟的
4. dharma [ˈdɑːmə]	n.	(佛教中的)达摩(指佛的教法、佛法、一切事物和现象);(印度教的)法则
5. eternity [iˈtəːnəti]	n.	来世,来生;不朽;永世
6. decorum [diˈkɔːrəm]	n.	礼仪;礼貌;端正;恪守礼仪
7. pedagogy [ˈpedəgɔgi]	n.	教育;教育学;教授法
8. apprentice [əˈprentis]	n.	学徒;生手
	vt.	使……当学徒
	vi.	当学徒
9. cluster [ˈklʌstə]	vi.	群聚;丛生
	vt.	使聚集;聚集在某人的周围
10. conspicuous [kənˈspikjuəs]	adj.	显著的;显而易见的
11. infinity [inˈfinəti]	n.	无穷;无限大
12. provocative [prəuˈvɔkətiv]	adj.	刺激的,挑拨的;气人的
13. eloquence [ˈeləkwəns]	n.	口才;雄辩;雄辩术;修辞
14. sycophant [ˈsikəfənt]	n.	谄媚者;奉承者
15. secularism [ˈsekjulərizəm]	n.	世俗主义;现世主义;宗教与教育分离论

Exercises

I Choose the correct letter A, B, C, or D.

1. What is the meaning of "juxtapose" in the first paragraph?
   A. to give some examples
   B. to put things together
   C. to compare the things
   D. to make things different

2. What is the meaning of "illustration" in the second paragraph?
   A. the truth or example
   B. a picture
   C. an article
   D. a book

3. The teachings emanating from India regard education as _____.
   A. dharma or duty
   B. a process of inculcating self discipline
   C. the life of the spirit
   D. a means through which men can prepare themselves for life, or for the life of the spirit

4. The role of education as a process of inculcating self discipline is _____.
   A. for human desires
   B. for the life of the spirit
   C. for human duty
   D. for the mind and the body

5. What is not Heaven for the Chinese?
   A. A given quantity.
   B. An accepted heritage.
   C. A system.
   D. An unquestioned heritage.

6. Teaching by example, by immersing oneself in the cultural heritage of the age became the model of _____.
   A. good living
   B. good pedagogy
   C. good spirit
   D. good living and good pedagogy

7. Western educational practices owe a great deal to _____.
   A. Plato and Aristotle
   B. Plato and Socrates
   C. Alexander and Socrates
   D. Alexander and Aristotle

8. Which of the following statements is not true according to Greek thought?
   A. The early Greek cosmologists were concerned with the nature of existence and with man's relationship to the universe.
   B. The concern with the cosmos prevented the Greeks from developing a scientific philosophy which arose alongside with the rationalistic conception of man as the

Unit 6　Educator & Educational Thoughts　教育家与教育思想

center of knowledge.

 C. The Greek philosophy recognized that the aim of education is to sensitize man both to the infinity, and to the business of social life on earth.

 D. Greek education remained for all times a model of activity of man as an idealistic and thinking, but also rational and political being adjusting himself through reason to social and spiritual levels of life.

9. Which of the following statements is not true of Quintilian?

 A. He concentrated on elaborating a system of education based on oratory as a means to restore the moral virtues.

 B. His tragedy was that he advocated eloquence and republican virtue at the time when it could no longer serve public good, but it could only be used by careerists and sycophants around the imperial throne.

 C. He emphasized both moral values and actual practice, experience of life and a natural interest in a nation whose claim to fame lay only in the powers of intellectual concentration.

 D. His precise pedagogical devices were deprived of the vigorous goals, in the service of which they could have been used in an earlier age.

10. What is the meaning of "surrender" in the last paragraph?

 A. to stop fighting   B. to give

 C. to control   D. to give up

II　Comprehension of the text.

Decide whether the following statements are true (T) or false (F) according to the passage.

1. Human desires, the quest for satisfaction of material needs, the thirst for fulfillment of the senses, these are the obstacles with which men must contend in their search for eternity.

2. Education became a means to inculcate good precepts, and a way to pass on ancient wisdom.

3. Both the heaven-centered and the earth-centered teaching resulted in practice in systems of formal education in which children were forced to memorize by writing.

4. That more practical preparation was less conspicuous or imparted on a family basis was the reason why the education of Asia was affected.

5. The teachings of Plato and Aquinas are best known parts of development of Greek thought and practice in education.

III Translate the following sentences into Chinese.

1. Education is a process of inculcating self discipline, so that the mind and the body can be freed from concern for life.
2. Both the heaven-centered and the earth-centered teachings resulted in practice in systems of formal education in which children were forced to memorize ancient writings by repetition by rote, while older students apprenticed or clustered informally around their teachers.
3. The Greek philosophy recognized that the aim of education is to sensitize man both to the infinity, and to the business of social life on earth.
4. His precise pedagogical devices were thus deprived of the vigorous goals, in the service of which they could have been used in an earlier age.
5. In the broadest sense man surrenders his curiosity and quest of the unknown to the overriding certainty that life on earth must be seriously cultivated.

Supplementary Reading

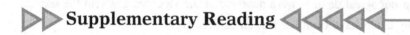

"Filling Bellies and Brains": the Educational and Political Thought of Frederick James Gould

Frederick James Gould, one of three children, was born into the impoverished lower middle-class family of an itinerant actor in Brighton on 12 December 1855. Between 1871 and 1896 he was a teacher, initially in two religious schools in Buckinghamshire, at Chenies, and then at Great Missenden, and later in two London School Board schools at Turin Street and Northey Street, in the Boroughs of Hackney and Tower Hamlets respectively. When he moved to London, in 1879, he also married. He left teaching in 1896 and moved to Leicester where he was elected to the school board in 1900. After he left Leicester in 1910 he became active in large number of educational associations and continued to write and publish on educational matters at a phenomenal rate until his death on 6 April 1938.

After his death two of his close associates, E. M. White, a lecturer on Civics, and F. H. Hayward, a one-time schools inspector, compiled a selection of his later writings under the title of *The Last Days of a Great Educationist*. His prolific output and his lifelong, tenacious and pioneering championing of moral education and educational reform probably merit this eponymous praise. However, this educational work has been badly served by historians. The period of his life that Gould spent in Leicester and his involvement in local politics there have been detailed by the separate works of Bill Lancaster and David S. Nash.

That Gould placed a very high emphasis on the power of education to change people's lives for the better must be beyond doubt. In 1891 he wrote a Utopian novel, *The Agnostic Isle*, in which the improved ordering of society was directly attributed to the education provided for the citizens. Gould placed moral education at the forefront of all his thoughts on education. He summarized the essential components of any good moral education system under four headings. These were order, beauty, service and progress, a list that barely changed during the course of his life. By order he did not mean discipline but rather the striving for an essential and natural order by the universe and all that lay therein, including human society. G. P. Gooch's introduction to one of Gould's earlier works noted that the message of the work was that service to one's fellows was "the highest glory, the crown of endeavor". The duty of a teacher was to show examples of progress in the fields of order, beauty and service, so as to inspire in the pupils the desire for yet more progress in the future. In 1899 he produced an outline syllabus to effect this overall scheme. Children, he argued, should be taught lessons based round moral themes rather than traditionally defined subjects. These new lessons would feature the concepts of self-respect and self-control, truthfulness, kindness, work and duty, mutual dependence, justice and cooperation, nature, and, lastly, art.

He advocated teaching through the use of stories that could be read to the children and which concluded with an obvious moral that Gould recommended be elicited from them. He produced 15 books of such tales during his life. The titles of the chapters in the series of four books Gould produced around the turn of the century called *Children's Moral Lessons* are indicative of this overall approach.

Gould had sketched out the broad parameters of how these lessons ought to be taught in a *Labor Prophet* article of 1893. Here he suggested that the children in socialist Sunday schools be divided into two groups, juniors and seniors, roughly on age lines, that classes begin at 3:00 p. m. with a socialist hymn and that lessons were as far as possible illustrated with pictures or, even better, magic lantern slides. Within this style of lessons Gould had very definite opinions on how his stories should be used to achieve his aims. He held out against what he called "lazy moralists", that is to say teachers who might have believed that simply presenting children with a good tale with a moral to learn at the end would ensure that the moral was adopted by its young audience. This type of activity, he argued, tended to present the children with a series of negative instructions, a list of "don'ts" and was, moreover, extremely boring. Rather than this pointlessness, Gould advocated a dramatic presentation using props and blackboard sketches to set the scene from which the truth would emerge "naturally and spontaneously".

In his 1900 publication *Moral Instruction* he laid out his general approach to methodology in the classroom, "Education must allow for more conduct and less lecturing, and the conduct must be transformed into neighborly conduct." To achieve this neighborliness he advocated exercises in four aspects of civic life. First, there was what he called "social alertness". This consisted of personal and environmental cleanliness, respect for public order, and an understanding of one's civic duties such as voting. Second, there was ordered recreation as opposed to a mere romp. Third, excursions were to be arranged to places that gave concrete examples of the organic nature of social life such as cathedrals, castles, local authority buildings, harbors, lighthouses, mines and factories. Fourth, the practice of charitable works and visits to the less fortunate was to be encouraged.

Unit 7 Educational Objective
教育目的

Text A Aims and Objectives of Education

导读：教育目的是根据一定社会的政治、经济、生产、文化科学技术发展的要求和受教育者身心发展的状况确定的。它反映了一定社会对受教育者的要求，是教育工作的出发点和最终目标，也是确定教育内容、选择教育方法、检查和评价教育效果的根据。目的不明确的教育就像一条无舵的船只。

1. Introduction

The importance of aims and objectives of education is recognized by all the educational, professional, political, nonpolitical and religious associations, organizations and groups at various levels in their memoranda, letters and brochures. It is said that education without clear cut aims is like a rudderless ship. The following comparisons emphasize this point fully well.

Every pilot has a route-chart and set timing of landing at predetermined destination. There is constitution or set of principles and traditions through which a country is governed. Similarly, there should be properly defined and declared principles, aims and objectives of education or the basis of which policies and programs of education have to be formulated to achieve the set goals without wasting scarce energies and resources in chasing the wild goose.

It is generally felt that our educational system has not followed the desired aims as a result that it does not produce ideal citizens in the country. It has followed rather a narrow aim of preparing individuals for livelihood, as mentioned in one of the documents received from an organization.

The main reason of failure of educational system is that it basically stands on pre-independence system. The main objective of its products was how to take degree and to earn money and to be careerist without consideration of ethical values and national spirit. It has also been pointed out that it is unreasonable to criticize educational system alone because it is based on the other subsystems accepted by us.

On the one hand, we are developing and cultivating the British given economy, judicial system and system of administration and parliament; and on the other, we are decrying and criticizing the education system which merely fulfils the needs of the British systems that we are propagating.

As pointed out in a memorandum of an association, "the main defect of the old Education policy is that it had completely ignored the Indian culture and the interest of the masses of India and has left them economically too backward and socially too fragmented to articulate their miseries...".

The aims and objectives of education, suggested in the documents, include individual as well as social aids, with emphasis of social transformation aiming at reconstructing society to make it modernized, productive, participative, and value oriented nation committed to its constitutional obligations.

2. Individual development

Development of an individual—physically, mentally and spiritually is well known as aim of education. Objectives related to this aim of individual development have been expressed in various ways in the memoranda:

Develop physical and mental faculties;

Acquiring the capacities of understanding, appreciation and expression through word and act is the fundamental aim of education;

Aim of education should be to make children self-confident and self-dependent, and to make them strong physically and mentally;

Education is meant to develop every child's character, personality and culture and as much knowledge as the child can assimilate instead of merely memorizing.

The best expression of complete development of an individual and the harmonious development of personality, however, is found in the following paragraph.

The policy should be directed to the aim of enlightenment of head and heart; illumination of consciousness for all-round development of individual personality. Education should enable a human being to attain the greatest possible harmony, internal and external, spiritual and material, for the fullest possible development of human potentialities and capacities.

3. Social and national development

Social aim of education is equally important because an individual lives in society and has his obligations towards his nation. There is a realization that, "The present education system does yield required results mainly because it is divorced from the real social content and social goals."

It has, therefore, been suggested that education should be able to discharge its natural functions and must correspond to its structure, goals and content in the interest of national development and social progress. It has also been suggested in this connection that students from young age should be made aware of the social responsibility cast on them.

At the same time, there are certain constitutional commitments, which are intimately related to this aim. We as the citizens of the republic, are constitutionally committed to democracy, social justice, equality of opportunity, secularism and above all to a welfare state. It has, therefore, been suggested that, "Educational policy and educational program should clearly reflect these commitments."

The objectives of developing a sense of national identity, unity and patriotism are advocated by many associations. It is pointed out that the national objectives of planning and programs and development with special emphasis on popular participation and the national problems that we face in different fields should be taught at relevant stages.

Individual and social aims of education are not contrary to one another. In fact they are complementary to one another. The following view strikes a balance between individual and social aims of education.

The purpose of education should be the development of the fullest possible capacities and potentialities physical and spiritual of a "total man". It should make a man capable of earning his livelihood reasonably well to enjoy a happy and secure life while making effective contributions to the society and national effort of making India strongly advanced and prosperous.

4. Social transformation

Education should not merely equip an individual to adjust with society to its customs and conventions, but it should enable him to bring desirable changes in the society. It has been, therefore, suggested that, "Every educational institution from secondary school to university college should be developed to become an agency of change..."

However, it is essential that we should be quite clear about the purpose of change. It is, therefore, natural to ask the question, "Reform and change to achieve what? What type of society we aim at and what type of citizens we wish to produce?" The following ideas give an indication of the kind of changes education is expected to bring about.

4.1　Modernization

Modernization of society in terms of scientific and technological advancement is a view which seems to be quite popular. It is thought that education should enable us to move with times and attain excellence in science and technology.

Scientific and technological advances are gaining momentum and conscious efforts are made to incorporate them into the development sectors. This calls for modernization of education in order to make it in conformity with the modern times and to keep pace with the advances in the world.

Modernization, however, is not interpreted and equated with westernization. In fact, lot of emphasis is given to "Indianness" while talking about modernization. One of the suggestions explicitly points out that, our education should integrate and unite the people of India, modernize society while preserving what is authentically Indian in our cultural and spiritual heritage.

The following suggestion beautifully reconciles the twin objectives of modern technical sophistication and the ancient spirituality.

"New education policy of India should be built on the foundation of ancient spirituality and modern culture and technical sophistication. It should develop scientific temper and spirit of enquiry in the students."

4.2　Productivity

Some documents have insisted on linking education with productivity and thus making individuals as productive citizens to build a productive society. One of the suggestions, in a memorandum, for example, says, "It should bring about a social transformation, and enhance greater efficiency and productivity in all sectors: agriculture, industry and service." It is in this context that Mahatma Gandhi's system of basic education is still considered as a basically sound system and a suggestion has been made that with necessary modification elements of basic education may form part of education not only at the primary stage but at all stages in our national system of education. These elements are:

Productive activity in education;

Correlation of the curriculum with productive activity and physical and social environment;

    Intimate contact between the school and the local community.

  4.3 Community participation

In a democracy education without community participation is barren. This aim of education is, therefore, voiced by a number of groups and organizations. The change that is envisaged on this front is that of integrating education with community in all respects. To quote a suggestion in this regard:

The education system in all its branches and sectors should get itself involved in activities related to problems of local community life and shall thus endeavor through the desirable community participation community involvement in the educational field to bring all education of its rightful place in community life.

5. Acquisition of values

Moral, cultural and spiritual values in education have been given immense importance in the Memoranda documents. One of the expressions emphatically point out that, "certain basic values as respect for others, responsibility, solidarity, creativity and integrity must be fostered in our children."

It is interesting that a number of specific values have been suggested in the documents. The values which are considered important are mentioned below:

Emphasis should be given in cultivating good qualities like cooperation, good will, forgiveness, tolerance, honesty, patience etc. in order to encourage universal brotherhood and to prepare students worthy citizens of the country;

Values of optimism and secularism, and service to the poor should be stressed on the young minds.

6. Summing up

It is worth reproducing what a document mentions about the aims of education.

The aim of education is two-fold: development of the individual in society; and consequent development of the society. The aim of education in relation to individual may be spelt out as follows:

To produce full human personality with courage, conviction, vitality, sensitivity and intelligence so that men and women may live in harmony with the universe;

To bring out the fullest potential of child and prepare him for life and its varied situations so that he becomes a cultured and responsible citizen dedicated in the service of community.

In relation to the society, the aim of education is to create:

A sane and learning society where material production will be such that no section of the society remains unemployed. In the Indian context such production will be necessarily based on a decentralized economy utilizing all available manpower;

A society where the conditions of work and general environment will offer psychic satisfactions and effective motivations to its members;

A society reconciling technological and scientific advancement with general well-being and security of its members, enhancing joy of life and eliminating all forms of exploitation.

The broad objective of education should, therefore, be to look beyond the existing society and to develop men and women amenable to the advent of a sane and healthier society of tomorrow.

While summing up, it may be pointed out that various dimensions of individual and social development, social transformation, value acquisition etc. have been well identified in the memoranda documents. The following words briefly summarize the various dimensions which are considered important indeed for marching into the 21st century: We are of the opinion that Indian education should aim at producing men and women of knowledge, character and cultural values and trained skills to achieve excellence in their career and life. Let us make it clear that we wish to prepare youth to march into the 21st century on the ideals of truth and non-violence as shown to us by our great leaders.

1. **Memorandum(备忘录)**: A memorandum or memo is a document or other communication that helps the memory by recording events or observations on a topic, such as may be used in a business office. The plural form is either memoranda or memorandums.

2. **Ethical Value(伦理价值)**: In ethics, value is a property of objects, including physical objects as well as abstract objects(e.g. actions), representing their degree of importance. Ethic value denotes something's degree of importance, with the aim of determining what action or life is best to do or live, or at least attempt to describe the value of different actions. It may be described as treating actions themselves as abstract objects, putting value to them. It deals with right conduct and good life, in the sense that a highly, or at least relatively highly, valuable action may be regarded as ethically "good" (adjective sense),

Unit 7 Educational Objective 教育目的

and an action of low, or at least relatively low, value may be regarded as "bad".

3. **Judicial System (司法制度)**: Judicial system is the system of courts that interprets and applies the law in the name of the state. It also provides a mechanism for the resolution of disputes. Under the doctrine of the separation of powers, it generally does not make law (that is, in a plenary fashion, which is the responsibility of the legislature) or enforce law (which is the responsibility of the executive), but rather interprets law and applies it to the facts of each case.

4. **Social Transformation (社会转变)**: One definition of social transformation is the process by which an individual alters the socially ascribed social status of their parents into a socially achieved status for themselves. However, another definition refers to large scale social change as in cultural reforms or transformations. The first occurs with the individual, the second with the social system.

5. **Modernization (现代化)**: In the social sciences, modernization refers to a model of an evolutionary transition from a "pre-modern" or "traditional" to a "modern" society. The teleology of modernization is described in social evolutionism theories, existing as a template that has been generally followed by societies that have achieved modernity.

New Words and Expression

1. objective [əb'dʒektiv]　　adj.　客观的;目标的;宾格的
　　　　　　　　　　　　　　n.　目的;目标
2. association [əˌsəusi'eiʃən]　n.　协会,联盟,社团;联合;联想
3. rudderless ['rʌdəlis]　　　adj.　无舵的;无指导者的
4. chase [tʃeis]　　　　　　　vt.　追逐;追捕;试图赢得
　　　　　　　　　　　　　　vi.　追逐;追赶;奔跑
5. propagate ['prɔpəgeit]　　vt.　传播;传送;繁殖;宣传
　　　　　　　　　　　　　　vi.　繁殖;增殖
6. fragment ['frægmənt]　　n.　碎片;片断或不完整部分
　　　　　　　　　　　　　　vt.　使成碎片
　　　　　　　　　　　　　　vi.　破碎或裂开

7. assimilate [əˈsimileit]   vt.   吸收;使同化;把……比作;使相似
   vi.   吸收;同化
8. enlightenment [inˈlaitənmənt]   n.   启迪;启蒙运动;教化
9. external [ikˈstəːnəl]   adj.   外部的;表面的;[药]外用的;外国的;外面的
10. discharge [disˈtʃɑːdʒ]   vt.   解雇;卸下;放出;免除
    vi.   排放;卸货;流出
    n.   排放;卸货;解雇
11. intimately [ˈintimitli]   adv.   熟悉地;亲切地;私下地
12. patriotism [ˈpætriətizəm]   n.   爱国主义;爱国心,爱国精神
13. relevant [ˈreləvənt]   adj.   有关的;中肯的;有重大作用的
14. prosperous [ˈprɔspərəs]   adj.   繁荣的;兴旺的
15. convention [kənˈvenʃən]   n.   大会;[法]惯例;[计]约定;[法]协定;习俗
16. desirable [diˈzaiərəbl]   adj.   令人满意的;值得要的
    n.   合意的人或事物
17. essential [iˈsenʃəl]   adj.   基本的;必要的;本质的
    n.   本质;要素;要点;必需品
18. indication [ˌindiˈkeiʃən]   n.   指示,指出;迹象;象征
19. incorporate [inˈkɔːpəreit]   vt.   包含,吸收;体现;把……合并
    vi.   合并;混合;组成公司
    adj.   合并的;一体化的;组成公司的
20. equate [iˈkweit]   vt.   使相等;视为平等
    vi.   等同
21. heritage [ˈheritidʒ]   n.   遗产;传统;继承物;继承权
22. sophistication [səˌfistiˈkeiʃən]   n.   复杂;诡辩;老于世故;有教养
23. barren [ˈbærən]   adj.   贫瘠的;不生育的;无益的;沉闷无趣的;空洞的
    n.   荒地
24. envisage [inˈvizidʒ]   vt.   正视,面对;想象
25. acquisition [ˌækwiˈziʃən]   n.   获得物,获得
26. sane [sein]   adj.   健全的;理智的;[临床]神志正常的
27. decentralized [ˌdiːˈsentrəlaizd]   adj.   分散的;分散化,分散式;分散管理的;去中心化

Unit 7 Educational Objective 教育目的

28. reconcile ['rekənsail]　　vt.　使一致;使和解;调停,调解;使顺从
29. amenable [ə'mi:nəbl]　　adj.　有责任的,应服从的;有义务的;经得起检验的
30. dimension [di'menʃən]　　n.　[数]维;尺寸;次元;容积
　　　　　　　　　　　　　　vt.　标出尺寸
　　　　　　　　　　　　　　adj.　规格的

I　Vocabulary.

Match the word in Column A to the correct definition in Column B.

Column A	
1. objective	2. relevant
3. convention	4. reconcile
5. in a close manner	

Column B
A. having a bearing on or connection with the subject at issue
B. be attained
C. way of approaching sb./sth.
D. something regarded as a normative example
E. bring into consonance or accord

II　Comprehension of the text.

Decide whether the following statements are true (T) or false (F) according to the passage.

1. Our educational system has followed the desired aims and it produces ideal citizens in the country.
2. The aims and objectives of education, suggested in the documents, include individual

as well as social aids.

3. Individual and social aims of education are contrary to one another and are complementary to one another.
4. Education should not merely equip an individual to adjust with society to its customs and conventions, but it should enable him to bring desirable changes in the society.
5. Modernization is actually interpreted and equated with westernization.

III Try to fill in the spaces with the suitable words.

1. The main reason for failure of educational system is that it basically stands on _____.
2. Acquiring the capacities of understanding, appreciation and _____ is the fundamental aim of education.
3. The present education system does yield required results mainly because it is divorced from the real _____.
4. Values of _____, and service to the poor should be stressed on the young minds.
5. The aim of education is two-fold: development of _____ and consequent development of _____.

Text B Education, Basics of Education and Educational Objectives

导读：教育是培养新生一代准备从事社会生活的整个过程，也是人类社会生产经验得以继承发扬的关键环节。20世纪50年代，布卢姆等人提出将教学活动所要实现的整体目标分为三大领域——认知领域、情感领域和动作技能领域。他们的教育目标分类强调指导教学过程和对结果进行评价，其实是一种教学目标分类。

Definition of education

Education can be defined as a continuous process that aims at bringing about desirable changes in the behaviour of learners on a relatively permanent basis and which are evident by way of acquisition of knowledge, proficiency of skills and development of values.

History of taxonomy of educational objectives

For a long time, organised educational system is facing difficulties with student evaluation. A group of educational psychologists took up the challenge of infusing transparency in teaching and evaluation. Thus, at the convention of American Psychological Association in 1948, a group of teachers decided to adapt

the model of taxonomy used in biology for educational practices. They described this classification Taxonomy of Educational Objectives. This informal group consisted of Benjamin Bloom, Max D. Englehart, Edward J. Furst, Walker H. Hill, David Krathwohl and Bertran B. Masic among others.

Their findings were published in the book—*Taxonomy of Educational Objectives: The Classification of Educational Goals, handbook 1: Cognitive Domain* in the year 1956. This group of psychologists identified that most of educational objectives can be grouped under three headings—cognitive, affective and psychomotor. The cognitive domain, according to this book includes such educational objectives as dealing with recall or recognition of knowledge and development of intellectual abilities and skills. The educational objectives in affective domain are concerned with "changes in the interest, attitudes and values, and the development of appreciations and adequate adjustments". The educational objectives belonging to psychomotor domain refer to "the manipulative or motor skill area".

Further, this book explained the various levels of cognitive domain. The hierarchy of objectives in affective domain was explained in *Taxonomy of Educational Objectives: The Classification of Educational Goals, Handbook 2: Affective Domain* that was published in the year 1964.

This group did not explore the hierarchy of educational objectives in psychomotor domain. Many others attempted to develop this hierarchy and in the year 1972, Elizabeth Simpson presented the levels of objectives in psychomotor domain. The taxonomy marked an important milestone in the field of higher education. Since learners in higher education are adults, and seek reasons and purpose for their learning, educational objectives and their hierarchy provide a useful benchmark.

Aims and objectives

Definition of aim

Aim can be defined as a broad statement of educational activity, e.g., to understand disease. It describes what one intends to achieve at the end of an educational activity.

Definition of objective

Objective is a precise point in the direction of aim, e.g. identifying uncommon symptoms. It can be defined as a statement of intent in an educational context. Other terms that are synonymous with educational objective are—teaching objectives, learning objectives, intended learning objectives, enabling objectives, instructional objectives, curriculum objectives, terminal objectives, operational objectives, performance objectives, outcomes, competencies, etc. Of these, the terms performance objectives and competencies refer more specifically to objectives in psychomotor domain.

Educational objective can be defined as a statement of intent in an educational context, which is demonstrable and measurable on predetermined parameters. Thus, educational objective is a statement that clarifies the complete range of activity and expected performance outcomes.

Functions of objectives

Purpose for teaching
- Direction to teaching
- Teaching made easy
- Structure for teaching

The sequencing of objectives not only makes it easy to teach, but also provides a comprehensive structure to teaching.

- Layers of educational objectives—core, intermediate, peripheral

Educational objectives determine learning contents. Because educational objectives determine what has to be learnt, it becomes necessary to know how much has to be taught/learnt. This classification of learning is made under three headings—must know, desirable to know and nice to know. This classification is equally applicable to each of the three domains of learning. The "must know" segment consists of educational objectives that represent the core competences of the discipline. The learner must acquire the knowledge, skill and attitude listed in this category, if he/she has to be certified as competent/successful. These comprise of 70% of the total statements of educational objectives in the discipline. The other category is "desirable to know", which constitutes 20% of educational objectives. This includes statements, which are not core competences, but something beyond it. These objectives complement the core competences and may become core objectives in higher levels of learning. "Nice to know" consists of objectives that are of "general knowledge" interest. The significance of must know category is to ensure that the student passing out with a health sciences degree must have the basic and necessary competences to practice and provide health services competently and comprehensively. The purpose of including desirable and nice to know components is to differentiate the exceptional learner from the average ones for awarding grades in certifying exams.

· Levels of educational objectives—institutional, departmental and specific learning

Educational objectives can also be classified at three different levels. The statements in this classification are more in the form of goals than objectives, as explained earlier to differentiate goal/aim and objectives.

The most broad and general form of goals are said to be institutional or course goals. These list the competences that a graduate has to acquire at the end of the course of study. These are mainly drawn from the national health policy and the strengths of the health sciences discipline for which the course is being prepared. While listing these goals, not only the current health needs, but also the future needs of the community have to be kept in mind, so that the course does not become obsolete or lose its relevance to society.

Departmental goals refer to the statements made for the subject/department in the context of the course. For example, anatomy is taught for various health science disciplines like medicine/dentistry, nursing, physiotherapy, etc. But the teaching of anatomy in each of these disciplines is determined by the course goals. There are situations, where goals of two or more departments within a course may overlap or complement each other. For example, the departments of Community Medicine and Paediatrics may share the goal for immunisation. Or the departments of Community Medicine and OBG may share the goals for Family Planning. Speaking of the homeopathic course, the departments of Community Medicine and Homeopathic Philosophy may share the goals of prevention of epidemics. The statements, which express these shared goals, are known as interdepartmental goals. These are at the same level as departmental goals.

Specific learning goals are same as instructional objectives. These are the specific statements, which are written for each departmental goal. These explain the precise and specific performance that is expected of the learner in the department at the end of a specified educational activity.

SLOs or Educational Objectives as they are more conventionally known are explained in three different domains—cognitive, affective and psychomotor. The significance of knowing domains of learning is the possibility to plan the educational activity in an accountable manner. Such a planned educational activity provides space to think, understand and justify teaching/learning. In the absence of planning, the entire exercise may become vague, opinion-based and dogmatic. As the saying goes, "If you fail to plan, you plan to fail."

Domains of education

Educational activity is broadly classified into three domains—cognitive, affective or psychomotor, depending on the type of intended learning objectives—whether it is acquisition of knowledge, development of attitude or proficiency of skill.

- Cognitive domain is about learning the behaviours that involve thinking, understanding or explaining. It ranges from simple recalling of facts to implementation and justification of ideas and concepts.
- Affective domain includes the learning behaviour that involves demonstration of feelings/values towards facts or concepts. It ranges from receptivity for people or events to automated empathy for them.
- Psychomotor domain includes all the skill-based performances like eye-hand / foot coordination.

Characteristics of educational objectives

Relevant—It is already noted that while stating educational objectives we have to keep in mind the national health needs. Any effort made towards realising such health needs adds relevance. It can therefore be said that relevance of educational objectives depends on the extent to which these statements conform to the national health needs. Relevance of educational objectives is a three tier process—first determine course goals, second the departmental ones and finally the specific learning goals. Thus, educational objectives that are written can be said to be relevant.

Valid—It is the degree to which the statement conforms to the domain to which it belongs.

Clear—The words must be precise and sentences clear. The idea is that message has to reach "clear and correct". There should be no room for confusion, misinterpretation or vagueness. The major ingredient of any educational objectives statement is an active verb. The entire statement revolves around explanation for the verb, which must be clear and unambiguous.

Feasible—The statement has to tell what is possible to do, both in terms of human capacity and resources/infrastructure available.

Observable—The very definition of learning is change in learner behaviour. Thus, to know whether learning has taken place, it is necessary to observe the changes that have taken place. Therefore, educational objectives have to be stated in terms that are observable.

Measurable—Measurability does not mean that learning has always to be quantitative. But to know whether learning has taken place, one has to measure the extent of change. Learning a skill could be qualitative, but the time taken to perform the skill before and after a learning session could be used as a benchmark to measure qualitative change.

Elements of educational objectives

Act—What the learner will be able "to do" at the end of a learning session. This could be in any of the three domains. Depending on the domain, the appropriate verb has to be identified to state the act.

Content—It is the performance that learner is expected to demonstrate.

Condition—The conditions under which the performance is done. It includes the enabling and restraining factors. It also denotes the range of manoeuvrability.

Act, Content and Condition together constitute the Task.

Criterion—This is the degree of freedom allowed for performance.

1. American Psychological Association(美国心理学协会): The American Psychological Association (abbreviated APA) is the largest scientific and professional organization of psychologists in the United States. It is the world's largest association of psychologists with around 150,000 members including scientists, educators, clinicians, consultants and students. The APA has an annual budget of around $115m.

2. Elizabeth Simpson(伊丽莎白·辛普森): Elizabeth Inchbald(née Simpson)(1753 – 1821) was an English novelist, actress, and dramatist.

3. OBG(牛津商业集团): Oxford Business Group

4. SLO(学生学习成果): Student Learning Outcome

New Words and Expression

1. proficiency [prəu'fiʃənsi]   n. 精通,熟练
2. taxonomy ['tæk'sɔnəmi]   n. 分类学;分类法
3. psychologist [psai'kɔlədʒist]   n. 心理学家,心理学者
4. transparency [træns'pærənsi]   n. 透明,透明度;幻灯片;有图案的玻璃
5. cognitive ['kɔgnitiv]   adj. 认知的,认识的
6. psychomotor [ˌpsaikə'məutə]   adj. 精神运动的
7. domain [dəu'mein]   n. 领域,域名;产业;地产
8. adequate ['ædikwit]   adj. 充足的;适当的;胜任的
9. hierarchy ['haiəˌrɑːki]   n. 层级;等级制度
10. milestone ['mailstəun]   n. 里程碑,划时代的事件
11. symptom ['simptəm]   n. [临床] 症状;征兆
12. synonymous [si'nɔniməs]   adj. 同义的,同义词的;同义突变的
13. parameter [pə'ræmitə]   n. 参数;系数;参量
14. peripheral [pə'rifərəl]   adj. 外围的;次要的
15. segment ['segmənt]   vi. 分割
    n. 段;部分
    vt. 分割
16. competence ['kɔmpitəns]   n. 能力,胜任;权限;作证能力;足以过舒适生活的收入
17. obsolete ['ɔbsəliːt]   adj. 废弃的;老式的
    n. 废词;陈腐的人
    vt. 淘汰;废弃
18. anatomy [ə'nætəmi]   n. 解剖;解剖学;剖析;骨骼
19. physiotherapy [ˌfiziəu'θerəpi]   n. 物理疗法
20. overlap [ˌəuvə'læp]   n. 重叠;重复
    vi. 部分重叠;部分的同时发生
    vt. 与……重叠;与……同时发生
21. immunization [ˌimjuːnai'zeiʃən]   n. 免疫
22. homeopathic [ˌhəumiə'pæθik]   adj. 顺势疗法的;同种疗法的
23. vague [veig]   adj. 模糊的;含糊的;不明确的;暧昧的
24. empathy ['empəθi]   n. 神入;移情作用
25. tier [tiə]   n. 层,排;行,列;等级
    vt. 使层叠
    vi. 成递升排列

Unit 7　Educational Objective　教育目的

26. misinterpretation [ˈmisinˌtəːpriˈteiʃən]　n.　误解；误释
27. unambiguous [ˌʌnæmˈbigjuəs]　adj.　不含糊的；清楚的；明白的
28. quantitative [ˈkwɔntitətiv]　adj.　定量的；量的，数量的
29. benchmark [ˈbentʃmɑːk]　n.　基准；标准检查程序
　　　　　　　　　　　　　　　vt.　用基准问题测试（计算机系统等）
30. manoeuvrability [məˌnuːvrəˈbiləti]　n.　机动性；可移动；操纵的灵敏性

I　Vocabulary.

Match the word in Column A to the correct definition in Column B.

Column A
1. proficiency　　　2. cognitive
3. adequate　　　　4. synonymous
5. vague

Column B
A. of or being or relating to or involving cognition
B. the quality of having great facility and competence
C. not clearly understood or expressed
D. enough to meet a purpose
E. (of words) meaning the same or nearly the same

II　Comprehension of the text.

Decide whether the following statements are true (T) or false (F) according to the passage.

1. This group explored the hierarchy of educational objectives in psychomotor domain in the year 1972.
2. Educational objectives determine learning contents.

3. The "must know" segment comprises of 60% of the total statements of educational objectives.
4. Specific learning goals are different from instructional objectives.
5. Any effort made towards realising such health needs adds relevance. It can therefore be said that relevance of educational objectives depends on the extent to which these statements conform to the national health needs.

III Try to fill in the spaces with the suitable words.

1. This group of psychologists identified that most of educational objectives can be grouped under three headings—cognitive, _____.
2. Educational objective can be defined as a statement of intent in an educational context, which is _____ on predetermined parameters.
3. _____ not only makes it easy to teach, but also provides a comprehensive structure to teaching.
4. Educational objectives can also be classified at three different levels. The most broad and general form of goals are said to be _____.
5. SLOs or _____ as they are more conventionally known are explained in three different domains—cognitive, affective and psychomotor.

Supplementary Reading

Knowing Your Learning Target

The article discusses the importance of using learning targets in education. The author suggests that learning targets help students understand what they are meant to be learning during a lesson. The impact of learning targets on helping students achieve educational goals and meet instructional objectives is addressed. Several real-life classroom examples are presented in which learning targets for lessons in subjects such as mathematics and social studies are explained to students, who then become more engaged in lessons and take a more strategic approach to lessons and classwork.

The first thing students need to learn is what they're supposed to be learning

One of Toni Taladay's students walked into Lenape Elementary School wearing a colorful tie-dyed shirt with a tiny bull's-eye shape in the lower front corner. That small design caught the eye of his classmate, who exclaimed, "Look, Joey, you're wearing a learning target!" In the Armstrong School District in southwestern Pennsylvania, learning targets are everywhere: in lesson plans, on bulletin boards, in hallways—and as this story illustrates—firmly on students' minds.

What is a shared learning target?

If you own a global positioning system (GPS), you probably can't imagine taking a trip without it. Unlike a printed map, a GPS provides up-to-the-minute information about where you are, the distance to your destination, how long until you get there, and exactly what to do when you make a wrong turn. But a GPS can't do any of that without a precise description of where you want to go.

Think of shared learning targets in the same way. They convey to students the destination for the lesson— what to learn, how deeply to learn it, and exactly how to demonstrate their new learning. In our estimation (Moss & Brookhart, 2009) and that of others (Seidle, Rimmele, & Prenzel, 2005; Stiggins, Arter, Chappuis, & Chappuis, 2009), the intention for the lesson is one of the most important things students should learn. Without a precise description of where they are headed, too many students are flying blind.

The dangers of flying blind

No matter what we decide students need to learn, not much will happen until students understand what they are supposed to learn during a lesson and set their sights on learning it. Regardless of how important the content, how engaging the activity, how formative the assessment, or how differentiated the instruction, unless all students see, recognize, and understand the learning target from the very beginning of the lesson, one factor will remain constant: The teacher will always be the only one providing the direction, focusing on getting students to meet the instructional objectives. The students, on the other hand, will focus on doing what the teacher says, rather than on learning. This flies in the face of what we know about nurturing motivated, self-regulated, and intentional learners (Zimmerman, 2001).

Students who don't know the intention of a lesson expend precious time and energy trying to figure out what their teachers expect them to learn. And many students, exhausted by the process, wonder why they should even care.

Consider the following high school lesson on Jane Eyre. The teacher begins by saying,

"Today, as you read the next chapter, carefully complete your study guide. Pay close attention to the questions about Bertha—Mr. Rochester's first wife. Questions 16 through 35 deal with lunacy and the five categories of mental illness. The next 15 questions focus on facts about Charlotte Bronte's own isolated childhood. The last 10 items ask you to define terms in the novel that we seldom use today—your dictionaries will help you define those words. All questions on Friday's test will come directly from the study guide."

What is important for students to learn in this lesson? Is it how to carefully complete a study guide, the five types of mental illness, facts about Bronte's childhood, meanings of seldom-used words, or facts about Mr. Rochester's first wife? Your guess is as good as ours.

Constructing a learning target

A shared learning target unpacks a "lesson-sized" amount of learning—the precise "chunk" of the particular content students are to master (Leahy, Lyon, Thompson, & Wiliam, 2005). It describes exactly how well we expect them to learn it and how we will ask them to demonstrate that learning. And although teachers derive them from instructional objectives, learning targets differ from instructional objectives in both design and function.

Instructional objectives are about instruction, derived from content standards, written in teacher language, and used to guide teaching during a lesson or across a series of lessons. They are not designed for students but for the teacher. A shared learning target, on the other hand, frames the lesson from the students' point of view. A shared learning target helps students grasp the lesson's purpose—why it is crucial to learn this chunk of information, on this day, and in this way.

Students can't see, recognize, and understand what they need to learn until we translate the learning intention into developmentally appropriate, student-friendly, and culturally respectful language. One way to do that is to answer the following three questions from the student's point of view:

What will I be able to do when I've finished this lesson?

What idea, topic, or subject is important for me to learn and understand so that I can do this?

How will I show that I can do this, and how well will I have to do it?

Beginning to share

When teachers in the Armstrong School District began sharing learning targets with their students, their early efforts were tentative and inconsistent. Not all teachers tried it, and some who tried did not share targets for every lesson. Some simply paraphrased instructional objectives, wrote the target statements on the board, or told students what they were going to learn at the beginning of a lesson. Yet, even their exploratory attempts became game changers. When teachers consistently shared learning targets in meaningful ways, students quickly became more capable decision makers who knew where they were headed and who shared responsibility for getting there.

At Lenape Elementary School, for example, teachers and administrators marveled at the immediate effect of shared targets and how quickly those effects multiplied. Principal Tom Dinga recalls a visit to a 1st grade classroom during the first week of sharing learning targets. The teacher, Brian Kovalovsky, led the class in discussing the learning target for the math lesson that day—to describe basic shapes and compare them to one another. When he asked his students how they would know when they hit that target, one 6-year-old replied, "I'll be able to explain the difference between a square and a rectangle."

Invigorated by the changes they were witnessing, teachers and administrators used e-mail, peer coaching, peer observations, focused walk-throughs and professional conversations to share what was working in their classrooms and buildings and supported these claims with evidence that their students were learning more and learning smarter.

Students are now more actively engaged in their lessons as full-fledged learning partners. Because they understand exactly what they are supposed to learn, students take a more strategic approach to their work. Students have the information they need to keep track of how well a strategy is working, and they can decide when and if to use that strategy again. In other words, students not only know where they are on the way to mastery, but also are aware of what it will take to get there.

The power of meaningful sharing

Learning targets have no inherent power. They enhance student learning and achievement only when educators commit to consistently and intentionally sharing them with students. Meaningful sharing requires that teachers use the learning targets with their students and students use them with one another. This level of sharing starts when teachers use student-friendly language—and sometimes model or demonstrate what they expect—to explain the learning target from the beginning of the lesson, and when they continue to share it throughout the lesson. Here are two powerful ways to do that.

Designing a strong performance of understanding

The single best way to share a learning target is to create a strong performance of understanding—a learning experience that embodies the learning target. When students complete the actions that are part of a strong performance of understanding, they and their teachers will know that they have reached the target.

When introducing the lesson, the teacher should explicitly share the learning target for the day and explain how each of the tasks that are part of the lesson will lead students toward that target. Remember the lesson on Jane Eyre? Consider this lesson introduction:

Today we will learn more about how Bronte uses her characters to explore the theme of being unwanted. Remember, a theme is an underlying meaning of the story. Yesterday, we examined Jane Eyre's life experiences as they relate to the theme of being unwanted. Today we will do the same for Adele, Mr. Rochester's ward. As you read, find examples of Adele being unwanted, unloved, uncared for, or forgotten. Then, in your learning groups, discuss your examples and your reasons for choosing them. At the end of class, use your notes to draft a short paragraph that answers the question, How does the character of Adele deepen Bronte's theme of being unwanted in the novel Jane Eyre?

Note how the teacher explains what students will learn that day and how each task explicitly connects to that target. If students perform all of these actions, they will better understand how Bronte uses her characters to explore the theme of being unwanted. The tasks clearly lead students to the target, and the students can see how each task leads them to their goal. A strong performance of understanding helps students understand what is important to learn, provides experiences that will help them learn it, and gives them a chance to observe their growing competence along the way.

Explaining the criteria for success

Success criteria are developmentally appropriate descriptions and concrete examples of what success in a lesson looks like. They are not the grades students should earn, the number of problems they must get right, or the number of times they should include something in a performance or product (for example, how many descriptive adjectives they should include in a paragraph).

"I can" statements, like those pictured on p. 67, are a great way to explain success. Another useful strategy is to ask students to examine work samples that represent various levels of quality and discuss what makes some samples better than others. Teachers can also use rubrics to define the elements of a successful performance or product and describe various performance levels for each element. An especially powerful way to do this is to have students apply a rubric's organized criteria to work samples with various levels of quality. Then ask students to explain their decisions using the language in the rubric. When students know the success criteria, they can be mindful of what success looks like as they use the rubric to guide their learning.

Empowering every student

Armstrong teachers began embedding learning targets into their lessons in October 2009. Now, almost a year and one-half later, shared learning targets guide lesson planning, formative assessment, and classroom walk-throughs. But the most impressive transformation is that of students into full learning partners. Now that students know where they are going, they are more motivated to do the work to get there.

It's just this simple. Do we want classrooms full of empowered, self-regulated, highly motivated, and intentional learners? If we do, then it is time to own up to the obstacles that educators create by withholding the very information that would empower learners. Students cannot regulate learning, use thoughtful reasoning processes, set meaningful goals, or assess the quality of their own work unless they understand what success looks like in today's lesson.

Unit 8 Teacher & Student
教师与学生

Text A The Teacher, the Student and the Classroom

导读：教师是学生在知识海洋中追随的灯塔，帮助学生明确目标，在学生遇到困难时及时地答疑解惑；而学生个人才是学习的主体，他们持有一把独一无二的钥匙，只有通过自身努力才能开启知识宝库和未来成就的大门。教师为学生铺路，学生沿着这条道路驶向目的地。然而，事情并不是这么简单。在学生成长的过程中，他们会遇到许许多多不确定因素诱使他们偏离原先的道路。因此，教师应该不断鼓励学生抵制诱惑，认清方向，奋发向前。

The talk mainly focuses on the job of a teacher in the classroom majoring on the relationship of the two. In the talk the presenter will loosely emphasize the fact that the teacher is the light which the students, living either in total darkness in some instances or in twilight, need to follow if they want to be enlightened. More so, the student is the sole holder of the key to personal glory and success in  school. The teacher paves the way and the student (already containing the fuel got from socio-economical backgrounds) moves along to the set direction. However, it has to be stated that the primary school student has many things that attract him/her off the road. Therefore, the teacher should be close enough to perpetually encourage the student to ignore the attractions and continue on his/her journey.

The road is not easy. We would acknowledge that what attracts children are small colorful details hardly noticeable to the adult eyes. Thus the onus is on the teachers to find a way to discover and then channel these attractions to the purpose of learning. The more we find how these minor details such as cartoons, games, jokes, songs, trivial chats etc. can be incorporated in our lessons with attached significance (teaching objective), the more we make the road more attractive to the student. Without this, there is nothing a student will look forward to in school.

Who then is a Good Teacher?

From the above discussion, we could state that a good teacher is an educator or facilitator who leads the learner into the untrodden paths of knowledge. In doing so, the teacher (who in this case is a leader) needs to fulfill certain conditions in relation to whom he/she is leading. The best analog for this situation is to compare a teacher to an army commander in the battlefield:

- Never leave anyone behind—a teacher must be ready to let all the students follow the lesson without any left behind. To concentrate on the fast learners on the expense of the slow coachers is unbecoming of a teacher. One must learn to strike a balance between the slow and the fast in a way that they are not boring to the fast or incomprehensible to the slow;
- Curry the weak/wounded—different lessons have different difficulties thus the teacher must be cautious of those fast or otherwise who might have special problems with the topic. It is absurd to think that clever students would always follow the teacher without problems and also that slow students would always be a step behind. To curry the weak or wounded in this case is to create equilibrium in the flow of knowledge with a concentration on these with difficulty;
- Encourage the discouraged—for one reason or the other, students tend to have their favorite subjects. If yours is not the one a particular student likes, try to find the missing link. A student might be discouraged by the absence of challenges or the level and type of difficulty. (e.g. A science-oriented student might find arts to be very way out of their track and thus might do badly and consequently be discouraged.) The teacher must, therefore, encourage the student and direct them to perceive the subject in question with a different attitude;
- Motivate the lazy—some students might find a particular subject too easy to their ability. In the long run, they tend to be lazy (or spend little time in their work, do their tasks rapidly and carefree) and eventually fall behind or start performing badly. The teacher must use other means possible to motivate them to use the required amount of concentration in the subject;
- Give hope to the hopeless—some students seem not to absorb the knowledge in particular subjects. They can't get it right. After a couple of tries, they lose all hope

and convince themselves that they can't learn that particular subject. Teachers should remember that psychology plays an equal amount of contribution towards anybody's performance and success. From this point of view, the teacher must find all viable means to give hope to the student. One way is to let the student work out simple tasks first(those his/her peers would scorn) and gradually increase the difficulty;

- Criticize less and praise often—some teachers seem to take criticizing and teasing as a hobby. Criticism, a more especially negative one, saps the criticized of all the self-confidence. The student would eventually fear or shudder when responding to even a known question. The contrary is also true: when you praise one for the effort they put in giving a wrong answer, they will confidently and zealously respond next time with greater chances of getting it right;
- Never shout but calmly chasten—a shout sends fear to the body but a calm whisper delivers wisdom to the heart. There are many ways of teaching a child but constant shouting is not one of them. The more one shouts, the more the recipient builds a wall of protection around oneself. This wall would be in form of cold shoulder, deaf ear, ignorance, etc. at the end the teacher might call the student stubborn not knowing that teachers create stubborn students (Stubborn children are not necessarily stubborn students);
- Let everyone be your favorite—it is human nature to have favorites within a given group. However, in a classroom situation, favoritism should only be tolerated in extra-curricular activities. In most cases, good students tend to win favor in the teacher's eyes. In extreme cases, those who are low achievers fall on the sidetrack and are left in darkness even where other activities are concerned. The teacher must treat all students equitably, giving total concern to the deserving;
- Never label—some teachers are in a habit of openly classifying, sub-classifying and categorizing the students. Whilst this should be done in the teacher's report book, the task goes even in the classes such that the students know, and tend to live with it, how the teacher thinks of them. Like in a marathon race, some are slow starters but that does not mean they will remain at the tail. The difference is in the instance where their trainer constantly tells them that they are slow, and if they assimilate it they might take it that any effort to win the race might be a sheer waste of energy. From the teaching experience we can concur that some slow starters sometimes finish first.

The school is the battlefield. The enemy is illiteracy. Everyone needs to have a good

Unit 8　Teacher & Student　教师与学生

start for them to survive in the race for life. If students don't have a good foundation, they are unlikely going to survive by the time they reach middle school. Thus we as teachers must be very careful with how and what we teach. We risk putting the future of the country in jeopardy. It is said, "Lack of education leads to elimination."

A good teacher is known by his/her ability to teach those who are slow or can't learn to learn and be able to apply the learned items in problem solving in their exams or real life. If you teach the able to do what they are able to without difficulties, it is hard to draw a line whether you are a good teacher or not. "A good tradesman is known by the product not by the tool." In fact, one who has the worst tool but up-to-date product is the master of them all.

Primary School Students

Building a foundation is the heaviest task, for it will determine how long a building will last. In education sense, primary school is the construction of the academic world foundation of the children. A carefree constructer(teacher) will cause the children to fall in times of rain and storm. All children(unless gifted) have the ability to benefit equally from the teacher. Thus, a strict yet captivating mode of instruction has to be used as teachers go about their teaching business. At this level, teachers must never consider students as grown-ups who know what they want from school. They should bear in mind that some children are just forced to come to school and thus the last person they would like to meet is a bully from a teacher. Others don't have a slightest clue of what is going on at this stage of life. Yet still others think school is a trick by parents to stop children from playing. Some take school as a drop in centre the community has devised to take care of children while parents are at work. To the rich children school could be an instrument poor people use to gain something, thus they see no reason to be there. The duty is for the teacher to construct a basic foundation on which all these contradicting thoughts are brought to book.

A primary school student is a child. Let's face it: The prime aim of children is "play". To be a teacher of this type of person, one must be very understanding and tolerant. In teacher training programs, there is an emphasis on teachers lowering themselves to the level of their students. It is common knowledge that we learn best when the information comes from a familiar source or one we can easily identify with.

To the primary school student:

- Play is the reason they exist—primary school age is a very delicate time for adventure and discovery. They want to explore and learn latest activities and tricks seen on TV, read in books and talk about among peers. All these collectively make up child play. A classroom deprived of these would be to the child a nightmare. All that the child would be looking forward to is break time. But if the teacher integrates these in his/her lessons, classroom would be a better place.

- Provoking/irritating others is a sport—students like making others for fun. If the teachers fall for this trap then the students would do everything to make the teacher angry. This requires a teacher to be at the same level with the students, to be able to take charge and enhance learning.

- Disobedience is a standard—there are many reasons which may lead a child to be disobedient. A forceful teacher is one of them. A teacher who wants something to be done in a given way at a given time, without considering the student's creative ability is inviting disobedience. To give room for personal creativity allows children to respect yours.

- Being directed is an offence—most children just like adults, don't like to be told what to do. Everyone wants to be seen as being able to think independently. A teacher should lead by example. The tendency of directing is: One shows the way without having to tread.

- Mischief is fun—getting in trouble is one way of being noticed so many children enjoy that. However, a teacher must encourage being noticed through hard work and other worth activities.

- Jokes are entertainment—if a teacher should encourage entertainment then the class will be interesting. An ever-serious teacher is hard to follow because no one would like to be in that state for hours.

- Being lazy is a "virtue"—in management psychology we learn that humans have an innate tendency of not wanting to do work. Therefore, instead of punishing them for their attitude, we must find ways to motivate them. The best ways to curb laziness are, therefore, through reward and motivation.

- Nothing is good enough—for most children at this age (school going age) they don't know what they want in life. They are at the breaking age of discovery and are still discovering themselves. What interests them today might not be tomorrow. What they need most is moderation. Accept them as they are while carefully giving the viable advice.

- Being underestimated is fatal—it is hard without proper assessment to determine what the children are capable of. However, to take thing for granted and make it general that they don't know ABC will be making a grave mistake. This might affect the child's perception of self. If the perception is duly negative, then the child will lose self-confidence and esteem.

Unit 8　Teacher & Student　教师与学生

We mentioned earlier that the student is the sole holder of the key to success. The question arises: How can someone who doesn't know what life is all about hold the key? The answer to the question lies in the understanding that one can never force a donkey to drink water. In the classroom situation, the teacher should win, through tricks if necessary, the confidence and interest of the students. Children, due to lack of understanding of consequences, are very good at giving deaf ears. They can even decide to "turn off" their minds from the teacher. This could be evident when they are tired or the teacher is "killing" them with boredom and the bell goes, one can see them jump and cheer while, as though planned, dashing to the door.

We should understand that while the teacher holds the key to imparting knowledge, the learner holds the key to receiving the knowledge. The teacher cannot learn on behalf of the student, thus he can never claim the key. Some teachers think they can beat, force or shout lessons into the students. The more they do it, the harder it is for the students to understand. They build numerous rules and rigorous regulations, standards and values for their classes which have little to do with teaching and learning. They use corporal punishments for academic flouting. In doing so, the relationship between the teacher and the students change to "cat and mouse". When the teacher goes away, all the students sigh.

The Classroom

If teachers are commanders and the students are soldiers, then the classroom is the battlefront. (Remember we are shooting down illiteracy not personality.) Unlike where the enemy is external, the teacher like a doctor must see the symptoms and use them to cure the infected person. The teacher must carefully scrutinize each case and find ways to help the victim. He should, however, also bear in mind that each case is unique and must be treated unequally.

Thus the classroom is a treatment area and every teacher must:

- Avoid taking in personal complaints—there is nothing sickening than a teacher who always has a personal problem and seeks sympathy from the students. In the long run the students may consider their teacher as their big baby they need to protect rather than someone they look up to for help.

- Avoid releasing frustrations on the students—we all have our sets of frustrations, but to release these to our innocent children will cause not only a bad relationship but also uncalled for tension between the teacher and the students. This causes a

blockage in learning.
- Avoid bringing in home issues—social problems, especially adult related, are not to be taken into the classroom (this we know). Most teachers, however, forget that the teacher's uniform shields them from portraying any social related problems (just as it is unbecoming of the doctor to show that he can too get sick). Though not perfect, a teacher can be well received and respected if they are blemish free.
- Avoid ignoring "simple" behavioral outbursts—the key to controlling a class lies in the way the teacher checks nonsensical behavioral attitudes. In language teaching, these attitudes include those that deal with student's verbal behavior, participation, response etc.
- Never release their anger to the students—there is no room for anger in the classroom. Consider a classroom as a dispensary; it would be absurd for a doctor to be angry at the patients. The students come to school to seek help in their world of knowledge. If they do any unbecoming thing, it is digging a pit to bury another pit if the teacher rages with anger to correct a child.
- Never tease lazy students—negative teasing which sends the child into self pity and sups confidence should be discouraged at all times. Some children don't know things not because they are dull but due to many other factors. A teacher should aim at correcting the child rather than play him or her for a fool. There are honest mistakes which must be taken seriously.
- Tell students that they will definitely fail—even to a nonstarter child, plain straightforward negative talk will send them back into their hole. However, they will be satisfied that at least people understand their situation and that even though they don't do anything about it is still okay.

However, as teachers we should expect students to come in the class with all of the above. The onus again is on the teachers not to castigate the children but to help them get over their many problems including age.

A good teacher always has good results and contributes positively to the general growth of the children and the nation as a whole. The classroom is a place for the dissemination of information and a treatment area for problems. Whether in or outside the four walls a teacher is still a teacher and must as though impelled, curry the classroom tendencies wherever they go. A student is a learner whether within or without the classroom and they address teachers as teachers even in the supermarket. This serves to mean that our classroom is not limited to the four walls but in the abstract sense to the world of teaching and learning. The students are the people that make the profession worthwhile. Without them, all that is called teaching would be useless. Thus to help them learn is the teacher's main objective and to do so with courtesy and dedication.

Verbal Behavior（言语行为）：Verbal behavior is a methodology that is based upon behavioral principles, but combines the functionality and generalization of Floortime.

New Words and Expression

1. perpetually [pə'petʃuəli]	adv.	永恒地，持久地
2. onus ['əunəs]	n.	责任，义务；负担
3. channel ['tʃænəl]	vt.	引导，开导；形成河道
	n.	通道；频道；海峡
4. trivial ['triviəl]	adj.	不重要的，琐碎的；琐细的
5. incorporate [in'kɔːpəreit]	vt.	包含，吸收；体现；把……合并
	vi.	合并；混合；组成公司
	adj.	合并的；一体化的；组成公司的
6. analog ['ænəlɔg]	n.	[自]模拟；类似物
	adj.	[自]模拟的；有长短针的
7. equilibrium [ˌiːkwi'libriəm]	n.	均衡；平静；保持平衡的能力
8. viable ['vaiəbl]	adj.	可行的；能养活的；能生育的
9. sap [sæp]	n.	[植]树液；精力，元气；活力；坑道
	vt.	使衰竭，使伤元气；挖掘以破坏基础
10. shudder ['ʃʌdə]	n.	发抖；战栗；震动
	vi.	发抖；战栗
11. zealously ['zeləsli]	adv.	热心地，积极地
12. chasten ['tʃeisən]	vt.	惩罚；磨炼；抑制
13. whilst [hwailst]	conj.	同时；时时，有时；当……的时候
14. assimilate [ə'simileit]	vt.	吸收；使同化；把……比作；使相似
	vi.	吸收；同化

15. illiteracy [iˈlitərəsi]	n.	文盲；无知
16. jeopardy [ˈdʒepədi]	n.	危险；(被告处于被判罪或受处罚的)危险境地
17. captivating [ˈkæptiveitiŋ]	adj.	迷人的；有魅力的
	v.	使……着迷(captivate 的 ing 形式)
18. provoke [prəuˈvəuk]	vt.	驱使；激怒；煽动；惹起
19. bizarre [biˈzɑː]	adj.	奇异的(指态度，容貌，款式等)
20. curb [kəːb]	n.	抑制；路边；勒马绳
	vt.	控制；勒住
21. moderation [ˌmɔdəˈreiʃən]	n.	适度；节制；温和；缓和
22. rigorous [ˈrigərəs]	adj.	严格的，严厉的；严密的；严酷的
23. corporal [ˈkɔːpərəl]	adj.	肉体的，身体的
	n.	下士
24. scrutinize [ˈskruːtinaiz]	vi.	细阅；作详细检查
	vt.	详细检查；细看
	n.	仔细或彻底检查
25. unbecoming [ˌʌnbiˈkʌmiŋ]	adj.	不适当的，不相称的；不合身的，不得体的
26. blemish [ˈblemiʃ]	n.	瑕疵；污点；缺点
	vt.	玷污；损害；弄脏
27. nonsensical [nɔnˈsensikəl]	adj.	无意义的；荒谬的
28. dispensary [disˈpensəri]	n.	药房；(学校、兵营或工厂的)诊疗所；防治站
29. castigate [ˈkæstigeit]	vt.	严惩；苛评；矫正；修订
30. courtesy [ˈkəːtisi]	n.	礼貌；好意；恩惠
	adj.	殷勤的；被承认的；出于礼节的

I Vocabulary.

Fill in the blanks with the most suitable words. Change the form when necessary.

| onus | trivial | shudder | zealously | illiteracy |
| captivating | provoke | blemish | nonsensical | courtesy |

Unit 8　Teacher & Student　教师与学生

1. The main task of our government is eliminating poverty, disease and _____.
2. It's very annoying and the most _____ business situation I have ever been involved in.
3. I still _____ when I think of that moment.
4. Who could look away from Suzanne Somers' sad but _____ efforts to turn back time?
5. The _____ is on the Government to create the necessary conditions for credible and inclusive elections.
6. Those measures sought to _____ a court challenge of the U. S. Supreme Court's 1973 Roe v.
7. Nevertheless, women of all ages still appreciate this _____.
8. A lawyer should represent a client _____ within the bounds of the law.
9. The extra security precautions are not _____ and affect most communication technology on the market.
10. That is no doubt my fault, and a great _____ in me.

II　Comprehension of the text.

Decide whether the following statements are true (T) or false (F) according to the passage.

1. What attract children are small colorful details which are also noticeable to the adult eye.
2. A teacher must be ready to let most of the students follow the lesson and can leave some students behind.
3. The school is the battlefield. The enemy is illiteracy. If students don't have a good foundation, they are still likely going to survive by the time they reach middle school.
4. Instead of punishing them for their attitude, we must find ways to motivate students. The best ways to curb laziness are, therefore, through reward and motivation.
5. We should understand that while the teacher holds the key to imparting knowledge, the learner holds the key to receiving the knowledge.

III　Try to fill in the spaces with the suitable words.

1. _____ is the sole holder of the key to personal glory and success in school.
2. The teacher should be close enough to perpetually _____ the student to ignore the attractions and continue on his/her journey.

3. From the above discussion, we could state that a good teacher is an educator or _____ who leads the learner into the untrodden paths of knowledge.
4. A student might be discouraged by _____ of challenges or the level and type of difficulty.
5. _____ is the heaviest task, for it will determine how long a building will last.

Text B Teacher-Student Attachment and Teachers' Attitudes towards Work

导读：无论是在课内还是在课外，教师都被认为是学生学习的榜样。罗丝曾经对教育者在正式或非正式场合所起到的榜样作用进行调查研究，并强调了榜样对群体的某些态度、观点和生活方式的影响；罗丝发现学生通常把教师视为与其父母同等重要的榜样。凯尔认为："不论一个教师教的是哪门学科，他都在孩子的教育过程中起到榜样的作用。教师应该为人正直，不赌博，不酗酒，不做荒淫的勾当，不与不道德的人为伍。"

Introduction

Teachers are expected to be positive role models for their students, both inside and outside the classroom. Rose(2005) has examined the role of educators as role models in formal and informal education, and stressed that role models can expose groups to specific attitudes, lifestyles and outlooks. Children often see teachers as important role models on a par with parents. According to Carr(2000), teachers, regardless of subject area, have a moral role to play in education. It is the teachers' duty to be socially acceptable by keeping themselves morally upright, refraining from gambling, abhorring drunkenness and other excesses, and avoiding immoral relations.

Referring to Sava(2001), teachers' actions could actually have some lasting negative effects on students. Unfortunately, on top of that, Kearney, Plax, Hays and Iveys(1991) reported that researchers often tend to overlook teachers as a potential source of problems in the classroom. Compared to the large body of literature that focuses on positive teacher communication behaviors, fewer studies have been done on negative teacher communication behaviors. Concurrently, educational reform tends to focus only on curricula, neglecting the importance of effective teacher-student interaction. Teacher support can be conceptualized similarly to social support in schools, which is strongly related to a student's psychological well-being (acceptance, care, encouragement and approval from others) and may improve students' self-esteem and self-evaluation. On the other hand, Bru, Boyesen, Munthe and Roland (1998) asserted that lack of teacher support would hinder students from developing a positive self-concept.

Despite all these compelling reasons to study teachers' behavior, researching negative teacher-student interactions is often considered a taboo, which can make study in this area difficult. Besides, according to Sava(2001), it is ironic to study a teacher's mistakes or faulty education when their primary aim is to be educational agents. Unfortunately, studying the characteristics of effective teachers will not give us all the elements necessary to understand teachers' misbehavior. However, it might give us a better understanding and provide a discussion frame for such problems in order to improve teacher training programs. In this paper, we examine the relationship of teacher-student attachment to teachers' attitude towards work.

Teacher-student attachment

Ainsworth and her colleagues were the first to provide empirical evidence for Bowlby's(1988) attachment theory. Using the strange situation procedure, Ainsworth and Bell classified infants into one of three categories: (1) secure, in which infants use the mother as a secure base for exploration and seek contact with her after separation; (2) anxious-ambivalent(later called "resistant"), in which infants are unable to use the mother as a secure base and are often angry and push her away upon reunion; (3) anxious-avoidant, in which infants fail to use the mother as a secure base for exploration and avoid the mother upon reunion or approach her only indirectly. More recent work presented a fourth category(disorganized-disoriented), in which infants have no predictable or effective pattern of eliciting care-giving behaviors when stressed. Each of these attachment classifications, across the lifespan, falls on a continuum of emotional regulation for managing effect, events, and relationships. This conceptualization places the anxious-avoidant style, with its overly organized strategies for controlling and minimizing affect, at one end of the continuum, and the relatively uncontrolled, poorly managed affect of anxious-resistant styles at the opposite end. Secure attachment, falling along the midpoint of the emotional continuum, reflects a balance of the two extremes of emotional regulation. Those with disorganized-disoriented attachment classifications may present a range of behaviors involving under-controlled emotional reactions such as impulsive verbal or physical aggression or over-controlled responses in which emotions are difficult to express and behavior may reflect withdrawal and difficulty handling conflict. Thus, their emotional reactions are unpredictable and typically maladaptive.

Bowlby(1988) suggests that attachment is a special emotional relationship that involves an exchange of comfort, care, and pleasure. Previous research has found that adults differ according to their own attachment style in their ability to act as a secure base for children in their care. Secure adults are typically better at realistically evaluating their own relationship histories and responding sensitively and appropriately to a child's attachment needs(Crowell & Feldman, 1988) than adults with an insecure attachment history. Pianta, Steinberg and Rollins(1995) define positive teacher-student relationships as "warm, close, communicative" and such relationships are linked to behavioral competence and better school adjustment. Teacher and student attachment has been identified as a significant influence on students' overall school and behavioral adjustment. According to Fisher and Cresswell(1999), interaction with other people (students, other teachers, and staff) is actually a major part of most teachers' school days. Therefore, it is important to study the naturalness and quality of teacher-student relationships, as it influences the quality of their relationships. According to researchers, the qualities that lead to effective teacher-student relationships are positive affection, warm attitude, tact in teaching, teacher immediacy and teacher power, teacher assertiveness and responsiveness, and low differential treatment. Lack of any of these traits may negatively influence teacher-student interaction.

According to Kennedy and Kennedy(2004), teachers with a dismissing(avoidant) attachment style may have difficulty recognizing their own lack of warmth, trust and sensitivity in their relationships with their students. These teachers may have unrealistic expectations for their students' maturity and independence, as they themselves may have learned to be overly self-reliant and distant in their own interpersonal relationships. Teachers with a dismissing status may generally respond to students by distancing themselves, demonstrating a lack of warmth and understanding. The teacher with a preoccupied(resistant) style may be intermittently attuned to students' needs and easily become involved in dealing with specific observable behaviors without addressing underlying problems. Kennedy and Kennedy(2004) furthermore reported that teachers, regardless of their attachment status, may perceive the anxious-avoidant student as passively aggressive, angry, withdrawn, and uncooperative and the anxious-resistant students as overly dependent and reactive, demanding of attention, and prone to impulsivity and acting-out behavior. The disorganized student may be viewed as aggressive, reactive, unpredictable, and difficult to manage. Because of their own relationship needs, teachers may be more accepting of students with one attachment style than students with another one(Kennedy & Kennedy, 2004). Teachers with preoccupied status, because of their own dependency needs, may be more supportive of the anxious-resistant student and rejecting of anxious-avoidant and disorganized students, bolstering the negative internal working model of relationships for these children. Teachers with a dismissing attachment style (with the need to maintain an emotional distance from others) would be expected to show less acceptance of anxious-resistant and disorganized students(who need too much help or supervision), but also fail to support avoidant children(who are reluctant to ask for assistance). Both dismissing and preoccupied teachers would be expected to work best with children secure in attachment style. The secure teacher, on the other hand, may recognize in the anxious-avoidant students' withdrawal and aloofness, the anxious-resistant students' dependency and the disorganized students' acting out behavior, the need to foster positive supportive interaction, trust, and relatedness in their relationship.

As Sava(2001) reported, the organizational climate in schools, teachers' ideologies, and their level of burnout(outcome of stress) could harm teacher-student relationships. Affected teacher-student relationships can in turn cause teacher-conflict-inducing attitudes (lack of teacher emotional support, teacher misbehavior or hostility). Sava (2001) reported that the quality of teacher-student relationships can influence students' educational and psychosomatic outcomes. Concurrently, high incidences of educational, psychological and somatic complaints are seen in students whose teachers they characterize as more hostile in their attitude towards them. Teachers who have lower morale due to school climate conditions and who are more likely to burn out tend to adopt conflict-inducing attitudes towards students, which will in turn lead to educational and psychosomatic complaints in students(Sava, 2001).

According to Abidin and Kmetz(1997), teacher-student relationships are one of the factors that influence teachers' stress, and the stresses developed by teachers are reflected in their behavior towards students. Teachers, as reported by Abidin and Kmetz(1997), have different perceptions and experienced different stress levels with regard to specific students in classroom (behaviorally challenging students and typical students). These perceptions and stress levels are linked to their classroom behaviors and may bias a teacher's behavior towards those students. In addition, teachers' behavior towards challenging students involved greater amounts of negative and neutral behaviors compared to the control students. Briefly, if teachers' stress levels increase, this will decrease their positive behavior towards the students, and the teacher will avoid contact or ignore the students. The more stress induced by the students, the less engaged the teacher will be with the students, which affects the teacher-student relationship.

Teachers' attitudes towards work

The word "attitude" is defined within the framework of social psychology as a subjective or mental preparation for action. It defines outward and visible postures and human beliefs. Attitudes determine what each individual will see, hear, think and do. They are rooted in experience and do not become automatic, routine conduct. Furthermore, "attitude" means the individual's prevailing tendency to respond favorably or unfavorably to an object (person or group of people, institutions or events). Attitudes can be positive (values) or negative (prejudices). According to Kreitner and Kinicki (2007), there are three components of attitudes: affective, cognitive and behavioral. The affective component is a feeling or an emotion one has about an object or situation. The cognitive component is the beliefs or ideas one has about an object or situation, whereas the behavioral component of attitude reflects how one intends to act or behave towards someone or something. In most situations, the three components appear concomitantly to shape teachers' classroom postures, through direct and indirect interaction between society, school and teachers. Moreover, teachers' styles and attitudes are strong context outcomes rooted in experience. They do not become automatic routine behaviors, in the sense that they are developed through very slow interactions (action and reaction), and become well-established constructs for each individual only after some time. In that sense, as noted by Carr (1990), attitudes can be modified only by each individual, when they become aware, through elements and evidence, that new postures would be better to deal with the surrounding world.

Attitudes towards work mean perceptions that affect how employees perform in their positions. In the mid-1970s, Brophy and Good (1974) reported that many educational researchers have supported the idea that teachers' attitudes and expectations can be self-fulfilling prophecies. Brophy and Good (1974) also proposed that once teachers develop a particular attitude or belief, they may begin to treat students differently in ways that help bring about the outcomes that they expect. On the other hand, according to Petty and Cacioppo (1986), attitude and behavior are defined comprehensively as individuals' general evaluations about themselves, others, other objects, events and problems. Briefly, attitudes do predict people's behavior. In order to understand teachers' attitudes and understand how attitude reflects teachers' behavior, we could examine many components of attitude in context of organizational behavior. In this study, we would like to focus on four components of attitude used to assess teachers' attitude towards work: job satisfaction, commitment, communication, and alienation.

According to Mitchell and Lason (1987), in the organizational behavior field, job satisfaction is the most important and frequently studied attitude. It reflects the extent to which people like their jobs. As expected, teachers' working conditions, assessed by their level of job satisfaction, affect teacher-student interaction. Hence, higher levels of job satisfaction improve teachers' morale, which students perceive positively.

"Commitment" is a term used to distinguish those who are "caring", "dedicated", and who "take the job seriously" from those who "put their own interests first". Commitment is an important work attitude, because committed individuals are expected to be willing to work harder to achieve their goal and remain employed. Nonetheless, according to Kelchtermans (2005), teachers do not all have the same level of commitment to their job. For some teachers, commitment is a major part of their lives, and they afford it extensive consideration and high priority. Others may perceive it differently, seeing teaching as just a job. Meanwhile, a reflexive account of research over a 20-year period with 54 primary school teachers indicated that the word "commitment" appeared in almost every interview. In a different context, Jackson, Boostrom and Hansen (1993), Goodlad (1990) and Sockett (1993) have reported the moral purposes of teachers, using words such as "courage", "integrity", "honesty", "care" and "fairness". It is easy to see how these words may be associated with commitment. The more obvious signs of commitment are enthusiasm for the job and for the people with whom one works. Individuals' commitment levels affect their performance at work. However, findings reported by Leung (1997) and Tett and Meyer (1993) on commitment outcomes, particularly turnover, absenteeism, tardiness, and work performance, are mixed, weak, or inconsistent.

Communication manifests itself in attitudes as accuracy and openness of information exchange. Effective communication is the heart of creating and maintaining an effective school. Communication that occurs within schools is crucial in shaping teachers' social reality. School excellence is directly related to what teachers think and do. Teachers' attitudes and behavior strongly rely on their perceptions about their schools.

The fourth component of attitude is alienation, meaning the extent to which staff members feel disappointed with their careers and professional development (Rafferty, 2003). On the whole, the concept of positive student-teacher interaction is multidimensional, as it involves organization, workload (difficulty), expected fairness of grading, instructor knowledge, and perceiving learning.

Teaching has been identified as a stressful profession. High stress among teachers has many negative consequences, including higher than average levels of anxiety and depression and a desire to quit the profession and to use drugs. Indeed, according to Bakewell(1988) and Kyriacou and Sutcliffe(1978), teachers' relationships with their students affect their stress levels significantly. According to Mancini et al. (1984), teachers with depersonalization(an "alteration" in the perception or experience of the self so that one feels "detached" from one's mental processes or body) will behave immorally and fail to give information to their students. These teachers tend to deny opinions and ideas from students as well as fail to interact or communicate with their students. Several studies show that teacher stress predicted negative teacher and student relationships. Significant correlations were found among teacher stress and negative relationships between teacher and student. Teacher stress arises from being unable to discipline pupils in the way they would prefer.

Referring to Day, Elliot and Kington's (2005) study, teacher commitment has been found to be a critical predictor of teachers' work performance, absenteeism, retention, burnout and turnover. Day et al. (2005) suggested that teachers remained committed to their beliefs throughout their professional life. Although their levels of engagement with particular practices were modified through various life events and activities, their commitment to their ideological positions did not diminish. However, some teachers' commitment might vary over time, because different people have different levels, and some can plateau earlier or later than others. Commitment was moderated through a range of factors; some of which were sustaining and some diminishing. Teachers were less likely to engage in particular activities or behave in particular ways at one point in time, depending on various work and life contextual factors such as school contexts, and relationships with students and colleagues. These seemed to be the major work and life factors that diminished commitment.

The relationship between job satisfaction and stress coping skills of primary school teachers has been studied extensively by Bindhu and Kumar(2007). Bindhu and Kumar's (2007) study shows a statistically significant difference in job satisfaction between male and female primary school teachers. However, in case of stress coping skills, they found no statistically significant difference. Bindhu and Kumar's (2007) study also shows a significant and positive correlation between job satisfaction and stress coping skills, which are self-reliance, pro-active attitude, adaptability and flexibility, and total stress coping skills. In brief, the ability to cope with stress can increase teachers' job satisfaction.

Role model(行为榜样): The term role model generally means any "person who serves as an example, whose behavior is emulated by others". The term first appeared in Robert K. Merton's socialization research of medical students. Merton hypothesized that individuals compare themselves with reference groups of people who occupy the social role to which the individual aspires.

New Words and Expression

1. abhor [əbˈhɔː] vt. 痛恨,憎恶
2. excesses n. 过分荒淫的行为;剩余额(excess 的复数)
3. assert [əˈsəːt] vt. 断言;主张;声称;维护;坚持
4. hinder [ˈhində] vt. vi. 成为阻碍
   vt. 阻碍;打扰
   adj. 后面的
5. compelling [kəmˈpeliŋ] adj. 引人注目的;强制的;激发兴趣的
6. ambivalent [æmˈbivələnt] adj. 矛盾的;好恶相克的
7. elicit [iˈlisit] vt. 抽出,引出;引起
8. avoidant [əˈvɔidənt] adj. 回避反应的
9. overly [ˈəuvəli] adv. 过度地;极度地
10. resistant [riˈzistənt] adj. 抵抗的,反抗的;顽固的
    n. 抵抗者
11. withdrawal [wiðˈdrɔːəl] n. 撤退,收回;提款;取消;退股
12. maladaptive [ˌmæləˈdæptiv] adj. 适应不良的;不适应的;不利于适应的
13. assertiveness [əˈsəːtivnis] n. 魄力,自信
14. responsiveness [riˈspɔnsivnis] n. 响应能力;有同情心
15. bolster [ˈbəulstə] n. 长枕;支持
    vt. 支持;支撑
16. aloofness [əˈluːfnis] n. 冷漠;高傲;超然离群
17. ideology [ˌaidiˈɔlədʒi] n. 意识形态;思想意识;观念学

18. hostility [hɔˈstiləti]		n.	敌意；战争行动
19. psychosomatic [ˈpsaikəusəuˈmætik]		adj.	身心的；身心失调的；身心治疗的
		n.	身心上有病的人
20. concurrently [kənˈkʌrəntli]		adv.	兼；同时发生地
21. hence [hens]		adv.	因此；今后
22. morale [mɔˈrɑːl]		n.	士气，斗志
23. dedicated [ˈdedikeitid]		adj.	专用的；专注的；献身的
24. reflexive [riˈfleksiv]		adj.	反身的；[物] 反射的
25. inconsistent [ˌinkənˈsistənt]		adj.	不一致的；前后矛盾的
26. manifest [ˈmænifest]		vt.	证明，表明；显示
		vi.	显示，出现
		adj.	明显的
27. alienation [ˌeiljəˈneiʃən]		n.	疏远；转让；精神错乱；[哲] 异化；[戏] 离间效果
28. depersonalization [diːˌpəːsənəlaiˈzeiʃə]		n.	[心理] 人格解体，人性之丧失
29. absenteeism [ˌæbsənˈtiːizəm]		n.	旷工；旷课；有计划的怠工；经常无故缺席
30. retention [riˈtenʃən]		n.	保留；扣留，滞留；记忆力；闭尿

I Vocabulary.

Fill in the blanks with the most suitable words. Change the form when necessary.

abhor	assert	hinder	compelling	maladaptive
assertiveness	hostility	concurrently	morale	manifest

1. Even now, I still believe the logic is _____.
2. Opposition to the war, he still thinks, explains much of the _____ to him.
3. They _____ all forms of racial discrimination.
4. "The suggestion that I've done anything to warrant criminal investigation, it is

_____ nonsense," said Muthaura.

5. _____, a serious diplomatic effort is needed to address the major anomaly of the Afghan war.

6. China's growing military reach and _____ are fuelling neighbors' uncertainty about its strategic intentions.

7. Schizophrenia—A group of disorders manifested in delusions, disturbances in language and thought, mood shifts, and _____ behaviors.

8. Its statesmen used to _____ that Germany had no independent foreign policy, only a European policy.

9. Low pay in recent years has led to low _____.

10. Officials say Williams' death could _____ the work of non-government groups in the country.

II Comprehension of the text.

Decide whether the following statements are true (T) or false (F) according to the passage.

1. Teachers are expected to be positive role models for their students only inside the classroom.

2. Ainsworth and Bell classified infants into one of three categories: ⋯ (3) anxious-avoidant, in which infants are unable to use the mother as a secure base and are often angry and push her away upon reunion.

3. Secure adults are typically better at realistically evaluating their own relationship histories and responding sensitively and appropriately to a child's attachment needs (Crowell & Feldman, 1988) than adults with an insecure attachment history.

4. Teachers with preoccupied status, because of their own dependency needs, may be more supportive of the anxious-resistant student and rejecting of anxious-avoidant and disorganized students, bolstering the negative internal working model of relationships for these children.

5. The word "attitude" is defined within the framework of social psychology as a subjective or mental preparation for action.

III Try to fill in the space with the suitable words.

1. Despite all these compelling reasons to study teachers' behavior, researching _____ is often considered a taboo, which can make study in

this area difficult.
2. Bowlby (1988) suggests that _____ is a special emotional relationship that involves an exchange of comfort, care, and pleasure.
3. Teachers with a dismissing status may generally respond to students by distancing themselves, demonstrating a lack of _____.
4. According to Abidin and Kmetz (1997), teacher-student relationships are one of the factors that influence teachers' stress, and the stresses developed by teachers are reflected in _____.
5. According to Kreitner and Kinicki (2007), there are three components of attitudes: affective, _____ and behavioral.

Supplementary Reading

New Teacher and Student Roles in the Technology-Supported Classroom

The focus of this paper is a preliminary analysis of how the roles of teachers and students in different classroom settings are altered as a result of computer-based technologies. We are particularly interested in how the capabilities of computer-based technologies can enable and constrain innovative pedagogical practices.

Powerful new capabilities of computers make it possible to access, represent, process, and communicate information in new ways. These capabilities make it possible to search and organize information, analyze data, represent ideas, simulate complex systems, and communicate with others in ways that were not practical or even possible previously. They also enable new ways of teaching and learning—new activities, new products, and new types of learning. The research literature (Means & Olson, 1997) documents a strong association between these new technology-based practices and changes in curriculum and pedagogy. For example, in many countries, the use of educational technology is part of an instructional shift toward project-based, constructivist approaches to teaching and learning within a context of school improvement or reform.

Instead of focusing solely on increasing the acquisition of facts related to specific subject areas, teams of students are engaged in solving complex, authentic problems that cross-disciplinary boundaries. Instead of dispensing knowledge, teachers set up projects, arrange for access to appropriate resources, and create the organizational structure and support that can help students succeed. This approach moves conceptions of learning beyond rote memorization of facts and procedures to learning as a process of knowledge creation. It moves education beyond the notion of a place where knowledge is imparted to one of classrooms, organizations, and societies as knowledge building communities. These are more appropriate constructs for the information society and knowledge economy of the future. Technology plays a role in this approach of providing students with tools and information that support their problem solving, communication, collaboration, and knowledge creation. It also provides teachers with new tools that can transform instructional roles, curricula, and practices. Plomp, Brummelhuis, and Rapmund (1996) define learning as a process in which four components interact: (1) the teacher, (2) the student, (3) curriculum content and goals, and (4) instructional materials and infrastructure—more specifically in our paper, the role of information and communications technology (ICT). In this paper, I will synthesize findings about changing teachers' and students' roles and classroom practices from twelve case studies in technology-enhanced classrooms across the U.S. In this paper, we will provide descriptive details of individual cases as well as analyze similarities and differences across cases.

  As in other studies, many of the innovative schools in this study used technology to support project-based or inquiry-based learning. Project-based learning was a predominant feature of the innovations in two of the schools: Walnut Grove Elementary School and Future High School. In two of the schools, Harland and Joshua, project-based learning was part of a larger reform effort. In Harland Elementary, the reform is part of a larger, "Basic School" philosophy in which technology was used to create a learning community with a coherent curriculum. At Joshua Junior High, the reform package is more eclectic and a theoretical and project-based learning is employed along with other approaches that include reduced class size, renovation of facilities, and retention of school staff. In the remaining two schools, Mountain Middle School and Pine City Middle School, project-based learning (inquiry-based learning, in the case of Pine City) are instructional approaches that are employed along with others with the primary goal of increasing student achievement. In the case of Mountain Middle School, student achievement is explicitly standards-based.

  Beyond this finding, what implications do these new instructional approaches have for the roles of students? What do new teacher roles complement those of students? How does technology support these roles? In the following sections, these questions will be addressed by analyzing interview and observational data I collected from the six case studies in the 2000 – 2001 academic year.

Student roles

New student roles

Looking across the six schools in our study, we identified three new roles for students that were often associated with project-based or inquiry learning: self-learner, team member, and knowledge manager. Each of these roles is, in turn, associated with typical activities.

The "self-learner" role is not only a major feature of Future High School but also at the elementary school, Walnut Grove. In the schools, students must select their own real-world projects and identify possible solutions. In this way, students help determine the content of the curriculum. Students in these schools must also organize their projects and manage progress made on them. This management task extends to managing student time. Time management was most pronounced at Future, where students moved from class to class within the open campus at their own discretion, unprompted by bells that marked class periods. At Joshua Junior High School the role of self-learner extended to that of helping others learn. As one teacher put it, "They definitely rely on each other instead of me. The focal point is on them and not on me." While students have always been divided into groups, the role of collaborator or "team member" is a relatively new one for students. The difference here is that the team in some way owns the project or investigation, and the team member is actively involved in advancing the project.

There is both shared and individual responsibility for the success of the project. Students work collaboratively to move it forward. This team work was most obvious in the projects observed in Mountain Middle School, where students collaborated in science class to publish a newspaper on the Alaskan ecosystem, called Tundra Times, or the cross-disciplinary "light rail" project in the 3rd grade of Walnut Grove. Sometimes the role of team member was a specialized one. For example in the "light rail" project, students rotated between different tasks given to a map committee, a research committee, and a field trip committee. For the 5th grade "flowers and plants" project at Walnut Grove, students performed specialized tasks such as collecting survey data on the preferences of potential customers, cultivating the plants, developing and implementing an advertising campaign for the plant sale, or conducting research on how to care for the different plant varieties. Sometimes, students share their expertise with other students, as at Joshua Junior High School.

The third role that we observed was that of "knowledge manager". This was, perhaps, the most prevalent role and the one most often associated with the use of technology to support project-based learning. The focus of the role is on the development of knowledge products. Examples of these products include a daily, student-produced, in house news TV program at Harland, a presentation on biomes at Pine City, student-published poetry on a website at Mountain, and a study of flowers and plants at Walnut Grove. Activities demanded of this role include formulating questions, searching for information, collecting and analyzing data, and designing reports and presentations. Perhaps the school that took this role most seriously was Future High School, which has as its mission "to prepare students to excel in an information-based, technologically-advanced society". Run as a high-tech start-up company, New Tech views students as knowledge-workers. At New Tech, students are engaged in extended projects consisting of complex tasks and long-term deadlines. The intent is to create technology-savvy citizens who are prepared for college and the world of work.

Technology supports for new student roles

A range of hardware and software applications support these new student roles. The most supported role is that of "knowledge manager". In this role, students have access to vast stores of information, either on the Internet or CD-ROM. In addition, they have a variety of tools that they can use to transform this information into knowledge, tools such as search engines, data analysis packages, word processors, spreadsheets, graphing and graphics packages, and presentation and web development software.

The role of "team member" is supported through the use of communications hardware and software. Two schools—Walnut Grove and Harland—are using wireless computers that support teamwork. With wireless laptops, students could assemble whenever and wherever needed (within the range of the network). Students were observed using their computers in classrooms, hallways, and libraries. Thus, groupings are based on what made the most sense for learning rather than on hardware constraints. Several schools provide students with email accounts that they used to exchange information with team members and teachers. Additionally, several schools used intranet applications such as Lotus Notes or Blackboard that support the exchange of documents. However, there was no use of software that was specifically designed for collaboration or shared construction of documents.

The least-supported role was that of "self-learner". This role is marked by the need for students to set their own goals, organize their own work, and manage their time. There were no student-equivalents to professional applications such as project management and time management software. This kind of software design for students engaged in project-based learning remains an open-market niche for educational software companies.

Teacher roles

New teacher roles

In terms of new teacher roles, the picture in the six cases we studied is much more complicated. Although teachers retained many of their traditional roles (e. g. class leader or director, lecturer, discussion leader), they negotiated multiple new roles in classrooms that utilized innovative technology-supported practices. The new teacher roles we identified were: instructional designer; trainer; collaborator; team coordinator; advisor; and monitoring and assessment specialist. Each role is associated with specific activities and is made possible by the use of technology in support of project-based learning and inquiry-based instructional methods. "Instructional designer" is one of the more common new roles taken on by teachers. Much like the "self-learner" role adopted by students, teachers in this role must design, plan, and organize themselves in order to effectively use and integrate technology in their classrooms. The instructional designer takes into account of all the resources available to meet the variety of needs his/her students have and implements well designed activities to address those needs. Teachers from Future High School are exemplars of this role. Since all the curricula are based on students creating interdisciplinary projects, teachers design and create instructional materials constantly. A teacher, describing a software tool (Tegrity) that allows a teacher to record and store digital web video on demand for students to view, explained, "I think it meets a variety of learning styles and I couldn't do that in the traditional classroom, but it's wonderful. I have kids, you know, begging me, hey Smith, you know, we need you to put that Tegrity lesson up because they go home and they can access these materials from home. It helps them access the material to decode their textbook to get through the lessons and it's a wonderful, wonderful tool⋯. " Support for this new teacher role can be found in those cases where remedial instruction occurred. At Mountain Middle School, for example, remedial instruction in mathematics using a drill and practice software tools is in an overall approach using technology to provide remediation and develop skills so that students may catch up and eventually achieve at high standards. Pine City Junior High School, with its use of "thin client" terminals, is able to differentiate remediation for each child using a skill-based software program that helps to diagnose and remediate students according to their individual deficiencies in mathematics and reading. Each child can receive additional help in an area of weakness, receive guidance from a computer-based tutorial, and work independently so that teachers have the flexibility to work with students individually or in small groups.

The role of "trainer" is one that was reflected in 3 of the 6 cases. "Trainers" give individual instruction to enable skill development. This training is accomplished through modeling the use of technology and helping students see how they might use software tools that can help them accomplish unique tasks. The teachers in Walnut Grove regularly model how ICT could be used in completing projects. Because all teachers own an Apple PowerBook laptop computer, many use a variety of software applications and multimedia programs in class to present material or to model an activity that students will undertake. In a 4th grade classroom that was observed, the teacher began the class by giving a multimedia presentation about fractions (1/2, 1/4, etc.) that showed squares being divided into halves and into fourths. The next day, the students worked at laptop computers around the classroom, using the same multimedia software the teacher used the day before to create slides of whole squares representing fractions. Teachers at Walnut Grove have received support from a job-embedded form of professional development in the use of a variety of software packages and computer-based learning activities. During the training, the teachers are encouraged to take what they are learning about spreadsheets, databases, and multimedia presentations and share it with their students. As one teacher put it, "I know I've learned a lot. It has improved my teaching, I think, especially taking the FutureKids (professional development) class. I'm creating things; it gives me the opportunity to create things along with my students so we're kind of learning together..." This role of "trainer" was also supported by observations and interview data from Future High School and Joshua Junior High School.

The collaborator role was evident in all six of the cases we analyzed. Collaborator refers to a variety of activities teachers undertake to work with their colleagues to improve their instruction. These activities include informal sharing with colleagues, team teaching, and grade level or interdisciplinary instructional activities conducted in conjunction with other colleagues. Team teaching is common in instructional approaches that utilize project-based learning and allow for additional time for students to explore some natural phenomenon in depth. For example, team teaching is an institutionalized feature of core content instruction at Future High school. It is less so at Joshua Junior High, although teachers in the English department collaborate with one another on lesson plans and content. Teachers at Harland, Pine City, Mountain, and Walnut Grove report that sharing of ideas among their grade-level colleagues is common as was team teaching.

"Team coordinator" is another teacher role supported by data collected at three of the six case study sites. The focus of this role is on the active assignment of individual students to project or study teams. In addition to opening up opportunities for collaborative learning activities, teachers who assume the "team coordinator" create opportunities for peer tutoring and support between students with mixed achievement levels. This role was evident at Walnut Grove, Future High, and Joshua Junior High. At Future High, students receive a grade for their level of collaboration from their project team members. Additionally, to graduate, all students must demonstrate and document their collaboration skills through the completion of an electronic portfolio that is evaluated by teachers and a review panel from the community. A teacher at Joshua Junior described how the use of technology enhances collaborative learning: "…when we went to technology, it was the highest form of collaborative learning. We didn't have all those obstacles in working with teams where one person was trying to force another person to work. The technology just lends itself to them working very much as a team…". Teachers at Joshua Junior and Walnut Grove employ heterogeneous grouping(i.e. placing students with different levels of ability together in the same group). Heterogeneous grouping is used to incorporate all students in small group collaboration. Provision is made to ensure that low performing students play a significant part in the group's work, especially true when using ICT. The role of "enabling advisor" refers to the teacher who gives assistance, advice, suggestions or poses questions in a way that enables students to make sound decisions and find the information they need to complete a particular task. The teacher adopting this role is apt to give students a great deal of autonomy so that they take greater responsibility for their own learning activities. A common term used sometimes to describe this role is the term "facilitator". This new teacher role was found in four of the six cases analyzed. At Joshua Junior High, one teacher described this role in this fashion:

I'm the facilitator! You know, I'll come back and say, oh, OK, here you might want to look at this, this, this, and this. Here you go. Here are three sites that I hope to address the question. Go ahead and read them and see if that's what you were looking for. Almost like a research person for them. But they don't even know it, which is, I mean, just absolutely fantastic. And they're just, you know, that's how I see myself. It's just there to assist them in their learning process…

Walnut Grove teachers link constructivist learning principles and project-based learning to this new teacher role. Here's how the technology coordinator described it:

As far as the role of the teacher, I think with the project-based learning, the traditional role of the teachers has definitely changed. I know when I entered into teaching it was kind of a more traditional role where the teacher stood up and taught the class. They taught the information and the child was responsible for regurgitating the information. It's more of a, I don't want to say, drill and practice, but it's more of memorization and exposure to information. Where now with the constructivist approach and project-based learning, the teacher pretty much takes a facilitating role and the child basically takes control and directs their own learning process...

Teachers expressed adopting this new role in Harland Elementary, Joshua Junior, and Future High, but less so at Mountain Middle School.

The "monitoring and assessment specialist" refers to the new role where teachers monitor student performance and attempt to assess and improve student performance. This role is reflected in a variety of ways among 4 of the 6 cases analyzed. In Mountain Middle School, a school where standards-based achievement was a vital priority, this role was reflected in teacher tracking of  individual student test scores. Teachers and administrators monitor test scores and provide written feedback and encouragement to students about how they might improve their scores on future examinations. At Pine City, the skills-based software for mathematics and reading provides "just-in-time" data to teachers about student performance. This enables the teacher to have a regular point of assessment. At Future High, teachers use rubrics that lay out the various components of the work being completed as well as assign a score or level of competence based on clearly articulated criteria. Students are regularly involved in a range of self-assessment and peer assessment activities using rubrics.

These various teacher roles align and exist in tandem with the new student roles seen in our analysis of these cases. Additionally, the new teacher roles appear to overlap the different student roles in the cases we analyzed. The student role of "self-learner" is complemented and supported by the roles that teachers play as "trainer", "instructional designer", and "monitoring and assessment specialist". This connection is nicely illustrated by the interaction of teachers and students in learning together and collaborating at Joshua Junior High School. The student role of "team member" appears to be linked to the teacher role of instructional designer, collaborator, and team coordinator. Walnut Grove, with its focus on teams working together on project-based learning activities, is an exemplar of how the new teacher and student roles operate. The knowledge manager, a creator of knowledge products, is related to and supported by the advisor, instructional designer, team coordinator, and the collaborator roles that teachers adopt. Future High, with its teachers adopting multiple roles, provides a setting where both the new student and teacher roles are present to support project-based, interdisciplinary learning with technology.

Technology supports for new teacher roles

A variety of technology supports these new teacher roles as they are adopted by teachers in all the school sites we visited. The instructional designer and trainer role are supported by a range of software tools that enable the differentiated instruction at Pine City and project-based learning occurring at Walnut Grove and Future High. The use of the Tegrity video software system at New Tech High, the utilization of application software tools, and the use of the CCC mathematics and reading software at Pine City are examples of how teacher can design an instructional program that can be used to develop skills and meet the needs of students of different learning styles and achievement levels. The collaborator and team coordinator roles are supported by the use of Internet browsing software and electronic mail software programs. Lotus Notes, used at Future High, enables teachers to plan appointments, communicate via email, compile agendas for weekly meetings, and obtain student information, add Internet hyperlinks to existing course documents, and store other digital learning resources. Telecommunications software permits efficient communication between team members (student teams or teaching teams) or between teachers, their students, and their parents. Electronic mail has been particularly supportive of these roles at Mountain Middle School, where teachers exchange email communication with students and parents. Additional support can also be found for the enabling advisor and monitoring and assessment roles in the skill development software and application tool software supporting projects in a number of the school sites analyzed.

Conclusions

The findings from this preliminary analysis of six cases reveal that technology is being used in a variety of ways to improve classroom instruction. Each of the six cases provides an example of how technology is enhancing instruction in variety of school types in different regions of the U. S. Additionally, teacher and student roles are being altered in ways that are reflective not only of the presence of technology, but also the efforts at systemic school reform. These findings highlight different roles that students and teacher adopt in the course of their interaction with technology-supported pedagogical practices that inquiry-based learning. These practices:

- Promote active and autonomous learning in students;
- Provide students with competencies and technological skills that allow them to search for, organize, and analyze information, and communicate and express their ideas in a variety of media forms;
- Enable teachers, students, and their parents to communicate and share information on line;
- Engage students in collaborative, project-based learning in which students work with other classmates on complex, extended, real-world-like problems or projects;
- Provide students with individualized or differentiated instruction, customized to meet the needs of students with different achievement levels, interests, or learning styles;
- Allow teachers and students to assess student and peer academic performance.

What is the significance of these role transformations? Although these changes in roles and technology-enhanced pedagogical practices can be linked with a number of factors, one stands out as noteworthy. The standards movement, which has resulted in schools throughout the U.S. adopting high performance standards, has had a significant impact on schools to prepare them to use technology. Coupled with the move toward challenging standards are the high expectations that schools have adopted, believing all children can achieve at high levels if given the necessary support. This environment has provided new opportunities for teachers and students to break out of old roles and patterns through the use of technology. Furthermore, technology has allowed teachers and students to adopt new behaviors and responsibilities consistent with the realities of a rapid technological society. Future analyses of all the data from the U.S. case studies will examine additional cases that will help to explain, identify, and describe additional role changes and derive implications for policy and improve practice.

Unit 9 School & Family
学校与家庭

Text A School and Family Cooperation Models for Reducing Social Problems

导读：社会排斥是拉脱维亚七到十五岁的学生可能遇到的成长问题之一。本文中的研究对象是寄宿学校的学生，寄宿学校的学生与综合学校的学生在团体关系方面是很不一样的。因为寄宿学校的学生通常来自不甚富裕的家庭，有些学生缺少父母的照顾，有些学生无家可归，有些学生达到上学年龄却没能上学，有些学生由于父母在外工作而被其他亲朋监护，也有些学生存在许多类似上述的问题……。

Pupils' (7-15 years old) social exclusion is one of contemporary problems in Latvia. The chosen target group for research is pupils living and studying in the boarding school. The membership of pupils in the boarding school highly differs from comprehensive schools in Latvia, because they usually are pupils from low-income and disadvantageous families, as well as children without parental care, those who have wandered for a long time, have not acquired education according to their age,

children being left under relatives' supervision because their parents have left for working abroad and also children with many similar problems. A large part of these pupils have not only limited possibilities to adopt themselves to the social life, to have exciting spare time, to contact with equals in age, to identify and develop their skills, abilities and interests, but also lack socially meaningful experience regarding the conventionalities and a moral, ethic model for imitation of these norms. The micro-society, life conditions in families where pupils live, unfortunately, do not develop conventionalities, but encourage anti-social behavior.

Admittedly, pupils in boarding schools have fair intellect, they are physically fit, with sufficient potential of energy being impossible to put into practice within the pedagogical context that could help them socialize and express themselves. Education is regarded as a value in the family, however, the socially-psychological characteristics also affect the learning process, because we can often notice explicit Attention Deficit Syndrome lowering their working capacity. In order to facilitate the reduction of pupils' social exclusion in the boarding school and their incorporation into the social life, as well as to prevent critical situations, these pupils and their parents need special support, because the pupil's identity development begins in the family, but improves at school.

Along with the country's economic situation, the parents' socio-economic situation has sharply worsened. Therefore, as a result of such changes, many families have experienced stressful situations. Consequently, parents often are full of their own problems forgetting about the child's needs, interests and peculiarities of development. Parents often do not take their child as an individual, and do not perceive their child as a value, because in their own childhood, they had felt themselves unplumbed, troublesome, cared, teachable, and pushed. Support for these children and their parents can be ensured by a complex of different educational measures and team work. One of the measures is promotion of cooperation between the school and the family, because the priority of boarding school pupils is their family, family members' opinion which is taken into account. But this cooperation must be insistent and permanent as only in this case positive results can be expected.

The research was carried on within the framework of doctoral thesis: holistic approach during process of socialization of social risk group pupils.

The report contains the analysis of the issue within two levels: *the theoretical level*, where the legislation of the Republic of Latvia related to social issues, children rights and parental duties as well as different models of school and family cooperation had been analyzed. Consequently, there proposed a triangular model referring to direct cooperation among school, NGO (non-governmental organization) and family; *the empirical level*, where the approbation of the proposed cooperation model (SCHOOL—NGO—FAMILY) was developed by interviewing the parents of the pupils. By the content-analysis, there analyzed the implementation of the cooperation model by the mediation of NGO "Liepna Boarding School and Pupils Support Families Union" in order to reduce social problems within the boarding school.

Analysis of cooperation between the school and the family and proposed solutions

Each person is an individual system, which functions in interaction by surrounding environment, creates correlated and interacted system and aggregate of structures. It is ecosystem approach and these conditions also refer to persons from social risk groups. In general, this thesis is basis for integrative and inclusive pedagogy. In accordance with scientific cognitions of U. Bronfenbrenner, microsystem is an aggregate of activities, roles and intermediate human relations, which is 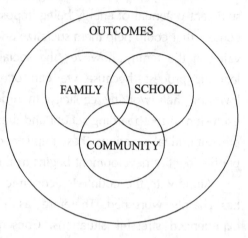 being experienced by the person with its characteristic physical and psychical features at some particular sphere of life by creating interaction with other persons. Accordingly, the child, his/her family and school are three microsystems.

In child's upbringing, the family has an important role. However, the function of upbringing is also performed by the school and it means that for child's development the cooperation between school and family is important. It should be well-thought-out and organized, because every family has different resources, skills, desires and needs. One approach of cooperation does not fit to everyone. Pupils, their parents and teachers usually have different desires, aims, opinions, values; it sometimes leads to disappointment and misunderstandings between school and pupils' families. If these differences are not being recognized and solved, there is developing lack of communication; consequently, there is impossible successful cooperation between school and family. This expression is often seen in boarding schools, where the parents of the pupils have different world outlook, because the majority of these families practice antisocial life-style. It is complicated to persuade and stimulate the parents to live more qualitatively; it creates necessity to include the parents:

- in active involvement into making decisions regarding school;
- in active school's activities as volunteers and members of parents' committee;
- leisure activities with their children;
- regular communication with school personnel regarding child's school and general progress;

Unit 9 School & Family 学校与家庭

- participation in opportunities of adults' education, offered by the school.

Families' involvement in school's activities can be one of the means to create cooperative, tolerant community. Nowadays, when schools become more and more open to the society, communication between parents and teachers is becoming not only more intensive but also more complicated. Teachers tend to recognize that work out of classroom in this case, it is the activity in the community and communication with parents is related emotional and intellectual efforts. As a result of communication between school and family, pupils' achievements, behavior, attitude towards studies and school are improving. The cooperation depends on families' education, family and society members, who are working together for consummation of united aims.

The features of cooperation between the school and the family in Latvia had changed by historical course of time. A. Baldins and A. Razeva mention that the older generation teaching children has grown and developed their identities in other socio-economic and political relations to a great extent being typical to the conditions of a primitive society. The grounds for these relations were social and economic safety and absolutization of the country's interests. Government ensured a single educational system for all children where the school became a partial performer of the family's functions. This experience regarding the school is familiar to parents, but the contemporary school realizes only its educational functions making the family realize its responsibility and importance of the upbringing function.

In its turn, the boarding school is an educational institution carrying out not only pupils' educating but also upbringing function. Pupils spend a majority of their life in the boarding school; as a result, the school mainly takes responsibility for pupil's development as individuality, but parents' responsibility stays apart.

Basing on the Children's Rights Protection Law passed by Saeima of the Republic of Latvia prescribing children's rights to clean environment for life (Article 46); basic provisions for the protection of children from negative influences in social surroundings (Article 47); children's protection from smoking and the influence of alcoholic beverages (Article 48); children's protection from the use of narcotic, toxic and other intoxicating substances (Article 49); protection from negative influence of games, films and mass media (Article 50); restrictions for children's involvement into events (Article 501); safety requirements in children's supervisory services (Article 503); children's protection from unlawful activities (Article 51); a child—a victim of violence or other unlawful activity (Article 52); quite often the children at high risk are being sent to a boarding school and thus being isolated from their families. As a result, parents' rights to bring up their children are limited. The connection between the child and his family is broken, also the obligations of parents prescribed in the Article 24 of the Children's Rights Protection Law of the Republic of Latvia determining: "to take care of the child and his property and represent him within his private and property relations"; "to prepare the child for an independent life in the society, as much as possible respecting his/her individuality, taking into consideration his/her abilities and inclinations"; "to safe-guard the child's rights and interests protected by the law"; as well as " upon failure to discharge parental obligations, or for the malicious usage of parental authority, physical punishing of a child, as well as cruel behavior against him/her, parents shall be held accountable as determined by the law" etc.

A part of parents' obligations is performed by the boarding school, and exactly by the school support measures. It is possible to maintain and improve the existent relations between the child, parents and teachers, but positive moral concepts being acquired at school are not always supported by the families of the social risk group, because in most cases parents have transferred their own negative experience regarding school to their children. The majority of parents are unemployed at the moment due to the economic crisis and they are followers of the anti-social environment, quite often these parents, when bringing their children to grade 1, give them for school's care and upbringing for over nine years. However, the positive result of child's upbringing can be reached only in case school efforts are being supported by the family. Otherwise, a child acquires different skills and habits; but consequently the positive influence in school often vanishes because of the lack of support in the family.

It creates the necessity to develop cooperation between the school and the family corresponding to school's intentions and motivating parents to arrive at school in order to see their child's growth. Frequently, the class teacher is the person informing parents about their children's interests, abilities, competences, needs, problems, friends, state of health. Usually it is quite difficult to involve parents into organization of the educational process, because there is a psychological barrier between the school and parents that is not easy to hurdle. The school visit mainly is connected to their child's bad behavior and insufficient success, the research shows that parents usually do not want to visit school and help its work due to the following reasons:

- They are not sure that their help is truly necessary;
- They are afraid to be mistaken;
- There is a lack of information regarding the form of the required support;
- low self-esteem, busyness;

- illness;
- alcoholism, drug addiction;
- They are undereducated and low-income people often with the inferiority complex.

As V. Senko notes, the time of negative experience accumulating for pupils in junior grades is noticeably shorter than for youngsters, therefore, the departure from the norm is not yet established. Their psyche is characterized by its flexibility and this feature facilitates the reformatory process. By the time when the child starts to attend school, a break of the dynamic stereotype happens and it goes quite easily, because the negative acquirements and habits have not become permanent. Therefore, the initiative of the pedagogical cooperation between the school and the family should be taken by the school without waiting for parents' interest. But families having pedagogical neglect require special attention and approach, because it is necessary to practise both the educating and the reformatory or reeducating function at the same time. It requires energy to improve educational conditions in families, help parents change their attitude towards their children and achieve a single influence of the school and the family upon the child.

As part of its effort to build the capacity of schools, the Network facilitates linkages among schools and between schools and other key institutional players that can support schools. The support for schools includes education departments at the district and state level, as well as universities and organizations, communities, and national school reform movements.

Indication of effective cooperation between school and family is unity in accomplishing purposes. Cooperation process requires uninterrupted planning of works, their drafting and evaluation. Schools have to undertake the leading role in organizing of the cooperation by providing environment and culture, helping families to perform their role of partnership.

Present situation in Latvian education, e.g. deep economic crisis and the life reality, shows that the school's support team often does not work in a body, because due to the economic crisis and structural modifications of the Latvian education system, there is a lack of funding for wages of qualified employees—organizers of interest-related education, out-of-class activities, psychologists, social pedagogues etc. wherewith the school has no opportunities to perform cooperation organizer's functions, as well as there is lack of funding for organizing of extracurricular activities and promotion of collaboration.

As the economic situation in the country is becoming worse, the social crisis has also deepened, because at the moment a great part of families where children attend boarding school faces some difficulties increasing social exclusion and problems related to it. As a result, the support is necessary for both—the pupils and their families. It creates circumstances and necessity for searching of new ways of collaboration.

1. **Social exclusion(社会排斥)**: Social exclusion is a concept used in many parts of the world to characterise contemporary forms of social disadvantage. Dr. Lynn Todman, director of the Institute on Social Exclusion at the Adler School of Professional Psychology, suggests that social exclusion refers to processes in which individuals and entire communities of people are systematically blocked from rights, opportunities and resources (e.g. housing, employment, healthcare, civic engagement, democratic participation and due process) that are normally available to members of society and which are key to social integration.

2. **Latvia(拉脱维亚)**: Latvia, officially the Republic of Latvia, is a country in the Baltic region of Northern Europe. It is bordered to the north by Estonia (border length 343 km), to the south by Lithuania (588 km), to the east by the Russian Federation (276 km), and to the southeast by Belarus (141 km). Across the Baltic Sea to the west lies Sweden. The territory of Latvia covers 64,589 km² (24,938 sq mi) and it has a temperate seasonal climate.

3. **NGO (non-governmental organization)(民间组织,非政府组织)**: A non-governmental organization (NGO) is a legally constituted organization created by natural or legal persons that operates independently from any government. The term is usually used by governments to refer to entities that have no government status.

New Words and Expression

1. contemporary [kən'tempərəri]　　n.　同时代的人;同时期的东西
　　　　　　　　　　　　　　　　　adj.　当代的;同时代的;属于同一时期的
2. comprehensive [ˌkɔmpri'hensiv]　adj.　综合的;广泛的;有理解力的
　　　　　　　　　　　　　　　　　n.　综合学校;专业综合测验

Unit 9 School & Family 学校与家庭

3. parental [pəˈrentl]   adj. 父母亲的,父母的;亲代的,亲本的
4. supervision [ˌsjuːpəˈviʒən]   n. 监督,管理
5. ethic [ˈeθik]   n. 伦理;道德规范
                                    adj. 伦理的;道德的(等于 ethical)
                                    n. 伦理;道德规范
6. admittedly [ədˈmitidli]   adv. 公认地;无可否认地;明白地
7. boarding [ˈbɔːdiŋ]   adj. 供膳的
8. incorporation [inˌkɔːpəˈreiʃən] n. 公司;合并,编入;团体组织
9. priority [praiˈɔrəti]   n. 优先;优先权;[数]优先次序;优先考虑的事
10. triangular [traiˈæŋɡjulə]   adj. 三角的,[数]三角形的;三人间的
11. implementation [ˌimplimenˈteiʃən] n. [计]实现;履行;安装启用
12. mediation [ˌmiːdiˈeiʃən]   n. 调解;仲裁;调停
13. in accordance with   依照,与……一致
14. aggregate [ˈæɡriɡət]   vi. 集合;聚集;合计
                                    vt. 集合;聚集;合计
                                    n. 合计;集合体;总计
                                    adj. 聚合的;集合的;合计的
15. intermediate [ˌintəˈmiːdiət]   vi. 起媒介作用
                                    adj. 中间的,中级的
                                    n. [化学]中间物;媒介
16. necessity [niˈsesəti]   n. 需要;必然性;必需品
17. intellectual [ˌintəˈlektjuəl]   adj. 智力的;聪明的;理智的
18. consummation [ˌkɔnsəˈmeiʃən]   n. 圆满成功;完成;成就;达到极点
19. provision [prəuˈviʒən]   n. 规定;条款;准备;[经]供应品
                                    vt. 供给……食物及必需品
20. beverage [ˈbevəridʒ]   n. 饮料
21. intoxicating [inˈtɔksikeitiŋ]   adj. 醉人的;令人陶醉的;使兴奋的
22. supervisory [ˈsjuːpəˈvaizəri]   adj. 监督的
23. prescribe [prisˈkraib]   vi. 规定;开药方
                                    vt. 规定;开处方
24. inclination [ˌinkliˈneiʃən]   n. 倾向,爱好;斜坡

25. correspond [ˌkɔːriˈspɔnd]　　　vi.　符合,一致;相应;通信
26. accumulate [əˈkjuːmjuleit]　　vi.　累积;积聚
　　　　　　　　　　　　　　　　vt.　积攒
27. reformatory [riˈfɔːmətəri]　　adj.　改革的;感化的;革新的
　　　　　　　　　　　　　　　　n.　少年管教所;妓女教养所
28. stereotype [ˈsteriəutaip]　　 vt.　使用铅版;套用老套,使一成不变
　　　　　　　　　　　　　　　　n.　陈腔滥调,老套;铅版
29. wherewith [hwɛəˈwiθ]　　　 adv.　用什么
　　　　　　　　　　　　　　　　pron.　用以……的东西
30. collaboration [kəˌlæbəˈreiʃən]　n.　合作;勾结;通敌

I　Vocabulary.

Fill in the blanks with the most suitable words. Change the form when necessary.

| contemporary | comprehensive | parental | supervision | ethic |
| admittedly | priority | necessity | intellectual | prescribe |

1. To pursue this vision, my administration conducted a _____ review of America's development programs.
2. "We cannot continue with costs that are out of control because reform is a _____ that cannot wait," he said.
3. "The International Monetary Fund should strengthen its _____ of capital flows between countries," he said.
4. I'm not prepared to _____ a drug to my patients that I wouldn't take myself.
5. The artist Michelangelo often stirred up the opposition of the _____ artists of his day.
6. The _____ is protecting the police and the public from their attacks.
7. The difference in _____ attitudes between first-borns and subsequent children is large and significant.

Unit 9   School & Family   学校与家庭

8. Optimism is an _____ choice.

9. Negativity gets on people's nerves and calls your work _____ into question.

10. _____, Mr. Yoon is no ordinary banker but a former engineer who designed the satellite communications network used in the US space shuttle program.

II Comprehension of the text.

Decide whether the following statements are true(T) or false(F) according to the passage.

1. The membership of pupils in the boarding school is the same with that of comprehensive schools in Latvia.
2. Each person is an individual system, which functions in interaction by surrounding environment, creates correlated and interacted system and aggregate of structures.
3. Families' involvement in school's activities can be one of the mean by creating cooperative, tolerant community.
4. As a result of communication between school and family, pupils' achievements, behavior, attitude towards studies and school are improving.
5. As the economic situation in the country is becoming worse, the social crisis has also deepened.

III Try to fill in the spaces with the suitable words.

1. In order to facilitate the reduction of pupils' social exclusion in the boarding school and their incorporation into the social life, as well as to prevent critical situations, these pupils and their parents need special support, because the pupil's identity development begins in the _____, but improves at school.
2. In child's upbringing the family has important role, however, the function of upbringing is also performed by the school and it means that for child's development the _____ is important.
3. Pupils, their parents and teachers usually have different desires, aims, opinions, values; it sometimes leads to _____ between school and pupils' families.
4. The positive result of child's upbringing can be reached only in case school efforts are being supported by _____.
5. The support for schools includes education departments at _____ level, as well as universities and organizations, communities, and national school reform movements.

Text B The Effects of Family, School, and Classroom Ecologies on Changes in Children's Social Competence and Emotional and Behavioral Problems in First Grade

导读：课堂是学生学习知识的场所，是学生与老师、学生与学生之间互动的平台；学校比课堂的空间更大，在学校里学生不单单是学习知识，还在学习做人，学校是社会的一个小小缩影，为学生从容走入社会做好准备；良好的家庭教育环境是促进未成年人健康成长的重要一环，父母是孩子的启蒙教师，父母的言行举止和教育方法，对孩子的成长有着重大影响。

Classroom-level influences on children's in-school behaviors

Although children's classroom ecologies can be characterized according to multiple perspectives and social and structural features, we consider the social atmosphere among classmates, as rated by the children themselves, to be particularly salient for children's social, emotional, and behavioral development in first grade. Growing evidence indicates that aggregate levels of peer behaviors within classroom groupings, including aggressive or victimizing behaviors, contribute to children's  adjustment in school, even after family-and school-level factors are accounted for. For instance, in an evaluation of a first-grade classroom intervention directed at reducing children's aggressive behaviors, Kellam et al. (1998) found that placement in first-grade classrooms with higher aggregate levels of physically aggressive peers (as rated by teachers) contributed to boys' (but not girls') behavioral problems in middle school, independent of family economic disadvantage and school disadvantage. Illustrating the connection between individual and peer group behavior, O'Connell, Pepler, and Craig (1999) showed that peers reinforce episodes of school-based peer victimization by watching or by physically or verbally joining the aggressors. Evidence also indicates that children's experiences of peer victimization in schools and classrooms are reciprocally linked to their social, emotional, and behavioral problems, such that children who show these problems are more likely to be victimized, which, in turn, can further elevate their level of problems. Clearly, aggressive and victimizing peer behaviors are not limited to dyads but rather function at the group level, and being in a classroom surrounded by a hostile group of peers who manipulate or harm other children may contribute to individual risks for developmental problems.

On the other hand, concentrated exposure to positive peer affiliations can reduce risks for social, emotional, or behavioral problems. Evidence shows that being competent in the social, emotional, or behavioral domain or having friends who can provide support and protection reduces children's risk of being victimized and increases their likelihood of receiving prosocial acts from peers. Vitaro et al. (1999) highlighted the importance of positive peer affiliations in their follow-up study of aggressive, second-grade boys who were targeted for an intervention program to improve social and problem-solving skills. Boys who associated with non-deviant peers showed lower risks for conduct disorder 4 years later than did program boys who associated with deviant peers. Having a stable group of well-adjusted, prosocial peers in the classroom increases children's exposure to more positive social learning experiences, which may, in turn, enhance their developmental outcomes. Although some research has shown that positive peer relationships and classroom environments can attenuate the negative effects of family-or school-level adversities on children's development, few studies have examined the ways that both positive and negative features of children's classrooms (particularly aggregate experiences of peer prosocial acts and victimization) shape children's behaviors in school in concert with markers of their family and school ecologies.

Family-level influences on children's in-school behaviors

Although family ecology is multidimensional and can affect children's development through many avenues, we focus specifically on indicators of family disruptiveness (household moves) and socioeconomic status (SES; mothers' education level) that can directly affect children's experiences in school. Evidence also suggests that these indicators may be linked. Research has documented that family disruptions, such as multiple household moves, contribute to social, emotional, and behavioral problems in children. Ackerman et al. (1999) observed that children who experienced high levels of family disruptions, including multiple household moves, in their early years were at higher risk for behavioral problems in preschool and for emotional problems in first grade than were children who experienced few disruptions. Although household moves may index changes in family SES (e.g. employment, income status), structure (e.g. divorce), or even opportunities, accumulating evidence indicates that the transitions necessitated by household moves represent an independent source of stress for children. Yet evidence on the mechanisms by which household moves affect school-age children's development is limited.

Shifts in household residences introduce disruptions into children's lives that can compromise the maintenance and accessibility of their social networks, particularly when parents' social and institutional ties are displaced. When children in a classroom have few bonds to one another outside the classroom or school environment because of residential instability, the supportive nature of the classroom climate may be threatened. On the other hand, the relation between household moves and children's behaviors may be attenuated in the presence of more constructive environmental experiences, such as classroom climates characterized by positive or supportive peer interactions.

Parental education has been positively linked to social competence and negatively related to emotional and behavioral problems in young children and may mediate the effects of household income on children's competent behaviors. Parental education indexes the human capital available to scaffold children's socialization and is less prone than household income to short-term financial fluctuations that can mask its effects, including seasonal unemployment or welfare spells. On the other hand, evidence suggests that poorly educated parents are more socially isolated, are less connected to the school system, and generate fewer social learning opportunities for their children outside of the school environment. If parents show limited engagement in their children's social experiences (e.g. rarely invite children's classmates over to play), their children may have few opportunities to develop interpersonal skills and may lack protective friendships with peers.

Evidence also indicates that low parental education can increase children's exposure to environmental stressors, including family and neighborhood poverty, family disruptions, and other adverse social conditions. When low parental education is coupled with other environmental stressors, such as high aggregate levels of poverty in schools and peer aggressiveness in classrooms, children's risks for developmental problems may be amplified. However, few studies have examined how mothers' education level and household moves influence children's in-school behaviors in the context of school- and classroom-related stressors.

School-level influences on children's in-school behaviors

Characteristics of children's school ecology are also varied and can operate on children's development through many avenues. We focus specifically on how school disadvantage (the proportion of poor students in the school) effects changes in children's in-school behaviors. Exposure to high aggregate levels of poverty (at the neighborhood and school levels) has been shown to adversely affect children's development. For instance, Kellam et al. (1998) found that high levels of school disadvantage (the proportion of children eligible for free lunch) in first grade increased children's risk for behavioral problems in middle school, independent of family economic disadvantage and classroom levels of physical aggressiveness. Schools that concentrate on children who are vulnerable to social, emotional, or behavioral problems together may reduce their exposure to competent peers and positive peer interactions. For instance, Simons, Johnson, Beaman, Conger, and Whitbeck (1996) showed that residing in poorer communities (which is, in turn, reflected in the economic characteristics of neighborhood-based schools) heightened adolescents' likelihood of associating with deviant peers, which, in turn, increased their risk for conduct problems. There is also evidence to suggest that episodes of peer victimization in classrooms are more common in disadvantaged schools than in more advantaged schools.

Associations between school disadvantage and poor developmental outcomes may also be altered by positive attributes of other salient environments, such as the prosocial or helping environment of children's classrooms. In the context of classrooms with high concentrations of prosocial, competent peer interactions, the negative influence of school disadvantage on children's development may be weakened. Yet surprisingly, few studies have explored how first-grade children's social, emotional, and behavioral trajectories are affected by the intersection of school disadvantage and the social environment of children's classrooms in the context of family-level risks.

The current study

In sum, the current study examined the independent and interactive contributions of classroom (concentrations of peer prosocial behaviors and victimization), family (household moves, mothers' education), and school (proportion of students receiving income assistance) factors to changes in children's in-school behaviors, as rated by their teachers during first grade. We expected (a) that increases in social competence across first grade would be predicted by higher levels of mothers' education and classroom prosocial behaviors, fewer household moves, and lower levels of school disadvantage and classroom victimization; (b) that increases in emotional and behavioral problems would be predicted by lower levels of mothers' education and classroom prosocial behaviors, multiple household moves, and higher levels of school disadvantage and classroom victimization;and(c)that the classroom-level variables would moderate the effects of the family-and school-level factors on changes in children's in-school behaviors. Specifically,the classroom concentration of prosocial behaviors was expected to buffer the effects of multiple household moves,low levels of mothers' education,and school disadvantage on changes in children's behaviors. The classroom concentration of victimization was expected to augment the effects of multiple household moves, low levels of mothers' education,and school disadvantage.

1. **Peer group(同辈群体;同龄群体)**: A peer group is a social group consisting of people. Peer groups are an informal primary group of people who share a similar or equal status and who are usually of roughly the same age, tended to travel around and interact within the social aggregate. Members of a particular peer group often have similar interests and backgrounds, bonded by the premise of sameness. However, some peer groups are very diverse, crossing social divides such as socioeconomic status, level of education, race, creed, culture, or religion.

2. **Victimization(欺负;牺牲)**: is the process of being victimized. According to Wiktionary, to victimize is to(1)make someone a victim or sacrifice, (2)punish someone unjustly, or (3) swindle or defraud someone.

3. **Socioeconomic status(SES)(社会经济地位)**: is an economic and sociological combined total measure of a person's work experience and of an individual's or family's economic and social position relative to others, based on income, education, and occupation. When analyzing a family's SES, the household income, earners' education, and occupation are examined, as well as combined income, versus with an individual, when their own attributes are assessed.

4. **Socialization(社会化)**: is a term used by sociologists, social psychologists, anthropologists, politicians and educationalists to refer to the process of inheriting norms, customs and ideologies. It may provide the individual with the skills and habits necessary for participating within their own society; a society develops a culture through a plurality of shared norms, customs, values, traditions, social roles, symbols and languages. Socialization is thus "the means by which social and cultural continuity are attained".

5. **Prosocial behavior**(亲社会行为,利他行为): is caring about the welfare and rights of others, feeling concern and empathy for them, and acting in ways that benefit others. Evidence suggests that prosociality is central to the well-being of social groups across a range of scales.

New Words and Expression

1. salient [ˈseiliənt]　　　　　　adj. 显著的;突出的;跳跃的
　　　　　　　　　　　　　　　　n. 凸角;突出部分
2. peer [piə]　　　　　　　　　　n. 贵族;同等的人;同龄人
3. aggressive [əˈgresiv]　　　　　adj. 侵略性的;好斗的;有进取心的;有闯劲的
4. reinforce [ˌriːinˈfɔːs]　　　　 vt. 加强,加固;强化;补充
　　　　　　　　　　　　　　　　vi. 求援;得到增援;给予更多的支持
5. episode [ˈepisəud]　　　　　　n. 插曲;一段情节;插话;有趣的事件
6. victimization [ˌviktimaiˈzeiʃən] n. 牺牲;欺骗
7. reciprocally [riˈsiprəkli]　　　 adv. 相互地;相反地;互惠地
8. elevate [ˈeliveit]　　　　　　　vt. 提升;举起;振奋情绪等;提升……的职位
9. dyad [ˈdaiæd]　　　　　　　　n. 双;[生物]二分体;一对;[化学]二价元素
　　　　　　　　　　　　　　　　adj. 双的
10. manipulate [məˈnipjuleit]　　 vt. 操作;操纵;巧妙地处理;篡改
11. affiliation [əˌfiliˈeiʃən]　　　 n. 加入;联盟;友好关系;从属关系
12. prosocial [prəuˈsəuʃəl]　　　 adj. 亲社会的;忠实于既定社会道德准则的
13. adversity [ədˈvəːsəti]　　　　n. 逆境;不幸;灾祸;灾难
14. disruptiveness [disˈrʌptivnis]　n. 破裂性
15. maintenance [ˈmeintənəns]　　n. 维护,维修;保持;生活费用
16. residential [ˌreziˈdenʃəl]　　　adj. 住宅的;与居住有关的
17. index [ˈindeks]　　　　　　　n. 指标;指数;索引;指针
　　　　　　　　　　　　　　　　vi. 做索引
　　　　　　　　　　　　　　　　vt. 指出;编入索引中
18. prone [prəun]　　　　　　　　adj. 俯卧的;有……倾向的,易于……的
19. stressor [ˈstresə]　　　　　　n. 紧张性刺激;光彩
20. trajectory [trəˈdʒektəri]　　　n. [物]轨道,轨线;[航][军]弹道

I Vocabulary.

Match the word in Column A to the correct definition in Column B.

Column A
1. peer   2. aggressive
3. reinforce   4. elevate
5. manipulate

Column B
A. give a promotion to or assign to a higher position
B. characteristic of an enemy or one eager to fight
C. influence or control shrewdly or deviously
D. a person who is of equal standing with another in a group
E. make stronger

II Comprehension of the text.

Decide whether the following statements are true (T) or false (F) according to the passage.

1. Aggressive and victimizing peer behaviors are limited to dyads and can not function at the group level.
2. Concentrated exposure to positive peer affiliations can reduce risks for social, emotional, or behavioral problems.
3. Shifts in household residences introduce disruptions into children's lives that can compromise the maintenance and accessibility of their social networks, particularly when parents' social and institutional ties are displaced.
4. Evidence suggests that poorly educated parents are more socially isolated but are better connected to the school system, and generate more social learning opportunities for their children outside of the school environment.
5. Yet surprisingly, few studies have explored how first-grade children's social, emotional, and behavioral trajectories are affected by the intersection of school

disadvantage and the social environment of children's classrooms in the context of family-level risks.

III Try to fill in the spaces with the suitable words.

1. O'Connell, Pepler, and Craig (1999) showed that peers reinforce episodes of school-based _____ by watching or by physically or verbally joining the aggressors.

2. Evidence shows that being competent in the social, emotional, or behavioral domain or having friends who can provide support and protection reduces children's risk of being victimized and _____ their likelihood of receiving prosocial acts from peers.

3. Having a stable group of well-adjusted, prosocial peers in the classroom increases children's exposure to more positive social learning experiences, which may, in turn, enhance their _____.

4. Schools that concentrate children who are vulnerable to social, emotional, or behavioral problems together may _____ their exposure to competent peers and positive peer interactions.

5. The classroom concentration of _____ was expected to buffer the effects of multiple household moves, low levels of mothers' education, and school disadvantage on changes in children's behaviors.

Supplementary Reading

Parent-Teacher Communication: Tips for Creating a Strong Parent-Teacher Relationship

Parent-teacher communication is essential to your child's success in school. Below are some important suggestions to help you create a strong parent teacher relationship that will serve your child's best interests. The hidden perk is that it will also make things easier and more enjoyable for you and your child's teacher.

Parents and teachers must agree to serve the same purpose which means serving the best interests of the child and the class as a whole. For instance, if a child's behavior disrupts the class, the parent and teacher can work together (from different fronts) to help the child express his needs in a way that serves him, the teacher and the class.

Parent teacher communication should be focused on the best interests of the child.

Parents and teachers must make a commitment to know the child. Socrates said, "Know thyself." I say, "Know the child." A child is much more than the sum of his behavior, his test scores or the grades on his report card. A child is a living being who has needs, hopes, interests and dreams. In order for parents and teachers to bring up a well-rounded individual, they must take the time to see who the child is, to draw forth what is inside and treat him with respect.

Parents must give teachers insights into their child's character, strengths, interests, needs and areas of concern. After all, the parent should know the child better than the teacher. To achieve this end, a teacher may send home a questionnaire at the beginning of the year which is designed to elicit this information. The answers help a teacher get to know the child, while revealing how the parent views her child and whether she acknowledges his strengths and is aware of areas of concern. Although this information can be helpful, the teacher needs to create her own relationship with the child that is based on her observations and interactions with the child.

Parents should discuss answers on the questionnaire with their child and set goals together, particularly with regard to pursuing areas of interest and improving skills that will help their child succeed in school and in life.

Parent teacher communication depends upon mutual disclosure. A parent must be willing to mention when there are struggles at home that might affect the child's ability to get along with others or dampen his enthusiasm for learning. Although parents may not choose to disclose personal details, it is important to alert the teacher when a child is experiencing undue stress at home. Teachers can use this information to provide empathy, support and guidance to a child who may not be getting all his needs met. Of course, disclosures should not be viewed as excuses for poor child behavior, but as a way for parents and teachers to work together for the benefit of the child.

Parent teacher communication is dependent upon mutual disclosure.

In the same vein, teachers must keep parents informed about what is happening at school. For instance, if a child is humiliated in front of the class while giving a report or is often taunted by his peers, parents need to know, so they can give the child support at home and teach him coping strategies and come-backs. (Of course, parents should create an open dialogue with their children, so they already know what is going on.) Keeping the lines of communication open so that parents and teachers can have a bigger perspective about what is happening in the life of the child, creates a supportive network that benefits everyone involved.

The parent teacher relationship is dependent on establishing a regular means for communication. Many teachers are accessible at school (and some even give out their home numbers), via email or school web sites. Find a way to communicate with your child's teacher on a regular basis, even if it means you have to use a payphone. If your child is struggling at school, either with homework or relationships with peers, be proactive and work with the teacher to create a two-pronged approach which encourages the child to discover ways to solve the problem using the guidance at home and school.

Establish a regular means of parent teacher communication.

Familiarize yourself with the school policies and rules specific to a teacher's class. Talk these over with your child, so he has a clear understanding of expectations for performance and guidelines for acceptable behavior. Although I have encountered a few school policies that were designed less to protect the children than to protect the school against a lawsuit, help your child understand the rules and how they contribute to a safe environment in which students can learn and interact positively with others. If your child understands how a rule benefits everyone, he is more likely to respect it.

Parent teacher communication tip: send your child's teacher a note of appreciation for all she does.

Teachers often hear from parents only when there are complaints or conflicts. On occasion, send your child's teacher a note or email to tell how much you value his or her influence in your child's life. Since teachers can be flooded with unwanted gifts during the holidays and on Teacher Appreciation Day, I think a note is more appropriate. Although teachers are paid for what they do, the best among them contribute far more to the children than their job description requires. Acknowledge and inspire teachers with your recognition and support.

Parent teacher communication is paramount to your child's success at school.

Create a strong parent teacher relationship by volunteering. Although many parents have to work, ask your boss if you can have some flex time once per month to volunteer or chaperone on field trips. If your children are anything like mine, they'll be tickled when you help out at school. In addition to supporting the teacher, you'll get to observe the dynamics of the class and get to know the cast of characters.

It takes a village to raise a child who is healthy, caring, and responsible. In school, this village starts with the network formed by parents, teachers and administrators who understand that their job is to work together to support and guide the development of each child.

Unit 10 Moral Education
道德教育

Text A   Education as a Moral Enterprise

导读:道德教育,我们应该怎样看待它所扮演的角色? 毫无疑问,在学生的成长过程中,道德教育有利于培养学生的良好品德,帮助其对有争议的良知问题做出理性的判断。

We trust it is uncontroversial to say that schooling is unavoidably a moral enterprise. Indeed, schools teach morality in a number of ways, both implicit and explicit.

Schools have a moral ethos embodied in rules, rewards and punishments, dress codes, honor codes, student government, relationships, styles of teaching, extracurricular emphases, art, and in the kinds of respect accorded students and teachers. Schools convey to children what is expected of them, what is normal, what is right and wrong. It is often claimed that values are caught rather than taught; through their ethos, schools socialize children into patterns of moral behavior.

Textbooks and courses often address moral questions and take moral positions. Literature inevitably explores moral issues, and writers take positions on those issues—as do publishers who decide which literature goes in the anthologies. In teaching history we initiate students into particular cultural traditions and identities. Although economics courses and texts typically avoid overt moral language and claim to be "value free", their accounts of human nature, decision making, and the economic world have moral implications, as we have seen.

The overall shape of the curriculum is morally loaded by virtue of what it requires, what it makes available as electives, and what it ignores. For example, for more than a century (but especially since A Nation at Risk and the reform reports of the 1980s), there has been a powerful movement to make schooling and the curriculum serve economic purposes. Religion and art, by contrast, have been largely ignored (and are not even elective possibilities in many schools). As a result, schooling encourages a rather more materialistic and less spiritual culture—a matter of some moral significance.

Educators have devised a variety of approaches to values and morality embodied in self-esteem, community service, civic education, sex education, drug education, Holocaust education, multicultural education, values clarification, and character education programs—to name but a few. We might consider two of the most influential of these approaches briefly.

For the past several decades values clarification programs have been widely used in public schools. In this approach, teachers help students "clarify" their values by having them reflect on moral dilemmas and think through the consequences of the options open to them, choosing that action that maximizes their deepest values. It is unjustifiable for a teacher to "impose" his or her values on students; this would be an act of oppression that denies the individuality and autonomy of students. Values are ultimately personal; indeed, the implicit message is that there are no right or wrong values. Needless to say, this is a deeply controversial approach—and is now widely rejected.

The character education movement of the last decade has been a response, in part, to the perceived relativism of values clarification.

Finally, we note what is conspicuous by its absence: Although all universities offer courses in ethics, usually in departments of philosophy or religious studies, very few public schools have such courses. Unlike either values clarification or character education programs, the major purpose of ethics courses is usually to provide students with intellectual resources drawn from a variety of traditions and schools of thought that might orient them in the world and help them think through difficult moral problems. As important as we all agree morality to be, it is striking that schools do not consider ethics courses an option worth offering.

Socialization, we suggested, is the uncritical initiation of students into a tradition, a way of thinking and acting. Education, by contrast, requires critical distance from tradition, exposure to alternatives, informed and reflective deliberation about how to think and live.

Not all, but much character education might better be called character training or socialization, for the point is not so much to teach virtue and values by way of critical reflection on contending points of view, but to structure the moral ethos of schooling to nurturing the development of those moral habits and virtues that we agree to be good and important, that are part of our moral consensus. This is not a criticism of character education. Children must be morally trained. But there are limitations to character education as a general theory of moral education; it was not designed to address critical thinking about those "ideologically charged" debates that divide us. Character education does appeal, as the Manifesto makes clear, to a heritage of stories, literature, art, and biography to inform and deepen students' understanding of, and appreciation for, moral virtue. Often such literature will reveal the moral ambiguities of life, and discussion of it will encourage critical reflection on what is right and wrong. But if the literature is chosen to nurture the development of the right virtues and values, it may not be well suited to nurture an appreciation of moral ambiguity or informed and critical thinking about contending values and ways of thinking and living(Of course, character education programs often nurture the virtues of tolerance, respect, and civility that play major roles in enabling educational discussion of controversial issues.).

One of the supposed virtues of the values clarification movement, by contrast, was its use of moral dilemmas and divisive issues; moreover, in asking students to consider the consequences of their actions, it required them to think critically about them. But the values clarification movement never required students to develop an educated understanding of moral frameworks of thought that could inform their thinking and provide them with critical distance on their personal desires and moral intuitions; it left them to their own inner resources.

Let us put it this way. Character education is an essential aspect of moral education, but a fully adequate theory of moral education must also address those morally divisive ("ideologically charged") issues that are sufficiently important so that students must be educated about them. Of course, one of these issues is the nature of morality itself; after all, moral education, it was not designed to address critical thinking about those "ideologically charged" debates that divide us. If students are to be morally educated—and educated about morality—they must have some understanding of the moral frameworks civilization provides for making sense of the moral dimension of life. After all, morality is not intellectually free-floating, a matter of arbitrary choices and merely personal values. Morality is bound up with our placs in a community or tradition, our understanding of nature and human nature, our convictions about the afterlife, our experiences of the sacred, our assumptions about what the mind can know, and our understanding of what makes life meaningful. We make sense of what we ought to do, of what kind of a person we should be, in light of all of these aspects of life—at least if we are reflective.

For any society (or school) to exist, its members (students, teachers, and administrators) must share a number of moral virtues: They must be honest, responsible, and respectful of one another's well-being. We agree about this. Public schools have a vital role to play in nurturing these consensus virtues and values, as the character education movement rightly emphasizes; indeed, a major purpose of schooling is to help develop good persons.

If we are to live together peacefully in a pluralistic society, we must also nurture those civic virtues and values that are part of our constitutional tradition: We must acknowledge responsibility for protecting one another's rights; we must debate our differences in a civil manner; we must keep informed. A major purpose of schooling is to nurture good citizenship.

What shape moral education should take depends on the maturity of students. We might think of a K-12 continuum in which character education begins immediately with the socialization of children into those consensus values and virtues that sustain our communities. As children grow older and more mature they should gradually be initiated into a liberal education in which they are taught to think in informed and reflective ways about important, but controversial, moral issues.

Character education and liberal education cannot be isolated in single courses but should be integrated into the curriculum as a whole. We also believe, however, that the curriculum should include room for a moral capstone course that high school seniors might take, in which they learn about the most important moral frameworks of thought—secular and religious, historical and contemporary—and how such frameworks might shape their thinking about the most urgent moral controversies they face.

K-12 (pronounced "k twelve", "k through twelve", or "k to twelve" 基础教育的年龄段): is a designation for the sum of primary and secondary education. It is used in the United States, Canada, Australia, and New Zealand where P-12 is also commonly used. The expression is a shortening of Kindergarten (K) for 4-6-year-olds through twelfth grade (12) for 16-19-year-olds, the first and last grades of free education in these countries.

Unit 10　Moral Education　道德教育

New Words and Expression

1. ethos ['i:θɔs]　　　　　　　n.　　　民族精神,道德风貌,气质
2. anthology [æn'θɔlədʒi]　　n.　　　选集,文选
3. initiate...into...　　　　　　　　　 传授某人奥秘
4. holocaust ['hɔləkɔ:st]　　　n.　　　大屠杀,浩劫
5. conspicuous [kən'spikjuəs]　adj.　明显的,显而易见的
6. orient ['ɔ:riənt]　　　　　　v.　　　使……适应,朝……方位
7. arbitrary ['ɑ:bitrəri]　　　　adj.　任意的,专制的
8. pluralistic [pluərə'listik]　 adj.　多元论的
9. capstone ['kæpstəun]　　　n.　　　顶层石,顶点
10. secular ['sekjulə]　　　　　adj.　世俗的,非宗教的

I　Vocabulary.

Fill in the blanks with the most suitable words. Change the form when necessary.

conspicuous　　ethos　　anthology　　arbitrary　　capstone

1. This _____ reveals a prejudice in favor of lyric poets.
2. I guess we're not used to your _____ standards, and you'd better change your plan.
3. Lincoln is a _____ example of a poor boy's success, whose experiences have encouraged and inspired numerous young people.
4. The day could not be far distant when naturalism would dominate the _____ of American literature.
5. He stood at the _____ of his political career.

II　Comprehension of the text.

Decide whether the following statements are true (T) or false (F) according to the passage.

1. It is often claimed that values are taught rather than caught; through their ethos, schools socialize children into patterns of moral behavior.
2. For the past several decades values clarification programs have been widely used in private schools.
3. The major purpose of schooling is to develop good persons and nurture good citizenship.
4. Character education and liberal education should be integrated into the curriculum for a moral capstone course in which school seniors learn about the most important moral frameworks of thought.
5. Moral education was supposed to address critical thinking about those "ideologically charged" debates that divide us and whose moral character we should hold onto.

III Discussion.

1. Does your school provide moral education for you? Is it effective?
2. What do you think are the major purposes of schooling? Try to name some.
3. One of the supposed virtues of the values clarification movement, by contrast, was its use of moral dilemmas and divisive issues. Do you think this method can be adopted here in China? Can it really work?

Text B Moral Education of Youth in the Information Age

导读：在中国，人们意识到学校教育的主要目的是教会学生做人，因此道德教育越来越被视为教育的重要部分。传统的道德教育无外乎正确道德观和价值观的反复灌输。而在信息时代，这样的教育方式，需要借助一定的信息技术，才能达到我们期望的效果。

(1) _____

Moral education in the Information Age is becoming an increasingly complex project because of the greater diversity of values that are present in our communities institutions, and life situations. When combined with the rapid pace of change that is characteristic of the Information Age, the variety of values that circulate in the communities and institutions challenge the general and uniformed applicability of moral principles that we have unquestionably accepted as truth. The emergence of values that are akin to the market and the keen competition that it generates, for example, has challenged the authority of certain time—honored values and practices, if not rendered them obsolete. Few moral principles can be exempted from the close scrutiny of moral educators who are urgently exploring ways to sustain the vitality and relevance of their work in the schools and beyond. Without beliefs and principles that are sound and lasting, moral education will have no intellectual and ethical footing. It will drift aimlessly in the sea of irrelevance.

The anxiety of moral educators has to be understood in today's context of cultural diversity and social change. The conception of cultural diversity is no longer confined within the boundaries of a country, for the Internet has quietly but effectively disseminated immense volumes of ideas, images, and artifacts of culture among citizens of any nations that have access to it. Moreover, interaction among people on the internet presents a kind of social change that challenges our ability to think morally in a real yet imaginary relationship. The absence of physical contacts in the "cyber world" often distorts our views on moral obligation toward others: If we do not even have eye-contact in making the transaction, how can we be obligated toward one another? Thus immoral acts such as the non-delivery of goods purchased, thefts of intellectual properties, intrusion into others "privacy, and even the deprivation of others" right to operate their computers normally, are buried behind a curtain of anonymity in the "cyber world".

Cultural diversity and social change in the Information Age warrant a new kind of understanding of the foundations of moral education. Diversity and change afford an opportunity for us to reflect on the aims of moral education and explore ways to facilitate the attainment of goals. If diversity of values has to be understood in specific cultural and social contexts, and change has become a constant factor in our lives, then it may be tempting to take no moral stance in our judgments and actions and submit ourselves to the command of moral relativism. When this happens, moral education loses it vitality, for it is no longer a principled exercise of our hearts and minds. For moral education in schools, upholding certain defensible moral principles, is a particularly important undertaking because it will determine whether moral education can continue to serve its educational purposes.

(2)_____

Fortunately for moral educators in schools, these moral principles can always be found in their schools' missions. While the continual interpretation and refinement of these principles can sustain their endeavors to a certain extent, lofty ideals that defy common wisdom may not be fully accepted by the students and their parents. For this reason, it should be the labor of moral educators to identify and uphold simple and enduring principles that can be readily embraced by all parties concerned. One of these principles is "respect for oneself and respect for others". "Respect" is a maxim in moral education that has been upheld by Chinese and western educators alike. As an essential element in any healthy social relations, "respect" refers not only to a desirable position toward others but also toward oneself. It affirms a person's worth, dignity, and rights. Because other persons have just as much worth, dignity, and rights as I, then it is reasonable for me to respect others as I should respect myself. As a guiding principle, "do not do to others what you do not want done to yourself" can be a simple but very useful constraint on one's desires and actions. More positively, "respect for others" provides an essential reference for one's attitude and conduct toward others, especially toward those persons that you do not know, or has no relations with. "Respect" magnifies the worth of a person. At the same time, it affords an axiological lens through which the worth and needs of "others" can be clearly recognized.

The students' capability of handling their relations with others can be enhanced if moral education is based on respect for others. From a social perspective, people's moral conduct is manifested in their relations with others; and moral education can only be effectively conducted with the "I-other" relationship as its epistemological and axiological basis. If our students can consider the dignity, rights, and welfare of others before they act, then it is much less likely that their actions would be harmful to others or to the common good. Moreover, if moral education call help the students to cultivate a thorough understanding of the "I-other" relationship and help them to nurture positive feelings toward others, then other important qualities such as compassion and empathy can be further developed. A desirable state in moral development is reached when altruism becomes an integral part of their character.

Given the aforementioned observation, the function of moral education is to help students handle their relations with others properly. Moral educators should guide students to appreciate the existence of others, care about their needs, understand their predicaments, empathize with their plight, and respect their rights and values. With this, the students will be able to gradually transcend their own self-interests and to give appropriate attention to matters of public interests. Their participation in the advancement of the common good will be a matter of course.

(3)_____

Many scholars and practitioners in education have assumed that the school is the only suitable sites for moral education. Indeed, as the social institution that is charged with the responsibility of teaching our children the basic literacy and social skills, the school seems to be the natural site for their moral education as well. However, today's formal schooling has lagged behind the developmental needs of the Information Age. This is especially true in terms of its requirements for human development. The examination-oriented pedagogy that is so prevalent in Chinese schools leaves little time and intellectual space for students to develop their social awareness and skills. Operating under the tyranny of an "audit culture" where "value-addedness" and academic achievement are the main concerns, our schools are consumed by the imperatives of performativity. The only emphasis of today's schooling is the demonstrable and measurable outcomes of education. Exploration of the inherent values of education is in large part being neglected by our schools; and, if such values are needed for ornamental purposes, the schools pay lip service to them and to moral education which embodies and expresses them.

Actually, the most natural site for moral education is the family. The family is considered to be the unit that consists of the most significant "others" in the lives of children and youths—their parents. The parents' influence on the moral development of their children is strong and lifelong. It is in the family where parental devotion to the well-being of the child can be considered a given, and where adult-child ratio in the educative process is definitely more favorable than that of the school. The home environment, moreover, affords a context in which intimate thoughts and feelings can be shared readily between parents and children without the social pressure and pretense that are often found in more formal social settings. Thus the family provides a more accommodating setting for moral education which warrants the exchange of ideas and inculcation of values that are personally derived. Among educators, the common concern about the family as a site of moral education is whether parents can truly understand the developmental needs of their children, and whether they are ready to engage their offspring in a knowledgeable and sensible way. Indeed, the needs of children for parental guidance and support differ from one stage of moral development to another. The manners of engagement, whether they are restrictive or supportive, in fact reflect the psychological basis on which moral education is conducted at home.

Other sites that can serve as platforms for moral education are the educational activities that are conducted outside the framework of the formal system of schooling. Rich in diversity, these activities afford a broad educational avenue through which the interests of growing children and adolescents can be served. Out-of-school programs which constitute what is known as "non-formal education" include a large variety of organized social and cultural activities that are organized by institutions and agencies such as youth palaces, cultural stations and museums, and by children and youth groups such as the Boys Scouts and Young Pioneers. In ways that are less rigid but more informal than classroom instruction, these out-of-school programs can be equally effective in inculcating desirable values and attitudes in the students. Their efficacy, however, remains to be tapped by moral educators.

Another possible site for moral education is the neighborhood. Compared to the schools and non-formal education programs, the neighborhood is much less structured. Compared to the family, it is more public; but for the social development of children and youths. It's potentiality for children's exploration and understanding of the "I-other" relations should not be underestimated. The neighborhood is where children and youths spend most of their time besides their homes and schools. Unlike homes and schools, which are highly controlled sites, neighborhoods are much less restrictive on behaviors. Thus whether neighborhoods are sites of opportunities for exploration and discovery or danger zones for indulgence and debauchery depends very much on the kind of activities that children and youths participate in. This in turn depends on the kind of peers that they choose to keep. Research has shown that risk-taking activities are more prevalent among youths in poorer neighborhoods than in densely populated urban areas. Research has also shown that youths, because they "inhabit a transitional middle-ground somewhere between childhood and adulthood", are excluded from many physical and social space in the community. For the purpose of moral education, the neighborhood can be a site where "respect for others" can be understood and practiced. If appropriate activities can be arranged, children and youths can practice neighborliness through participation in community service and observe first-hand the effects of their own contribution to the well-being of others.

(4) _____

A site for moral education that is unique to the Information Age is the "cyber world" that embodies numerous networks which serve to facilitate instant communication among users of information technologies. For moral educators, the emergence of the "cyber world" can be unsettling because of all the "demons" that lurk within a world that we cannot see. There can be little protection of the young minds if the corrupting effects are not readily discernible from their behavior. This kind of disorientation brought on by the presence of the "cyber world" poses the most serious challenge to moral education, regardless of its sites of application. This is because the "multidirectional networks" are transforming the structure of our economic and social institutions and our established system of beliefs and values would have to be able to maintain its validity and relevance

Unit 10 Moral Education 道德教育

in order to survive. The challenges to the established system will be multidimensional, intense and swift, because the global onslaught of axiological persuasions is projected through so many powerful lenses of informational technologies. Our world is now connected in global networks of the information and images that travel throughout the world instantly. Without a clear and strong epistemological and axiological anchor, moral education will drift in the sea of contentious ideas and values.

If we accept that moral education is an enterprise that should undergo constant review and revival, then the waves of new information that are generated from the multidirectional networks should not be feared; that is, if we can derive wisdom and insights from them. As a matter of fact, it is in this newly found wisdom that we can identify the impetus to the constant revival of moral education. New information and ideas challenge us to reflect on our own values; and if we can develop new notions of justice, rights, fairness, equity and harmony that we can uphold, and then we can confidently use them to guide our children and youths through the stages of their development with renewed interest and relevance. Moral educators should embrace the current phenomena of uncertainty and attempt to negotiate new notions of morality and education so that they do not fall too far behind the developmental needs of our children and youths. In fact, educators in other areas are attempting to do just that. The efforts of language educators to derive new meanings of literacy from the internet, for example, should serve as a useful reference for moral educators if they indeed wish to reestablish their bearings and resituate notions of morality in the realities of the "cyber world".

New Words and Expression

1. render ['rendə] v. 提供,表现,使成为
2. anonymity [ænə'nimətɪ] n. 匿名,笔者不明
3. warrant ['wɔ:rənt] v. 担保,给……正当理由
4. axiological [æksɪə'lɔdʒɪkəl] adj. 价值论的
5. epistemological [ɪpɪstəmə'lɔdʒɪkəl] adj. 认识论的
6. predicament [prɪ'dɪkəmənt] n. 困境
7. plight [plaɪt] n. 困境,苦境
8. lip service   说的好听的话,空口的应酬话
9. inculcation [ˌɪnkʌl'keɪʃn] n. 教授,谆谆教导
10. debauchery [dɪ'bɔ:tʃərɪ] n. 放荡,沉湎酒色
11. discernible [dɪ'sə:nəbəl] adj. 可辨别的

I Read the following subheadings and put them in the blank in this text appropriately.

a. The "cyber world" as a site of moral education
b. Respect as a guiding principle for moral education
c. Sites of moral education
d. Whither is the moral education drifting?

II Comprehension of the text.

Decide whether the following statements are true (T) or false (F) according to the passage.

1. The conception of cultural diversity is limited in a nation, for people immigrate and emigrate more often than before.
2. Lofty ideas defy common wisdom should not be fully acknowledged by students, so educators labor to uphold some simple principles.
3. Home and neighborhood are two ideal places for children to cultivate and nurture moralities.
4. Due to measures taken by the government and serious policies devoted to the protection of young minds when they are online, we totally don't have to worry about "demons", which lurk in a virtual world.
5. We need to develop new notions of justice, rights, fairness, equity and harmony that we can uphold, and then we can confidently use them to guide our children and youths through the stages of their development with renewed interest and relevance, because they need various help during different steps.

III Discussion.

1. How do your parents help you to cultivate your morality in different developmental stages?
2. Why do you think it is very important for us to focus on "cyber world" morality?
3. How can we make full advantage of the Internet to let it serve to the morality purpose?

Supplementary Reading

Moral Education and Improvement of Coexistence in Spain

Coexistence and moral education are areas of great interest in Spanish compulsory education, especially in the period that comprises between 12 and 16 years of age, named "compulsory secondary education" in Spain. With the aim to improve the processes of coexistence within this level, this research team on education from the University of Salamanca has conducted an experimental study, implementing a program to provide moral education through ICTs (information and communication technologies). So as to verify the positive influence of the programme, a series of means have been applied with consideration for two groups-control and experimental and certain stages of pre-test and post-test assessment. The first results denote that there has been an improvement in social-personal values in the students that were involved more actively in the programme.

Cava and Mositu (2002) supported that improving the coexistence allows to help adolescents generate autonomy, improve the self-esteem, make easier the work of the teachers, improve academic learning and defend as a strategy cooperative work among other reasons, because it allows favorable interpersonal relationships. What is more, through collaborative learning, competencies are developed and knowledge is gained (Waldegg, 2002). If we reflect on the potentialities of technologies in this field, as Winther and Balsley (2004) have stated, collaborative work is encouraged, especially through the use of blogs.

In the US, it was evidenced that the use of ICTs (information and communication technologies) for the teaching of conflict resolution is all appropriate alternative. After the application of a program, it was qualitatively and quantitatively demonstrated that adolescents manifested more abilities to solve and prevent conflicts.

Ryan, Sweeder and Bednar (1998), after running a program that developed empathy towards people with AIDS through the use of chat rooms, briefly pointed out that educational technology is a specially effective tool to develop values, such as solidarity, responsibility, equity and self-control in class.

The values that rule coexistence, solidarity, honesty, equality, responsibility, freedom, love, respect towards life, difference and human rights, cooperation and peace and justice must be promoted in the everyday life of the educational institution and in the curricula areas. Therefore, if it is evident that there is an urgency to undertake a moral and attitudinal education, we should join forces in order to educate people committed to the above-mentioned values.

The aim of the essay is to prove that the implementation of a program for moral education through the use of new technologies enhances the social values for the coexistence of adolescents in secondary education classrooms. In order to confirm the hypothesis, a quasi-experimental methodology has been set out, with the design of non-equivalent groups, and with a pre-and post-test assessment. A manipulation and control of variables through the assignation of an experimental and a control group has been carried out. Likewise, interfering variables that could affect the studied dependents will be considered to prove the impact of the program, diverse instruments of assessment were applied. In this paper, we present the results obtained in the questionnaire on socio-personal values.

We worked with a total of 50 students, of which 12 belong to the experimental group that was selected by the punctuations that had been granted to them as they participated in the different activities of the program.

The implemented program is called VES (values in situation, "Valores En Situation"). Its starting point is the everyday life of the secondary school and the acknowledgement through an express congratulation in a blog because of having performed actions or positive conducts that reflect one of the values. Taking these actions into account, we put forward the theory about that value and questions to encourage the reflection and participation in the comments on the blog. The duration was 9 weeks, working in each one of them with a different value.

Participants expressed a more favorable opinion in the post-test about the suggested statements. In this way, people who were more involved in the program show results denoting that they had a greater capacity to recognize their own success. On the other hand, a person who is grateful for a favor done is somebody that has developed empathy, being this one of the most worked values in the program. The capacity to give thanks, kindness, education and good manners were favored. Moreover, a positive influence of the program on the perception of the value of "justice" is observed. Finally, the sense of respect and solidarity was stressed and the students interiorized these values. This is made obvious, because those who were more involved in the program agreed more in that helping others is satisfactory and that respecting others avoids problems and makes life nicer.

Unit 10 Moral Education 道德教育

Prior results have allowed US to state that the application of specific programs in order to improve coexistence through the development of socio-personal values offers indications of positive results in compulsory secondary school students.

Studying school coexistence to find models of intervention and consolidated research constitutes an important challenge due to that it is a field of research relatively new and is of great concern in present-day society. As stated by Ortega(2006), it has been studied in Spain for barely 20 years. This previous research made it possible to structure some of the approaches, methods and strategies implemented nowadays to deal with this problem.

In this sense, we chose moral education as strategy to enhance coexistence. It is complex to visualize "moral education" from the perspective of intervention as we place ourselves in a field dealt with by literature, philosophy, and even politics. In spite of this, a psico-pedagogic approach has tried to be developed, so as to allow implementing a program of educational intervention.

To contextualize this intervention in our present society, we introduced the strategy and medium given by ICTs. In a society of knowledge and information, and working with adolescents, we find that ICTs not only offer a great motivational potential but also are structuring the thought and learning of the students, as well as transmitting knowledge in an attractive and creative way. These characteristics positively influence the attitudes and the feelings of the subjects in whose personality, when they do not forget the pedagogic objectives, knowledge is more easily integrated.

After the application of the program, we can conclude that reflection and moral learning has been encouraged to achieve the improvement of coexistence, even when statistically significant differences were not obtained in the coexistence variable, as they were obtained in that of socio-personal values. This data allow us to consider that the objectives of the program referred to moral education were achieved. Possibly, if a more extensive program were developed, with a greater implication of the whole education community, the results would be promoted as well.

Our research coincides with that of Perez(2007) in which, after carrying out a similar study to ours, no statistically significant differences were found either in the area of coexistence. However, both their research and ours permit to conclude that there have been some modifications in the classroom atmosphere, favoring social relationships.

Another coinciding research is Goldworthy, Schwartz and Barab's(2007), in which they also use ICTs as a tool to transmit knowledge that leads to learning how to resolve conflicts. In both studies, it is possible to conclude that those experiences which relay on these mediums allow a cognitive development and learning from experience which produces a great impact on personality and has repercussions on people's behavior and sociability.

Using Fernandez's (2008) words, we believe that creating programs to intervene in coexistence demands a design based on values that guide future actions. It is also believed that a research, such as this, can be useful as a first stage towards a deeper intervention to educate the education community in values that can structure school coexistence.

Authors with ample experience in the field of school coexistence (Ortega, 2008) pointed out moral education as valid strategy. This study hence becomes an innovative contribution that responds to the demands, not only of the research community, but also of education institutions and society as a whole.

Unit 11 Extra-curricular Activities
课外活动

Text A   Extra-curricular Activity and the Transition from Higher Education to Work

导读:根据对英国毕业生的一份大规模调查研究显示,课外活动对毕业生从学校走向工作岗位这一过程的转变有着重大的影响。可以总结出两种情况:一种是频繁的课外活动使毕业生在转变期的表现比平均水平好;另一种是比平均水平差。为什么会这样是一个值得研究的课题。

Extra-curricular activity is important because of its potential to reinforce and market the outcomes of the education system. Any particular involvement in a certain type of extra-curricular activity may influence a graduate's transition process to the labor market, for instance, by speeding up or slowing down access to employment. Therefore, it is essential that students and graduates understand the impact of extra-curricular activity and appraise the role it may play in their strategies for transition from higher education to employment.

Analyzing the effects of extra-curricular activity is also important to guidance services. As was stressed in a recent international report, most guidance activities in higher education concentrate on course choices and on psychological counseling to deal with students' emotional and study problems. However, as educational institutions are faced with increasing competition for students and resources, the labor market outcome of graduates is becoming a key marketing argument. Therefore, as a contribution to develop knowledge on the process of transition from higher education to the labor market, analyzing the effects of extra-curricular activities is crucial to guidance services and to their host institutions.

Research attention to date has been focused on the influence of extra-curricular activity on college choice decision making, personality and social behavior and alumni generosity. Factors affecting participation in extra-curricular activities have also been studied. In contrast, little attention has been paid to the influence of extra-curricular activities on the outcome of the education-to-work transition process. Eide and Rona (2001) have shown that, in the United States, participation in varsity sports may have positive effects on earnings, although these effects may vary according to graduates' ethnic background. But researchers have generally ignored the role of other types of extra-curricular activities as well as the effects of these activities on non-salary conditions of labor market entry. Therefore, this study should be of interest to readers involved in higher education, especially students, guidance researchers and practitioners, and educational administrators interested in rethinking the place of extra-curricular activities in higher education.

This study is based on a survey of graduates in UK. The paper is divided into three sections. Section one presents the interpretative framework. Section two is devoted to the methodology adopted. Section three presents and comments upon the main results obtained.

Interpretative framework

Economic theory, especially statistical discrimination theory, posits that employers pay particular attention to the non-market activities of job applicants. On the one hand, some employers value the non-market activities of job applicants. These employers consider that having been involved in non-market activities is an indicator of an applicant's responsibility, citizenship and maturity which they think will be of advantage to the firm. On the other hand, other employers consider that non-market activities have a negative effect. The main concern of this second type of employer amounts to excluding high turnover rate ("*high-quit-rate*") candidates, because turnover is costly to firms. Since the turnover propensity of an applicant cannot be observed directly, these employers divide applicants into two groups: a high-attrition-rate group and a low-attrition-rate group. These employers negatively associate worker turnover with non-market activities. Two reasons may explain this perspective. First, involvement in family life or in leisure or social activities may indicate low professional commitment resulting in low productivity and eventually firing. Second, family and social life can expand or become more important to such an extent that the employee resigns from the firm. In both cases, extra-professional life would appear to be a source of turnover. Consequently, applicants considered as belonging to the high-attrition-rate group are faced with stricter employment criteria, lower wages and fewer interviews, and may therefore be excluded altogether from the recruitment process, even when they are as qualified as other candidates. The statistical discrimination theory is not but one of the multiple ways to explain restricted access to employment. A lot of alternative approaches have been developed, especially by labor economists, which take into account such diverse determinants as employers' preferences, job-searchers' strategies, the behavior of labor market intermediaries, economic structures or labor market public policies. But statistical discrimination is of particular interest because it provides a framework to interpret extra-curricular activities. Within this framework, students' leisure and social activities can be interpreted as non-market activities, which employers consider positively or negatively. In that respect, the statistical discrimination approach helps us to better understand the relationships that might be observed between extra-curricular activity and labor market entry.

Method

This study uses data from a survey conducted in 2004. The survey was designed within the Research Laboratory in Theoretical and Applied Economics (Beta) at Louis Pasteur University of Strasbourg (France). Associations, offices, and networks of alumni from higher education were contacted in the UK and were requested to invite their members to respond a questionnaire on the survey website.

The questionnaire had three parts. Part one focused on personal details and education, part two on the respondents' extra-curricular non-market activities while students, and part three on their experiences during the transition process from higher education to the labor market. The transitional period was defined as the three years immediately following graduation.

One hundred nineteen individuals responded to the questionnaire. These respondents constitute the sample of the study. This is clearly a small sample. The effects of extra-curricular activity were investigated by means of regression analysis. Five explanatory variables were taken into account: the involvement in extra-curricular activities, the type of activity, and the time spent in the activity, the intensity of the involvement and the context of practice. In addition, the degree levels and subjects were included as independent variables in the estimates too, in order to clearly make the difference between their own effects and those of the five extra-curricular factors mentioned above. Three degree levels (bachelor, master and doctorate) and four degree subjects were distinguished. Given that different variables can yield similar effects because of intercorrelations between variables, intercorrelations were checked. No case of strong intercorrelation among the independent variables could be observed. The effects of these potential factors were investigated on five categories of dependent variables: job security, occupational status, access to large firms, wages and unemployment. For each outcome variable, several alternative specifications were used in order to avoid missing any significant effect. It was also checked that these outcome variables were uncorrelated. Linear regression analysis (ordinary least squares) was used when the dependent variables were quantitative while logistic regression analysis was used when they were qualitative. A two-step estimation procedure was adopted. The first step consisted in estimating the effects of involvement within the whole sample. The second step consisted in estimating the effects of all other factors put together within the group of respondents with extra-curricular experience.

Results and comments

Extra-curricular experience has a twofold influence on the outcome of the transitional process. On the one hand, having been involved in extra-curricular activity creates an advantage in terms of occupational status. As compared with graduates who were involved in extra-curricular activities, those who did not participate were almost three times more likely to begin their careers as office employees rather than as managers. On the other hand, graduates without extra-curricular experience had been unemployed for a significantly shorter period of time before getting their first jobs. These findings show that involvement in extra-curricular activities makes a difference. Further investigations demonstrate that within the group of the graduates who decided to be involved, the nature of the extra-curricular experience matters.

Job security

Within the group of graduates with extra-curricular experience, 93.75 per cent obtained an open-ended employment contract before the end of the transitional period (78.12 per cent right from the first job on). The most important factor favoring job security is participation in cultural activities.

As compared with other respondents, those who participated in cultural and spiritual activities were more likely to get open-ended contracts. Conversely, three characteristics were strongly linked with job insecurity. The first one has to do with the depth of the involvement. Graduates who engaged in an activity for a long period of time or at leadership level had fewer chances of getting open-ended contracts. Additionally, participation in the social sector led to fixed-term rather than open-ended contracts. Finally, the graduates who had practiced with their families or as clients were less likely to be employed under open-ended contracts within the transitional period.

Occupational status

Of the respondents with extra-curricular experience, 71.87 per cent reached a managerial position within the transitional period (59.37 per cent right from the first contract on). The access to a managerial position mainly depends on the depth and length of the involvement in activities as well as of the context of practice. A leadership experience gives more chances of reaching managerial positions. However, the whole extra-curricular experience should be kept in reasonable limits: The longer the experience, the fewer the chances of reaching managerial positions. Practice with family or with friends is also significantly correlated with becoming a manager. The types of activity play a role too.

Although no type of extra-curricular activity gives particular chances of becoming a manager, it seems that participation in student associations or in cultural activities are especially inadequate and tend to shift the graduates towards lower supervisory or office employee positions, at least for the first jobs.

Access to large firms

Of the respondents with extra-curricular experience, 51.56 per cent were employed in large firms during the transitional period (42.18 per cent right from the first job on).

Participation in sports was the less efficient extra-curricular activity as regards beginning one's career in a large firm. In comparison with participation in sports, involvement in student associations, in the social sector or in cultural activities gave better chances of joining a large firm right from the first job on. Graduates with an experience in citizenship activities also began their careers in larger firms. And at the end of the transitional period, graduates who had been participating in student associations or in citizenship activities were working in larger firms than those who participated in sports. Only the type of activity seems to matter. No other extra-curricular factor seems to have an influence on the access to large firms.

Wages

Wages are influenced by the context of practice and by the type of activity. Two observations may be made. The first one is that, as compared with practice within associations, practice with family seems to be more closely linked with better wages at the end of the transitional period. The second observation is that the graduates who participated in student associations or in the social sector had lower first-job wages than those who participated in sports.

Unemployment

Fifty per cent of the respondent graduates with an extra-curricular experience have been unemployed at some time within the transition period (46.87 per cent before the first job). The risk and length of unemployment depend on the four extra-curricular factors. On one hand, two characteristics lower the risk and length of unemployment. First, the graduates who had been leaders in their extra-curricular activities had a lower risk of experiencing unemployment before the first job. Second, as regards the length of unemployment, the graduates who had practiced their activity with their family were unemployed during a significantly shorter period of time than others both before and after the first job. On the other hand, some other characteristics increase the risk and length of unemployment. First, participation in cultural activities and long-term involvement increase the risk of experiencing unemployment before the first job. Second, practice with friend or as a client lengthens the spells of unemployment.

Extra-curricular profiles

It thus can be seen that within the group of graduates with an extra-curricular experience, the nature of the extra-curricular activity makes a difference to entry into the workforce. Although most extra-curricular factors have a twofold influence, three clear-cut profiles could finally be distinguished.

Profile 1 comprises "Leaders and Citizens". The graduates who engaged at leadership level had better access to managerial positions and the lowest risk of unemployment before the first job. Those who participated in citizenship activities had access to large firms right from the first job on, and all along the transition period. Their spells in unemployment also seem to have been shorter.

Profile 2 represents the "Sportspersons". This profile corresponds to the most frequent extra-curricular behavior, which consists in practicing sports as simple participant within associations. Profile 2 appears to be generally associated with average transition outcomes.

Profile 3 comprises "Activists and Clients". This profile features long-term participation and practice as a client. It could be observed that the graduates who practiced for a long period or as clients had fewer chances of getting open-ended contracts or managerial positions, and were at more risk of unemployment. According to the interpretative framework of this paper, this means that most employers considered long-term extra-curricular involvement and practice as a client as predictors of low professional commitment, low productivity, and high risk of turnover either by firing or by quitting.

These results emphasize the strategic potential of extra-curricular activity for students and graduates wishing improved transition to the labor market. Of course, extra-curricular activity is not only a matter of career development. It surely has much to do with personal development. But insofar as employers take account of the non-market involvement of job applicants, neither students nor education and guidance institutions should ignore the professional dimension of extra-curricular activity. Thus, for instance, it might be suggested to graduates to highlight in their resumes their "Profile 1" features. Awareness of the strategic potential of extra-curricular experience should also encourage guidance institutions to survey employers' extra-curricular preferences at the local level in order to assist graduates in building university-to-work transition strategies including effective extra-curricular participation. Furthermore, reconsidering the position and recognition of extra-curricular activities within higher education and their links with regular curricula might be of advantage to educational institutions facing competition in the higher education market. However, these results also raise the question of the way employers derive turnover and resignation probabilities from the nature of any extra-curricular activity. Why should employers unanimously appreciate involvement in citizenship activities but have diverging perspectives regarding participation in the social sector or in cultural and spiritual activities? A better understanding of employers' rationale and preferences regarding extra-curricular experience surely calls for further investigation.

OECD(经济合作与发展组): The Organization for Economic Co-operation and Development is an international economic organisation of 34 countries founded in 1961 to stimulate economic progress and world trade. It is a forum of countries committed to democracy and the market economy, providing a platform to compare policy experiences, seek answers to common problems, identify good practices, and co-ordinate domestic and international policies of its members.

New Words and Expression

1. alumni[ə'lʌmnai]   n.   (男)校友;(男)毕业生
2. propensity[prəu'pensiti]   n.   倾向;习性
3. criteria[krai'tiəriə]   n.   (criterion 的复数)(批评、判断的)标准,准则,尺度
4. regression[ri'greʃən]   n.   回归
5. quantitative['kwɔntitətiv]   adj. 数量(上)的;量化的;定量性的
6. twofold['tu:fəuld]   adj. 两倍地,双重的
7. supervisory[ˌsju:pə'vaizəri]   adj. 管理的,监督的
8. correspond[ˌkɔ:ri'spɔnd]   v.   相符合,相一致
9. insofar[ˌinsəu'fɑ:]   在这个范围;到这种程度
10. derive[di'raiv]   v.   得到;(从……中)获得
11. estimate['estimeit]   n.   估计,估价

I Vocabulary.

Fill in the blanks with the most suitable words. Change the form when necessary.

| propensity | insofar | derive | correspond | estimate |

1. Your account of events does not _____ with hers.
2. _____ as I can see, the representatives are all satisfied with the arrangement.
3. I can give you a rough _____ of the amount of wood you will need.
4. She _____ great pleasure from painting.
5. He has a _____ to exaggerate.

II Comprehension of the text.

Decide whether the following statements are true (T) or false (F) according to the passage.

Unit 11 Extra-curricular Activities 课外活动

1. Much attention has been paid to the influence of extra-curricular activities on the outcome of the education-to-work transition process.
2. Some employers consider that having been involved in non-market activities is an indicator of an applicant's responsibility, citizenship and maturity which they think will be of advantage to the firm.
3. Graduates who engaged in an activity for a long period of time or at leadership level had more chances of getting open-ended contracts.
4. The graduates who engaged at leadership level had better access to managerial positions and the lowest risk of unemployment before the first job.

III Translate the following sentences into Chinese.

1. Therefore, it is essential that students and graduates understand the impact of extra-curricular activity and appraise the role it may play in their strategies for transition from higher education to employment.
2. Consequently, applicants considered as belonging to the high-attrition-rate group are faced with stricter employment criteria, lower wages and fewer interviews, and may therefore be excluded altogether from the recruitment process, even when they are as qualified as other candidates.
3. Five explanatory variables were taken into account: the involvement in extra-curricular activities, the type of activity, and the time spent in the activity, the intensity of the involvement and the context of practice.
4. However, the whole extra-curricular experience should be kept in reasonable limits: The longer the experience, the fewer the chances of reaching managerial positions.
5. Furthermore, reconsidering the position and recognition of extra-curricular activities within higher education and their links with regular curricula might be of advantage to educational institutions facing competition in the higher education market.

Text B Extra-curricular Physical Activity and Socioeconomic Status in Italian Adolescents

导读：体育活动和健康状况之间的关系已经被人们深入研究过,而体育活动和社会经济状况之间的关系较少被涉及。本文以对意大利几个地区高中生展开问卷调查的形式,来探讨青少年的体育活动和他们家庭的社会经济地位之间的关系。调查结果证实了青少年课外体育活动和其家庭的社会经济地位之间的关系,并对教育管理者及政治家们如何弥补贫富家庭子女的隔阂提供了帮助。

The relationship between physical activity and health status has been described extensively in several studies. Active lifestyles are often associated with better health status and quality of life, however, the relationship between socio-economic status(SES) and physical activity has been investigated less. In regards to this subject, the definition for SES seems to be extremely variable. Giles-Corti et al. , evaluates SES according to residence in low, middle or high income geographical areas; Lindstrom et al. , considers employment exclusively; while Gordon-Larsen et al. , distinguishes between the different socio-economic levels based on family income, for example, low(up to \$26,200), middle(between \$26,200 and \$50,000) and high(>\$50,000). Anyway, most of the studies on socio-economic determinants influencing physical activity choices consider education as a discriminating factor.

In Italy there isn't an individual SES classification available, territorial data(ISTAT data) is based on personal economic consumption rather than income and education. Another possible classification of personal income comes from the Italian financial acts and the different levels of income tax rates. However, this data is not easily inferable from statistical sampling including adolescents. The aim of the present study was to investigate the relationship between adolescents' extra-curricular physical activity and the SES of their families.

The survey was carried out by submitting an anonymous questionnaire in junior high school students who were randomly selected in regions in Italy, during the school year 2002 – 2003. Sample size calculations(alpha = 0.05; beta = 0.20) suggested to sample 2,502 students. We obtained informed consent for interviewing minors in our study from their parents. Students absent during the first submission were given the questionnaire in the days following. 2,411 students(96.4% of the eligible individuals) agreed to participate in the study. The research was conducted according to the Declaration of Helsinki.

The questionnaire, already validated in a pilot study, contained information about the following areas:

-scholastic physical activity;

-extra-curricular physical activity;

-physical activity attitudes;

-lifestyle habits;

- parents' physical activity, education and work activity;
- students' socio-demographic data.

As far as it concerns physical activity of the adolescents, the questionnaire investigated whether or not extra-curricular physical activity is conducted, which type of physical activity is chosen by, how many hours per week are devoted to this activity. Concerning attitudes toward physical activity, it was asked if physical activity is considered useful in preventing obesity, in socializing, and in character-building. Moreover, we collected information on the following lifestyle habits, as dichotomous variables(yes/no): cigarette smoking, coffee and alcohol drinking. The following data from students' parents were collected: weekly physical activity, described as intense (more than two times per week), regular(two times per week), scarce(once per week) and absent; educational levels, indicating the level reached: Degree, Senior High school, Junior High school, Primary school; regarding work activities, we used a classification cited in another study: Managers/ Professionals, Office workers/Skilled workers, Non-skilled workers, Unemployed, Pensioners. In this classification housewives were considered equivalent to non-skilled workers.

Certain information about family income was impossible to obtain from the students. Therefore, SES was estimated considering parents' educational levels and work activities. The families' socio-economic levels were classified as: Very high, High, Middle, Middle-Low and Low.

Data from the questionnaires was collected in a suitable relational database and analyzed with SPSS statistical package.

Chi-square(χ^2) and chi-square for trend test for qualitative variables and student t-test for quantitative variables were applied to test the differences between the groups, considering $p < 0.05$ as statistically significant.

Furthermore, multiple logistic regression analysis was performed, using two different models. The first verified the influence on the variable "extra-curricular physical activity" of the following covariates: age group(reference group: 10 – 12 years), sex(reference group: males), educational level of both parents(reference group: primary school), father's job(reference group: unemployed), parents' physical activity(reference group: no physical activity), student's opinions about sport as a means of socialization, character-building and prevention of obesity(reference group: negative responses).

The second regression analysis model evaluated the influence of the same covariates used in the first model(with the exception of the father's job) and that of socio-economic level (reference group: low socio-economic level) on the variable "extra-curricular physical activity". Analysis was performed using the Hosmer and Lemeshow method.

Participants were 1,121 males(46.5%) and 1290 females(53.5%), aged between 11 and 17 years(median age 12 years). 33.7% of the students attended the first class, 38.5% the second and 27.8% the third one, 86.4% of them participated in school-based physical activity for two hours per week and 13.6% for three hours per week or more.

The types of school-based physical activity undertaken were as follows: 71.1% did gymnastics; 81.7% volleyball; 37.8% basketball; 10.7% football; 36.8% handball; 22.3% long jump; 21.6% high jump and 48.8% running.

71.1% of students declared to participate in extra-curricular physical activity with the following breakdown: 20.2% for one-two hours per week, 23.8% for three-four hours per week, while 56% stated they did five hours or more per week.

Concerning extra-curricular sports, 30.1% of the students played football, 19.7% did dancing/aerobics/gymnastics, 14.5% swam, 14.2% played volleyball, 5.8% played basketball, 5.4% did fitness/body-building, 3.9% did martial arts, and 1.8% cycled.

370 students (15.3%) state to take nutritional supplementation before or after physical activity. 68.2% of students practicing extra-curricular physical activity stated that they paid a monthly fee.

Concerning attitudes toward physical activity, 79.9% of participants considered constant physical activity useful in preventing obesity, 5.6% did not and 14.5% were unsure. 82.7% of students considered physical activity important in socializing, 5.9% did not and 11.6% remained unsure. 56.1% of responders considered physical activity important in character-building, 15.8% did not and 19.1% did not know.

As for unhealthy lifestyles, 37.8% stated that they were smokers or had started smoking, 43.8% drank coffee and 43.4% drank alcohol, especially beer, wine, alcoholic lemon drinks and vodka.

With regards to parental physical activity levels, fathers were significantly more active than mothers ($\chi^2 = 15.41; p = 0.001,5$). However, there were not significant differences between parental education ($\chi^2 = 4.113; p = 0.249$).

The main parental work activities were: Office workers/ skilled workers (36.5%) and Non-skilled workers (34.3%) for fathers and housewives (59.3%) and office workers (28.3%) for mothers. According to our SES classification adolescents' families were categorized in the following way: very high 16.8%, high 14.5%, middle 37.2%, middle-low 30.1% and low 1.4%.

In relation to the SES of the students' family, the variables parents' educational levels and work activities were considered. The educational level attained by the father seems to considerably influence the student's physical activity. Students with fathers who graduated with a Degree practice extra-curricular physical activity more frequently ($\chi^2 = 64.764; p < 0.000,1$) and more intensively ($\chi^2 = 21.091; p < 0.000,1$) than those with fathers characterized by lower educational attainment.

86.3% of students with fathers graduated with a degree considered constant physical activity helpful in preventing obesity, compared to 85.2%, 80.7% and 69.4%, of students respectively, with fathers holding a diploma, a secondary-school leaving certificate or a primary school leaving certificate ($\chi^2 = 35.421; p < 0.000,1$). 86.7% of students with fathers graduated with a Degree considered constant physical activity helpful in socializing, versus 84.5%, 88% and 75.5% respectively, of students with fathers holding a diploma, a secondary school-leaving certificate, a primary school/leaving certificate ($\chi^2 = 11.155; p = 0.084$).

Mother's educational level also seemed to considerably influence the determinants of the student's physical activity and the total number of extra-curricular weekly physical activity hours. Students with mothers graduated with a Degree were more likely to practice extracurricular physical activity ($\chi^2 = 55.512; p < 0.000,1$) and undertook physical activity, for more than three hours per week ($\chi^2 = 19.65; p < 0.000,1$), than those whose mothers have a lower educational level.

86.4% of students with mothers graduated with a Degree and 86.5% of those whose mothers have a diploma considered physical activity important in socializing, compared to 84.6% and 78.1%, respectively, of students whose mothers have a secondary-school leaving or a primary school-leaving certificate ($\chi^2 = 12.817; p = 0.046$).

83.5% of students with graduated mothers considered constant physical activity useful in preventing obesity, compared to 85.3%, 80.4% and 77%, respectively, of students with mothers holding a diploma, a secondary school leaving certificate, a primary school-leaving certificate ($\chi^2 = 15.11; p = 0.019$).

Furthermore, extra-curricular physical activity is related to the parents' work activity. Students whose fathers are Managers/Professional or Office-workers/Skilled workers showed a significantly higher level of extra-curricular physical activity than students with fathers who were non-skilled workers, Unemployed or Retired from work ($\chi^2 = 39.029; p < 0.000,1$).

The mother's work activity also considerably influences the students' extra-curricular physical activity ($\chi^2 = 64.319; p < 0.000,1$). Adolescents with mothers who are Non-skilled workers/Housewives or Unemployed undertake less extra-curricular physical activity than those with mothers who were Managers/Professionals or Office workers/Skilled workers.

Weekly hours of extra-curricular physical activity show a similar trend: percentages of students practice physical activity for three hours per week or more. Frequency of extra-curricular physical activity performed during the week appears to be related to the work activity level of both parents, with a statistically significant difference for fathers ($\chi^2 = 8.229; p = 0.048$) and even more so for the mothers ($\chi^2 = 28.321; p < 0.000,1$).

Several studies show evidence of a relationship between socio-economic level and health status. As demonstrated by Lowry et al., higher family income is associated with lower alcohol and cigarette consumption and a lower level of sedentary behavior. In Anglo-Saxon countries slums represent an obstacle to the practice of physical activity for several reasons ranging from absence of pavements, public parks and gardens to excessive traffic.

The likelihood of undertaking adequate physical activity is low for subjects who have a low family income and for not skilled Workers or Unemployed.

Studies on the relationship between physical activity and parents' educational level show that higher educational levels are determinant factors for children's physical activity. In particular, it is showed that demographic variables are good predictors of children's physical activity, and ethnic and SES differences are potential correlates of physical activity among adolescents. In a previous study, in 1,357 students in Central Italy, we found a strong relationship between weekly physical activity of adolescents, their BMI levels (overweight and obesity) and parents' educational levels and nutritional status, with a higher participation in physical activity shown above all in children with highly educated parents.

Results of our study confirm the relationship between family socio-economic, parents' educational levels and physical activity of adolescents.

Moreover the classification of socio-economic index used in this survey, derived by the combination of the parents' work activities (Very High, High, Middle, Middle-Low and Low), appears to be comparable to the distribution of family income levels.

Given these results, which are in agreement with other international surveys conducted in USA, South Africa, and Canada, we can say that family SES plays a key role in determining extra-curricular physical activity of students: the highest educational levels and the most remunerative work activities are directly related to the sporting practices of adolescents. Children with parents characterized by higher educational levels are encouraged more than others to practice constant and demanding extra-curricular sport. It is, demonstrated that among minority and low-SES adolescents (high school population) in USA, the prevalence rate of vigorous exercise tends to decrease with age or when this kind of population is not required to participate in school physical education. It is found that South African children belonging to the highest SES quartile were highly physically active, watched less television and had greater lean tissue than children in lower quartiles. In Canada, among adolescents aged 12–20 years, individuals from low income families had a 30% higher probability of being inactive than those from high income families. Families with high SES consider physical activity useful both in preventing chronic and degenerative diseases and for socialization, and essential for the correct physical and psychological development of adolescents.

SES is therefore clearly related to parents' educational levels, and parents' low educational levels and low remunerative work activities can negatively influence the participation of children in extra-curricular physical activity.

In addition, it must be considered the inadequate knowledge about benefits of physical activity, related to low socio-economic and cultural levels.

The present study has some limitations. As far as concerns internal validity, we sampled randomly the participants, and used a validated questionnaire. Misclassification bias could arise if incorrect information on both exposure (SES status) and outcome. The accuracy of self-reported physical activity of adolescents should have been avoided, given the reliability of the tool we used, which had been validated in previous studies. Moreover, we collected detailed information on potential confounding factors and took it into account in the analysis of possible effects.

As far as external validity, a potential selection bias could have been avoided, even if we used a cross-sectional type of study design. Finally, the precision of the estimates is comparable with that had been designed for.

Nevertheless, to our knowledge this is the first attempt in Italy to evaluate the relationship between SES, based either on a family income index or parents' educational status, and adolescents' extra-curricular physical activity.

In our study, parents' physical activity is a good predictor of adolescents extra-curriculum physical activity, accordingly to previous studies. In a recent review on correlates of physical activity of children and adolescents, it is demonstrated that for children, among other factors, parental overweight status, physical activity preferences, intention to be active and program/facility access were statistically associated to physical activity. For adolescents, variables consistently associated with physical activity were perceived activity competence, intentions, but also sports conducted at community level, parent support, sibling physical activity, direct help from parents and opportunities to exercise. In that sense, social, cultural and economic deprivation has an effect on extra-curricular physical activity participation. A strong help in this task could derive from school. In fact, in Italy the vast majority of scholastic building and infrastructures belong to municipalities and provinces, and are currently underused. A way to improve adolescents' participation in physical activity could be involving them in extra-curricular activity carried out within the schools. As an example, childhood obesity prevention might be achieved considering a variety of interventions targeting built environment, physical activity, and diet. As suggested, some of these potential strategies for intervention in children can be implemented by targeting preschool institutions, schools or after-school care services as natural setting for influencing the diet and physical activity. In this sense, the outcomes from this study will be useful to school administrators in their bid to bridge the gap between those children who are the most and least deprived.

1. **ISTAT(意大利统计局)**: The Italian National Institute of Statistics is a public research organization. It has been present in Italy since 1926, and is the main producer of official statistics in the service of citizens and policy-makers. It operates in complete independence and continuous interaction with the academic and scientific communities.

2. **Declaration of Helsinki(赫尔辛基宣言)**: The Declaration of Helsinki is a set of ethical principles regarding human experimentation developed for the medical community by the World Medical Association(WMA). It is widely regarded as the cornerstone document of human research ethics.

3. **SPSS("统计产品与服务解决方案"软件)**: It is a computer program used for survey authoring and deployment(IBM SPSS Data Collection), data mining(IBM SPSS Modeler), text analytics, statistical analysis, and collaboration and deployment(batch and automated scoring services).

4. **Hosmer-Lemeshow**: It is a statistical test for goodness of fit for logistic regression models. It is used frequently in risk prediction models. The test assesses whether or not the observed event rates match expected event rates in subgroups of the model population. The Hosmer-

Lemeshow test specifically identifies subgroups as the deciles of fitted risk values.

New Words and Expression

1. remunerative [ri'mju:nərətiv]   adj.   酬报的,报偿性的
2. inferable [in'fə:rəbl]   adj.   能推理的,能推论的
3. variable ['vɛəriəbl]   n.   变量
4. respectively [ris'pektivli]   adv.   分别;各自;顺序为;依次为
5. validate ['væli‚deit]   v.   证实;确证;使生效;使有法律效力
6. municipality [mju‚nisi'pæliti]   n.   自治市;自治区;自治市或区的政府当局
7. degenerative [di'dʒenərətiv]   adj.   退步的,变质的,退化的
8. sedentary ['sednteri]   adj.   (人或动物)定居的;定栖的;不迁徙的

I Vocabulary.

Fill in the blanks with the most suitable words. Change the form when necessary.

| degenerative | validate | inferable | sedentary | respectively |

1. People in _____ jobs need to take exercise.
2. The ticket has to be stamped by the airline to _____ it. I'm sorry I can't help you more.
3. My husband and I got pay rises of 8% and 10% _____. Let's celebrate!
4. _____ changes of the myocardium occur in many diseases.
5. Is the rightness of actions _____ from the goodness of their consequences?

II Comprehension of the text.

Decide whether the following statements are true (T) or false (F) according to the passage.

1. The relationship between socio-economic status (SES) and physical activity has been investigated in several studies.

2. Students with mothers graduated with a Degree were more likely to practice extra-curricular physical activity and undertook physical activity, for more than three hours per week.
3. As demonstrated by Lowry et al., higher family income is associated with higher alcohol and cigarette consumption and a higher level of sedentary behavior.
4. Families with high SES consider physical activity useful both in preventing chronic and degenerative diseases and for socialization, essential for the correct physical and psychological development of adolescents.

III Translate the following sentences into Chinese.

1. In Italy there isn't an individual SES classification available, territorial data (ISTAT data) is based on personal economic consumption rather than income and education.
2. Concerning attitudes toward physical activity, it was asked if physical activity is considered useful in preventing obesity, in socializing, and in character-building.
3. Mother's educational level also seemed to considerably influence the determinants of the student's physical activity and the total number of extra-curricular weekly physical activity hours.
4. Studies on the relationship between physical activity and parents' educational level show that higher educational levels are determinant factors for children's physical activity.
5. In this sense, the outcomes from this study will be useful to school administrators in their bid to bridge the gap between those children who are the most and least deprived.

 Supplementary Reading

Discussion and Conclusion of Correspondence Hypothesis

Evidence partly confirms the correspondence hypothesis: The persuasive effectiveness of democratic rather than authoritarian influence styles is affected by the initial position of the targets of influence. We need to stress that the targets' position was not expressed in terms of social status or competence, but as an attitudinal position, as expressed at the beginning of the interaction, as regards the very object of discussion: i.e., the presumed advantage of completing one's academic training with the attainment of the European Computer Driving License.

More specifically, results confirm that the predicted interaction affects the direct agreement with the message statements. As expected, students who have previously elaborated an autonomous orientation toward the proposed extra-curricular activity are more likely to concur with the source when this latter adopts a flexible, rather than a coercive, influence style. The complementary effect is not verified, as we expected, but we do not find that the rest of the students, initially less inclined to attain the ECDL, are persuaded more by a coercive rather than by an obliging approach.

When we turn from the evaluative agreement with the source to the behavioral intention to act as the source suggests, single planned contrast shows a complementary influence pattern.

For instance, authoritarian style is proved to increase students' intention to attain the ECDL when this intention has not been previously elaborated by students' themselves. Anyway, when students' position is already coherent with the subsequent source request, i.e., when they are already inclined to undergo the ECDL exams, a flexible approach does not enhance their commitment in the task more than an authoritarian one. For instance, this effect might be due to a measurement artifact, since these latter students might not have perceived a need to increase their agreement with the source, as their behavioral intentions are already adequate to meet the source's expectations.

A theoretical explanation of the difference between direct and indirect influence patterns could refer to the Conflict Elaboration Theory, from which the correspondence hypothesis is drawn. This postulates that direct or indirect persuasive outcomes are the consequence of the processes by which the target solves their conflict with the source. Briefly, the acceptance of the source's point of view at a direct level allows the targets to work out superficially, without any further message elaboration, its relational conflict with the source; in this case, a socio-cognitive paralysis prevents any indirect or deeper influence to appear, in particular for those subjects who are already close to the source's position. On the contrary, the rejection of an explicit direct agreement with the source leaves the conflict unsolved, thus compelling the target to elaborate the conflicts at a deeper level; in this case, an indirect change could appear, as a consequence of the more profound socio-cognitive activity.

What we observe here is that a democratic style produces the highest message acceptance, at a direct level, by targets who are attitudinally closer to the source, and that this explicit agreement is not followed by any indirect change in behavioral intentions. In a complementary way, an authoritarian style gives rise to a shift in behavioral intentions to attain the ECDL (indirect influence) only by students who were not previously orientated to act as the source demanded, despite (or thanks to) the fact that these targets show no significant direct agreement with the source's statements. What is new, and is predicted by the correspondence hypothesis, is that both authoritarian or democratic styles prove to be effective, the former at a direct and the latter at an indirect level of influence, only when they are appropriate to the specific relational context, i.e., when they are addressed to targets who actually expect that kind of communication style to be used. If this condition is not satisfied, any influence outcome is definitely prevented.

In this study we proposed an application of the correspondence hypothesis to the negotiation of innovative conducts in educational settings, following recent interest toward the ecological implications of social influence models to the innovation fields.

Here, evidence confirms that communication rhetoric may affect the outcome of these situated negotiation processes: for our purpose, different influence styles prove to facilitate or to prevent students' orientation toward innovative academic practices, depending on the students' positions in the influence interaction.

Interestingly, the correspondence hypothesis predicts that under some circumstances authoritarian styles may eventually induce a greater consensus by the targets, despite the social value normally devoted to respectful communication behaviors. In fact, it is stated that some interactions require coercive rhetoric, owing to the communication rules (i.e., the communication contract) that partners expect to be used in that context. This is the case of highly asymmetrical relationships between targets in a low social position and sources provided by much higher psychosocial resources. Under similar conditions, it is hypothesized that targets themselves expect sources to recur to assertive rhetoric, and perceive the use of a more obliging style as inconsistent, as regards the ruling communication contract.

It may easily be guessed that empirical findings supporting the correspondence hypothesis need to be discussed at different explanation levels. Contrary to Moscovici's first studies about influence style, whose predictions result from attributional processes, i.e., from an inter-individual level of explanation, the correspondence hypothesis refers to positional aspects (the psychological and/or social distance between the source and the target/s), and most of all to the level of representations (shared expectations about the context and the partner's role) and norms (the activation of specific communication contracts and rules).

Alternative explanations to our main findings may be found in the reactance theory, which states that an assertive persuasive effort, limiting the targets' perceived freedom of choice, motivates the targets themselves to restore their threatened autonomy. One of the easiest ways to restore one's threatened freedom is often to shift away from the source's request, although this shift may induce the devaluation of a response that was previously considered desirable. Maybe this is what happens, in our study, to students already orientated to the ECDL achievement: When the source addresses them with an authoritarian message, they evaluate the ECDL itself in less positive terms, despite the fact that they were previously inclined to attain the certificate.

Nevertheless, it seems difficult to explain, in terms of reactance, why students who define themselves as farther from the source position are eventually persuaded more by an authoritarian rather than by a respectful style. Despite the fact that these students may not perceive a threat to their freedom neither under a coercive nor under a flexible persuasive attempt, as the source is legitimated to suggest an extra-curricular task, it seems difficult to account for their authoritarian preference (at least at the level of declared behavioral intentions).

What the correspondence hypothesis suggests is that such "paradoxical" preference has to do with the significance that people attribute to relationships they are involved in, rather than to the influence style itself; both acceptance of the sources' proposal, and activation of counter-persuasive reactance or defensive motivations, arise from situated representations of the social context in which persuasive information is delivered.

It has to be underlined that the correspondence hypothesis predictions were not unequivocally and fully fulfilled, as it was in similar previous studies. Quiamzade et al. (in press) pointed out that the correspondence hypothesis was studied in various socio-cultural contexts (France, Suisse, Romania, and Italy in our case), so that a reference to the different cultural backgrounds could help to explain the diverse extent to which students submit to authority, or alternatively valorize their decisional autonomy. In fact, a systematic cross-cultural approach to the influence style issues seems to be essential.

A possible limit of this study lies in its purposely academic connotation: The setting and object of influence are explicitly related to academic tasks and to the relational conditions which enable university teachers and students to engage in educational innovations. A prominent academic connotation as this increases our findings' ecological validity, even though it reduces their extensive generalization to different relational and institutional contexts.

Research development should eventually explore the relational conditions under which authoritarian communication contracts are used in influence exchanges, possibly avoiding any reference to school and educational settings. Renewed interest in authoritarianism may provide useful links with the study of coercive influence styles in many contexts of daily life, such as in public communication campaigns (information, prevention, social marketing, and so on), influence attempts in different organizational settings (enterprises, institutions, etc.), and also informal face-to-face interactions outside of educational bounds.

Unit 12 School Management
学校管理

Text A   What is School-based Management?

导读: School-based Management 是何种管理方法? 为什么会被引进学校? 相比于旧式的管理方法, 它有哪些优势, 有哪些注意点? 引入此种管理机制的学校又该如何提高学校的"产出"? 本文将为你解答这些疑问。

Despite the clear commitment of governments and international agencies to the education sector, efficient and equitable access to education is still proved to be elusive for many people around the world. Girls, indigenous peoples, and other poor and marginalized groups often have only limited access to education. These access issues are being addressed with great commitment in international initiatives, such as Education for All, in which resources are being channeled to low-income countries to help them to achieve the Millennium Development Goals for education. However, even where children do have access to educational facilities, the quality of education that is provided is often very poor. This has become increasingly apparent in international learning tests such as Trends in International Mathematics and Science Study (TIMSS), in which most of the students from developing countries fail to excel. There is evidence that merely increasing resource allocations will not increase the equity or improve the quality of education in the absence of institutional reforms. Governments around the world are introducing a range of strategies aimed at improving the financing and delivery of education services, with a more recent emphasis on improving quality as well as increasing quantity in education.

One such strategy is to decentralize education decision-making by increasing parental and community involvement in schools—which is popularly known as school-based management (SBM). The argument in favor of SBM is that decentralizing decision-making authority to parents and communities fosters demand and ensures that schools provide the social and economic benefits that best reflect the priorities and values of those local communities. Education reforms in Organization for Economic Co-operation and Development (OECD) countries tend to share some common characteristics of this kind, including increased school autonomy, greater responsiveness to local needs, and the overall objective of improving students' academic performance. Most countries whose students perform well in international student achievement tests give local authorities and schools substantial autonomy to decide the content of their curriculum and the allocation and management of their resources.

An increasing number of developing countries are introducing SBM reforms aimed at empowering principals and teachers or at strengthening their professional motivation, thereby enhancing their sense of ownership of the school. Many of these reforms have also strengthened parental involvement in the schools, sometimes by means of school councils. Almost 11 percent of all projects in the World Bank's education portfolio for fiscal years 2000–2006 supported school-based management, a total of 17 among about 157 projects. This represents $1.74 billion or 23 percent of the Bank's total education financing.

The majority of SBM projects in the Bank's current portfolio are in Latin American and South Asian countries. In addition, a number of current and upcoming projects in the Africa region have a component focused on strengthening school-level committees and SBM. There are also two Bank-supported SBM projects in Europe and Central Asia and one each in East Asia and the Pacific (the Philippines), and in the Middle East and North Africa (Lebanon). The few well-documented cases of SBM implementation that have been subject to rigorous impact evaluations have already been reviewed elsewhere. In this paper, we focus on the concept of SBM and its different forms and dimensions and present a conceptual framework for understanding it. We define SBM broadly to include community-based management and parental participation schemes but do not explicitly include stand-alone, or one-off, school grants programs that are not meant to be permanent alterations in school management.

SBM programs lie along a continuum in terms of the degree to which decision-making is devolved to the local level. Some devolve only a single area of autonomy, whereas others go further and devolve the power to hire and fire teachers and authority over substantial resources, while at the far end of the spectrum there are those that encourage the private and community management of schools as well as allow parents to create schools. Thus, there are both strong and weak versions of SBM based on how much decision-making power has been transferred to the school.

The World Bank's World Development Report 2004 presented a conceptual framework for SBM. The WDR argues that school autonomy and accountability can help to solve some fundamental problems in education. While increasing resource flows and support to the education sector is one aspect of increasing the access of the poor to better quality education, it is by no means sufficient.

The SBM approach aims to improve service delivery to the poor by increasing their choice and participation in service delivery, by giving citizens a voice in school management, by making information widely available, and by strengthening the incentives for schools to deliver effective services to the poor and by penalizing those who fail to deliver.

SBM is the decentralization of authority from the central government to the school level. It is said that School-based management can be viewed conceptually "as a formal alteration of governance structures, as a form of decentralization that identifies the individual school as the primary unit of improvement and relies on the redistribution of decision-making authority as the primary means through which improvement might be stimulated and sustained. Thus, in SBM, responsibility for, and decision-making authority over, school operations are transferred to principals, teachers, and parents, and sometimes to students and other school community members. However, these school-level actors have to conform to or operate within a set of policies determined by the central government. SBM programs exist in many different forms, both in terms of who has the power to make decisions and in terms of the degree of decision-making that is devolved to the school level. While some programs transfer authority only to principals or teachers, others encourage or mandate parental and community participation, often as members of school committees (or school councils or school management committees). In general, SBM programs transfer authority over one or more of the following activities: budget allocation, the hiring and firing of teachers and other school staff, curriculum development, the procurement of textbooks and other educational materials, infrastructure improvements, and the monitoring and evaluation of teacher performance and student learning outcomes.

Good education is not only about physical inputs, such as classrooms, teachers, and textbooks, but also about incentives that lead to better instruction and learning. Education systems are extremely demanding of the managerial, technical, and financial capacity of governments, and, thus, as a service, education is too complex to be efficiently produced and distributed in a centralized fashion. Hanushek and Woessmann (2007) suggest that most of the incentives that affect learning outcomes are institutional in nature, and they identify three in particular: (i) choice and competition; (ii) school autonomy; and (iii) school accountability. The idea behind choice and competition is that parents who are interested in maximizing their children's learning outcomes are able to choose to send their children to the most productive (in terms of academic results) school that they can find. This demand-side pressure on schools will thus improve the performance of all schools if they want to compete for students. Similarly, local decision-making and fiscal decentralization can have positive effects on school outcomes such as test scores or graduation rates by holding the schools accountable for the "outputs" that they produce. The World Development Report 2004, Making Services Work for Poor People, presents a very similar framework, in that it suggests that good quality and timely service provision can be ensured if service providers can be held accountable to their clients.

In the context of developed countries, the core idea behind SBM is that those who work in a school building should have greater control of the management of what goes on in the building. In developing countries, the idea behind SBM is less ambitious, in that it focuses mainly on involving community and parents in the school decision-making process rather than putting them entirely in control. However, in both cases, the central government always plays some role in education, and the precise definition of this role affects how SBM activities are conceived and implemented. SBM in almost all of its manifestations involves community members in school decision-making. Because these community members are usually parents of children enrolled in the school, they have an incentive to improve their children's education. As a result, SBM can be expected to improve student achievement and other outcomes as these local people demand closer monitoring of school personnel, better student evaluations, a closer match between the school's needs and its policies, and a more efficient use of resources. For instance, although the evidence is mixed, in a number of diverse countries, such as Papua New Guinea, India, and Nicaragua, parental participation in school management has reduced teacher absenteeism.

SBM has several other benefits. Under these arrangements, schools are managed more transparently, thus reducing opportunities for corruption. Also, SBM often gives parents and stakeholders opportunities to increase their skills. In some cases, training in shared decision-making, interpersonal skills, and management skills is offered to school council members so that they can become more capable participants in the SBM process and at the same time benefit the community as a whole.

Unlike in developed countries where SBM is introduced explicitly to improve students' academic performance, how school decentralization will eventually affect student performance in developing countries is less clear. This section tries to define the ways in which SBM can increase participation and transparency and improve school outcomes.

First, the SBM model must define exactly which powers are vested in which individuals or committees and how these powers are to be coordinated to make the plan workable within both the school culture and the available resources. However, the structure of authority needs to remain flexible enough to enable school managers to deal with any unexpected events, which always seem to emerge during implementation.

Second, the success of SBM requires the support of the various school-level stakeholders, particularly of teachers. Also vital to the success of SBM is for school principals to support the decentralization reform. This is not a foregone conclusion, as principals will remain personally accountable for the performance of their school but will no longer have complete control over its management. In effect, they are being asked to give up some authorities without a corresponding decrease in personal accountability. Once SBM is in place, principals can no longer blame the policies of the school district when things go wrong.

The support of both local and national governments is also required. SBM by definition requires these governments to surrender some power and authority to the school level, but they retain the right and ability to reverse their earlier decision in favor of SBM if they feel their power is being usurped.

The final and most important source of necessary support is from parents and other community members. It is important, however, to distinguish between parents and other community members. While parents are always part of the community that surrounds a school, school councils do not have to include parents as members. For instance, in the United States, many schools are locally controlled in the sense that a school board of local residents officially sets policy, but there may be no parental participation in these schools. In some cases, wealthy individuals in a community may be members of a school council simply because they financially support the school.

Particularly in developed countries, parental participation as members of school councils or of the group that is implementing SBM is distinct from community participation. However, in developing countries, in particular in isolated small or rural communities, parental participation tends to be synonymous with community participation, since in these small communities almost everybody has a family member in school.

The expectation underlying SBM is that greater parental involvement will mean that schools will be more responsive to local demands (for example, for better teaching methods or more inputs) and that decisions will be taken in the interests of children rather than adults. A further hope is that involved parents will become unpaid or minimally paid auxiliary staff who will help teachers in classrooms and with other minor activities. Furthermore, even if parents are too busy working to help in the classroom, they can still encourage their children to do their homework and to show them, in this and other ways, that their family really values schooling and academic achievement. Since parents are networked in various ways with community leaders, the further hope is that parental support for SBM will encourage local community leaders to put schools higher on their political agendas and thus provide the schools with more material resources.

Once the nexus of autonomy-participation and accountability has been defined and a realistic management plan has been drawn up that has the support of all stakeholders, then it becomes possible to expect better school outcomes. Thereafter, the hope is that the school climate will change as the stakeholders work together in a collegial way to manage the school. However, there is little evidence that this really happens in practice. Also, the possibility exists that teachers and principals will come to resent being constantly monitored by parents and school council members, which will cause relations within the school to deteriorate.

At the same time, the teaching climate of a school is predicated on, among many other factors, how motivated teachers are to teach well, whether they know how to teach well, how good the various curricula are, how eager pupils are to learn, and how much parents actually support their children's learning in whatever ways are practical for them. Any school that wants to improve its academic record will have to work actively on some or all of these factors. Sometimes, the obstacles to improve the quality of instruction are motivational, sometimes they are cognitive in the sense of what teachers know, and sometimes they are social in the sense of petty personal matters that can prevent teachers from behaving professionally. Ideally, under SBM, because those who run the school are intimately acquainted with the individuals who work there, they will be able to identify the specific problems that need to be fixed and use their authority to find and implement solutions.

Some caveats must be mentioned about SBM. Decentralization or devolution does not necessarily give more power to the general public because it is susceptible to being captured by elites. As for the relationship between decentralization, proper growth, and reduced corruption, the evidence is mixed. Bardhan and Mookherjee (2000 and 2006) and Bardhan (2002) suggest that there may be numerous reasons why local control over resource allocation or decision-making may not yield the desired outcomes. First, local democracy and political accountability are often weak in developing countries and can lead to capture of governance—at the various levels—by elite groups. Second, in more traditional and rural areas with a history of feudalism, the poor or minorities may feel the need for a strong central authority to ensure that services are delivered to them and not just to the more powerful local citizens. Third, and related to this, is the issue that there may be no culture of accountability within communities, meaning that no one would think to question any actions taken by the group running the school (De Grauwe, 2005). This can be a problem in places where the teacher is regarded as the ultimate authority by the virtue of being the only "highly" qualified individual in a community. Finally, those given the responsibility for managing the school may not have the capacity to do so, which points up the need to build the capacity of education stakeholders at the grassroots level to ensure that SBM reforms do not fail in their execution.

These caveats help to strengthen our understanding of the pattern of SBM in developing countries (as discussed above). In particular, the caveats strengthen the notion that the specific type of SBM introduced in any given country depends (or should ideally depend) on the political economy of the particular country. For instance, strong SBM reforms have been introduced, and have been quite successful, in those countries where communities have been forced by some calamity such as war or a natural disaster to come together as a group to find ways to deliver basic services, including education.

Notes

1. **Education for All (全民教育):** The Education for All movement took off at the world conference on Education for All in 1990. Since then, governments, non-governmental organizations, civil society, bilateral and multilateral donor agencies and the media have taken up the cause of providing basic education for all children, youth and adults.

2. **Millennium Development Goals (千年发展目标):** The Millennium Development Goals are

eight international development goals that all 193 United Nations member states and at least 23 international organizations have agreed to achieve by the year 2015. They include eradicating extreme poverty, reducing child mortality rates, fighting disease epidemics such as AIDS, and developing a global partnership for development.

3. Trends in International Mathematics and Science Study(国际教育评价研究和评测活动): The Trends in International Mathematics and Science Study(TIMSS) is an international assessment of the mathematics and science knowledge of fourth-and eighth-grade (Year 5 and Year 9) students around the world. TIMSS was developed by the International Association for the Evaluation of Educational Achievement (IEA) to allow participating nations to compare students' educational achievement across borders. The IEA also conducts the Progress in International Reading Literacy Study (PIRLS). TIMSS was first administered in 1995, and every 4 years thereafter. In 1995, forty-one nations participated in the study; in 2007, 48 countries participated. Another similar study is the Programme for International Student Assessment.

4. Organization for Economic Co-operation and Development(经济合作与发展组织): It is an international economic organisation of 34 countries founded in 1961 to stimulate economic progress and world trade. It is a forum of countries committed to democracy and the market economy, providing a platform to compare policy experiences, seek answers to common problems, identify good practices, and co-ordinate domestic and international policies of its members.

New Words and Expression

1. indigenous [in'didʒənəs]　　adj.　土产的,土著的
2. marginalize ['mɑːdʒinəlaiz]　　v.　使局限于社会边缘;排斥;忽视
3. portfolio [pɔːt'fəuliəu]　　n.　投资组合
4. spectrum ['spektrəm]　　n.　系列;范围;幅度
5. incentive [in'sentiv]　　n.　刺激;鼓励;动机
6. auxiliary [ɔːg'ziliəri]　　adj.　辅助的,备用的
7. accountability [əˌkauntə'biliti]　　n.　负有责任;应作解释;可说明性
8. caveat ['kæviæt]　　n.　警告

Unit 12　School Management　学校管理

I　Vocabulary.

Fill in the blanks with the most suitable words. Change the form when necessary.

marginalize　incentive　auxiliary　spectrum　caveat

1. The _____ units are called in only when the main force has been overtaxed.
2. We must not _____ the poor in our society.
3. There is a wide _____ of opinions on this question.
4. But there is a crucial _____ : how much worse might the politics get.
5. The child has no _____ to study harder because his parents cannot afford to send him to college.

II　Comprehension of the text.

Decide whether the following statements are true(T) or false(F) according to the passage.

1. Increasing resource allocations will increase the equity or improve the quality of education in the absence of institutional reforms.
2. Good education means merely physical inputs, such as classrooms, teachers, and textbooks.
3. How school decentralization will eventually affect student performance in developing countries is apparent.
4. In developed countries, parental participation as members of school councils or of the group that is implementing SBM is the same as community participation.
5. The specific type of SBM introduced in any given country depends (or should ideally depend) on the political economy of the particular country.

III　Read the text and answer the following questions.

1. What's School-based Management?
2. What are the benefits of SBM?
3. What does SBM need to improve school outcomes?
4. Apart from the benefits, SBM may fail to achieve school outcomes. What's the major caveat about SBM?

Text B Comparative Case Study on School Management Practices in Two Schools in the United States and Turkey

导读：全球化和信息革命使得各个国家和地区的学校管理制度趋于一致，但是在这种大的趋势下，有些地区的学校管理方法却是截然不同的。本文选取了美国和土耳其这两个国家各一所学校，对比两者的学校管理制度以及两者在教学上的效率，希望给现在的学校一些管理上的参考。

The issue of centralized-decentralized governance structures and their influences on education systems have received a great deal of attention in recent decades. National education systems show great variation in certain respects because of the dissimilar historic paths they have followed. On the other hand, many believe that world education systems are converging because of increasing learning capabilities of systems from each other. Globalization and information revolution have brought the continents closer, along with making the educational practices less different. The American and the Turkish school systems, for example, are clearly distinct and have indicated signs of moving in opposite directions. The education system in Turkey is centralized, which means that the policy-making function is in the hands of the Ministry of Education that has power over all educational matters. The Ministry determines the personnel policy and arranges training, certifying, appointment and salary schedules of teachers. On the other hand, the public school system in the U.S. is governed by an open decentralized system. State legislatures are responsible for public education. Their task is to authorize funding and give legislative support for the schools. All states have state boards of education, which deal with policy development, personnel recruitment, budgeting and the law.

This study attempted to examine and compare Turkish and American school administrative processes and practices shaped by the national political traditions by using two schools, one in each country, as research sites. The two national political traditions correspond to two administrative paradigms: the Napoleonic tradition which connotes centralization and the Anglo-Saxon tradition which connotes decentralization. The researchers believed that looking at the administrative processes in the two schools, one in Turkey and one in the U.S., would provide some insights into how the administrative processes supported or impeded the change process in both systems.

Turkish school: the case study in Turkey was conducted at a state basic education school (grades 1-8). At this school there are 62 teachers, five administrators (one principal and four assistant principals), two counselors, one secretary, two cleaning personnel and 1,750 students. The school covers an area of 9,361m^2 and has 52 classrooms with one computer laboratory and a music room. This school was founded in 1967 and became a Curriculum Laboratory School in 1994. These were organized with the collaboration of the World Bank and established in the 23 provinces of Turkey. New educational approaches are piloted in these schools before they are put into general practice. This school was also selected to be a CLS, among other schools, by the Ministry of Education in order to try out new educational approaches with the aim of raising Turkish education to the OECD standards. In line with this aim, a working team called the School Development Committee was involved in initiating strategic planning and total quality management activities at the school. This committee was under the guidance of the Ministry of Education.

American school: the case study in Madison, the Wisconsin state capital, was conducted in an elementary school founded in the fall of 1958. It is located in a prosperous neighborhood on the southwest side of Madison, where upper and upper middle class families reside. The school shares the building with a middle school and uses the rooms and grounds on the building's east side.

This school has a total K-5 enrolment of approximately 300 students and 31 regular classroom teachers. Because the school has fewer than 500 students, there is only a school principal, but no assistant principal. In the school there are two custodians, one kitchen staff and one librarian, two nurses, one "outreach" person, and three administrative staff. Recently the school was involved in a five-year School Improvement Plan (SIP). SIP activities are monitored by a facilitator from the Metropolitan Madison School District. The goals and objectives of the SIP plan were mainly to increase students' proficiency in literacy and mathematics.

Sample

Neither case schools of this study are "average schools". They are both located in prosperous neighborhoods and are involved in undertaking change initiatives as part of the recent reform activities in the education systems of both countries. Despite the atypical characteristics of these schools, the researchers believe that this comparative case study manages to build a holistic description of activities and situations under investigation. Therefore, this study is significant for depicting the administrative styles and practices of both schools in relation to managing educational reform.

The participants in the study comprised 14 teachers and four administrators (one principal and three assistant principals) in the Turkish case, and 10 teachers and one principal in the American case. The researchers chose the maximum variation as a sampling strategy. According to Patton (1987) the maximum variation sampling helps researchers in selecting a small sample with great diversity. This sampling strategy will yield two kinds of findings: (1) high-quality, detailed descriptions of each case which are useful for documenting uniqueness, and (2) important shared patterns which cut across cases and which derive their significance from having emerged out of heterogeneity. The maximum variation sampling strategy enabled the researchers to work with teachers with different demographic characteristics (such as working experience, their subject areas, and gender).

Data collection and analysis procedures

Two of the sample questions in the schedule were:

(a) What can you say about your motivation and that of your teacher colleagues at work?

(b) Please identify some of the factors that helped or hindered your motivation.

The researchers collected data through semi-structured interviews. The interviews took on average 30 – 35 minutes. The researchers tried to elicit information about the participants' perspectives on the administrative processes (motivation, decision-making, leadership communication, organizational change) practiced in their school.

The Turkish version of the interview schedule was reviewed by three experts, experienced in qualitative studies, from the Department of Educational Sciences at the Middle East Technical University in Ankara. The draft interview schedule was later piloted with three teachers from a school that is equivalent to the case school. The instrument was revised in the light of the comments and the pilot study.

For the American school the researchers translated the interview schedule into English. In the U.S., feedback on the translated interview schedule was obtained from two experts from the Department of Educational Administration, University of Wisconsin-Madison.

The researchers transcribed the tape-recorded interviews verbatim. Content analysis was used to determine where the greatest emphasis was placed in the interview data. The data were broken down into manageable categories followed by thematic coding. Coding categories for both Turkish and English versions of the interview schedules emerged after the review of the relevant literature. The data collection during the first week of the interviews generated new categories and the coding was revised accordingly.

Findings
The Turkish school

The results related to "motivation" as perceived by teachers and administrators showed that some external factors such as poor physical conditions of the school, excessive paperwork, the education system, and the excessive involvement of parents and of the central authorities in the school's affairs and low enthusiasm for their work affected the teachers' motivation negatively. The administrators complained about the lack of autonomy and responsibility to undertake initiatives, and stated that school staff attempted participatory and collaborative work. This was interrupted by bureaucracy and centralization. The principal said:

> "The impossibilities that arise from poor physical conditions, poor communication within the administration, the education system, and the environment affect us negatively. We have efforts for collaboration, sharing, but there is no implementation. Why? Because centralized structure forms barriers to it, on one hand, it is said that the principal administers the school; on the other hand, I am deprived of autonomy. To say the least, whatever I want to do, I need to get permission from the central authorities."

The results concerning "decision-making" at the Turkish school showed a trend towards participatory decision-making. All administrators and teachers said that they made decisions through some committees concerning school issues such as strategic planning and total quality management. Yet most teachers complained that their decisions were not considered. They added that they were allowed to make decisions collaboratively, yet the principal still acted as the highest decision-making authority. Some teachers related this situation to the bureaucratic structure of the Turkish education in which administration was seen as the powerbase that can override participative decisions. On the other hand, the administrators complained about the reluctance of teachers in taking an active role in decision-making and avoiding taking responsibility in the application of the decisions.

Concerning the third administrative process, "leadership", most of the teachers viewed their administrators as effective leaders. They had sufficient administrative knowledge and experience to administer the school. However, administrators felt they lacked resources. The principal, for instance, complained about the system which, he said, did not provide the school with the financial resources or physical environment to take part in and use in-service training. Administrators stated that in the leadership process they had financial problems because insufficient budgets provided by the

Ministry for their school led to them asking for financial contributions from parents. This is illegal since public schools are free of charge in Turkey. The three administrators saw their needs of in-service training to keep up with new development in the administrative field.

Results related to "communication" indicated that most of the teachers complained about the lack of communication between teachers and administrators for various reasons. Two related this problem to the hierarchical structure of the school. The principal was the highest decision-making authority. Although teachers did participate somewhat in decision-making through reform initiatives, some saw this as lip service rather than an indication of real participative management. Some teachers complained that the administrators rarely visited the teachers' room and did not know what was happening in the school building. The principal mentioned that hierarchical tradition of Turkish school management formed barriers to communication.

He complained that the principal was seen as the highest authority in the school and was expected to do everything.

Concerning communication at this school, we saw the traces of the authoritative administrative system. The principal knows everything. In fact the principal does not have to know everything. Ninety percent of what the principal knows should also be known by other administrators.

The administrators highlighted the hierarchical and centralized structure of the system which caused communication problems between the school and the Ministry of Education. They added that communication through the "grapevine" was sometimes more effective and reliable than official communication channels.

With respect to the last process, "organizational change", respondents emphasized the strategic planning and TQM efforts that school committees were currently undertaking as required by a CLS. Some saw these activities as positive reform attempts that were failing because of the ineffective cooperation between the central government and the school. One assistant principal stated:

"These activities are conceptually very useful. Yet they do not have concrete results. In other words, the people who represent the decision-making authority for these activities do not encourage the others towards an effective collaboration. They do not do it intentionally. These things are only done for the sake of doing it, not to get any results or to improve anything. No-one keeps track of these activities or prepares a convenient setting for them."

The principal supported strategic planning and TQM efforts but they failed because teachers did not seem to understand that they are also partners in this process. They assumed that the principal was responsible for everything at the school. One assistant principal said that these reforms should be site-based and planned according to the needs of that particular institution. Another assistant principal also stated that these reforms should be decentralized to the local educational directories and financed by the municipalities. The general conclusion that could be drawn from the participants' comments would be stated as such that reform initiatives which were undertaken at this school failed because of the centralized character of the education system in Turkey.

The American school

The following results relate to administrative processes at the American school. The data concerning "motivation" revealed that all teachers at the American school seemed willing to work hard, and look for new ways and methods to help children learn. Some teachers related their high morale to the in-service training opportunities provided for them. They enjoyed the in-service classes where they could learn new things and share them with their co-workers. One said:

"One thing that helps us become motivated is the fact that we have many in-service classes so we are introduced new things and we get to try them. We also have some book clubs that, when there are new programs coming, we can discuss them and we try things in the classroom and we try to share our professional experiences."

The American principal also said that he was happy to work hard, especially for children, the environment was comfortable, and he had good relationships with his staff.

Concerning "decision-making" processes, all teachers said this was promoted by committees (vision committee, data gathering committee, best practices committee, and leadership committee), each established for the recent reform initiatives undertaken at the school. Every teacher had a voice in decision-making, and their opinions and input were sought by the principal before he reached final decisions. Yet they stated that whatever decisions they made at the staff meetings, the principal made the final decision in line with what he had in mind. Participants added that their committee decisions and activities were controlled by the district office. This was similar to the Turkish school where staff complained about the bureaucratic central office control over the school.

Teachers were content with the shared decision-making process fostered through the committees that they sat on. Some complained that certain factors hindered decision-making. Five thought that during this process everybody gave their opinion but it was difficult for them to sift the ideas and reach consensus. The principal saw the master bargaining agreement between the union and the school as the greatest factor that hindered the decision-making process. This agreement decreased his autonomy in making decisions about certain educational issues.

The master bargaining agreement is between the union and the school. This is an agreement that we have to follow with teachers. It tells things like how much time the teacher must use as planning time or how often the school should hold staff meetings. They also set rules on job postings. This limits my decision-making in the school.

Findings concerning "leadership" showed that all the teachers perceived their administrators as hardworking, diligent, receptive to new ideas, open to criticism, friendly and approachable. He visited homes of the students in crisis, tracked their progress and dealt with their behavioral problems. One teacher said that he was enthusiastic about learning new things, building on his knowledge by attending some classes as part of the professional development program. However, the principal saw some weaknesses in himself as an administrator. He said that after the summer holiday he would give teachers a chance to evaluate him.

As regards results concerning the "communication" process, most of the teachers complained that they did not have enough time for communication. Teachers said that, due to the recent mandates from the district office, they had little time to speak to each other. Yet all teachers said that communication among teachers teaching the same grade level was good. Teachers would come together, sharing their classroom materials, handouts, and their classroom experiences either at the grade level meetings or through visits to each others' classrooms. All teachers were content with the communication tools that the principal used. Among these tools were e-mail, newsletters, bulletins, voice-mail, and telephone. Teachers said that the principal was always accessible through these and by appointment.

Teachers did not know how communication took place between the central district office and the school. Three teachers mentioned a move in the education system towards centralization and standardization which would limit their freedom in their classrooms. They also complained that because of the new governor, the state had far more weight in making educational decisions. The principal was also concerned about increased centralization and bureaucracy:

We operate under the guidelines of the School District. Our SIP (School Improvement Program) committee submits things to my supervisor for approval.

We report to the assistant superintendent. Federal government barriers to what we do, making mandates. In Madison, 20 years ago it was pretty much a local building business. It became much more centralized in the last five years. Our teachers do not like that. Now everything is decided by the school district. There used to be 30 report cards for 30 different schools. Now there is one that everybody should follow.

This made it clear that increased centralization and bureaucracy in the American education system made communication between the district and the school more centralized and hierarchical.

Findings about the administrative process of "change" revealed that all the American teachers were very positive about the new initiatives the school has recently undertaken. The biggest organizational change attempt in the school was the SIP program designed by a committee. This year's plan was different because it had a five-year planning and implementation process. Most teachers agreed that although SIP was mandated by the district office, schools had autonomy in designing the organization and the components of their own improvement plan. But the principal said that the SIP was strategic planning developed by the district, so each school's plan had to fit in with the district's strategic planning. One teacher said that, outside the SIP, the school was involved in other activities which also contributed to school improvement:

There are other things we do. We had family fun night that did not come up under SIP where we invited parents to come and do activities with their kids. We do plan reading days when we devote all of our day and we invite guest readers to come in, especially on Dr. Seuss' birthday. So there are other things that are done outside SIP.

The interviews concerning the change process revealed that most participants were quite positive about the change process. They believed that the change initiatives undertaken at the school were going to be successful over the next five years.

1. Kentucky(肯塔基): The Commonwealth of Kentucky is a state located in the east-central United States of America. As classified by the United States Census Bureau, Kentucky is a Southern state, more specifically in the east-south-central region. Kentucky is one of four U.S. states constituted as a commonwealth (the others being Virginia, Pennsylvania, and

Massachusetts). Originally a part of Virginia, in 1792 it became the 15th state to join the Union. Kentucky is the 37th largest state in terms of total area, the 36th largest in land area, and ranks 26th in population.

2. **Wisconsin(威斯康星州)**: It is a US state located in the north-central United States and is considered part of the Midwest. It is bordered by Minnesota to the west, Iowa to the southwest, Illinois to the south, Lake Michigan to the east, Michigan to the northeast, and Lake Superior to the north. Wisconsin's capital is Madison, and its largest city is Milwaukee. As of 2010 the state has 5,686,986 residents. The state contains 72 counties.

3. **TQM(全面质量管理)**: Total quality management or TQM is an integrative philosophy of management for continuously improving the quality of products and processes. It is used around the world. TQM functions on the premise that the quality of products and processes is the responsibility of everyone who is involved with the creation or consumption of the products or services offered by an organization. In other words, TQM capitalizes on the involvement of management, workforce, suppliers, and even customers, in order to meet or exceed customer expectations.

New Words and Expression

1. paradigm [ˈpærədaim]	n.	范例,师范,典范
2. connote [kɔˈnəut]	v.	意味着,隐含,暗示
3. impede [imˈpiːd]	v.	防止,阻碍
4. verbatim [vəːˈbeitim]	adj. / adv.	逐字的(地),一字不差的(地)
5. bureaucratic [bjuə͵rəuˈkrætik]	adj.	官僚的,繁文缛节的
6. grapevine [ˈgreipvain]	n.	小道消息
7. mandate [ˈmændeit]	v. / n.	命令,指令,要求
8. bulletin [ˈbulitin]	n. / v.	公告,公示

Exercises

I Vocabulary.

Match the word in Column A to the correct definition in Column B.

Unit 12   School Management   学校管理

Column A
1. bureaucratic   2. impede
3. mandate   4. verbatim
5. bulletin

Column B
A. to order sb. to behave, do sth. in a particular way
B. to delay or stop the progress of sth.
C. exactly as spoken or written
D. involve complicated official rules which may seem unnecessary
E. an official statement about sth. important

 Read the text and answer the following questions.

1. What are centralized-decentralized governance structures' influences on education systems?
2. What do you think has contributed to the lack of autonomy and responsibility to undertake initiatives?
3. Why do most teachers in America think the Sip program is helpful?

 Supplementary Reading

Evaluating School-based Management

For more than 20 years, policymakers, educators, and academics have advocated participative leadership as a key ingredient in school improvement and reform. Two fundamental assumptions underlie the logic of participative leadership: (a) Schools are most effective when stakeholders from across the school community are meaningfully involved in core school decision making, and (b) participative leadership reflects democratic practice and, as such, is justified as a valid management strategy. In practice, participative leadership can be referred to as school-based management, participative decision-making or democratic leadership. Although, the practice of participative leadership can vary somewhat across different models, participative leadership typically revolves around a school-level management team comprised of administrators, teachers, staff members, parents and community members. These teams have articulated roles and responsibilities. They often are granted decision authority in core school decisions pertaining to learning and teaching, management, budget, and resources. Teams typically include elected members as well as non-elected representatives, who serve on various subcommittees. For example, teaching and non-teaching staff members, who are not elected as full members of the management team, typically are required (or are given opportunity) to serve on one of several subcommittees. The subcommittee structure facilitates and maximizes the inclusion of all staff in school decision-making. This participatory structure is intended to distribute decision authority across the school community and is purported as a means to improve the quality of school-level decision-making. To this end, the potential benefits of participative leadership are difficult to refute and as such it has become a popular and widespread school management style.

The impetus for the current study came from the observation that, although prior research has provided substantial information on what constitutes effective teams as well as strategies for successful implementation, concomitantly, there is a paucity of research on team evaluation. Specifically, what strategies can teams use to self-monitor or evaluate their goals, outcomes, and overall effectiveness? Teams ultimately are accountable to their larger school community and to this end must be conscious of the degree to which their goals, objectives, and values align. The purpose of this study was to propose a practical evaluation tool—the values Inquiry checklist—for management team self-review and evaluation. It is posited that the information derived from the checklist will enable teams to evaluate the degree to which their values align with those of the school community as a whole and as a result, increase the transparency of team decision-making and improve team accountability.

The evaluation guide proposed in the current study is founded on values inquiry evaluation research (Mark, 2001), which was posited as an appropriate melding of evaluation theory to the field of school management. As defined by Mark (2001), a values inquiry approach to program evaluation is one in which value positions are important to social programs and policies are identified and incorporated into the evaluation plan. Values inquiry is intended to be transparent, with differing values acknowledged early in the evaluation process and included as evaluation findings. Such findings are believed to have an impact on the nature of the evaluation information and subsequent judgments regarding the merit of programs. For example, Mark (2001) uses the example of whether parents of young children in a preschool program would see the program as successful if it promoted academic outcomes but did not emphasize social skills. In such a case, in spite of the fact that academic achievement and social skills both are valid goals of preschool programs; differing values within the parent group would potentially impact judgments on program success. Acknowledging differences in values at the onset of the evaluation and incorporating this information into subsequent evaluation activities are the basis of values inquiry evaluation.

From the perspective of evaluation, school-management teams primarily are accountable to their constituents—the larger school community. Effective management teams are aware of their constituent needs. Therefore, team effectiveness should be gauged by the degree to which team decisions reflect and/or address constituents' needs. To this end, the purpose of values inquiry evaluation is to increase team accountability by increasing transparency in team decision-making. If teams are able to articulate the values that drive their decisions and align these articulated values with those of the larger school community, in theory, the teams will be more effective and more accountable. In practice, teams that perceive themselves as effective, competent, and cohesive, concomitantly can be perceived by the larger school community to be ineffective or even in opposition to the needs of their constituents. In such cases, it is likely that goals prescribed by the team either misalign with the expectations of the larger school community or are misunderstood. Such misalignment is the focus of values inquiry evaluation.

The values inquiry approach to evaluating team effectiveness outlined in the following section proposes that stakeholder values on all important issues related to team accountability should be identified, addressed, and incorporated into team decision-making. Based on findings from educational research on school-based management, a list of 30 questions was developed that represent core aspects of team functioning, operations, and decision authority (see Table 1). In theory, team values and individual team member values are reflected in the way these 30 questions are answered and, in turn, incorporated into team decision-making.

The list of questions in Table 1 has been organized like a checklist for use with individual team members and aggregated to the team level. Collectively, the questions address choices that teams must make. These choices reflect dominant team values. Conversely, answers to these questions gauge which values are tradeoffs. For example, in the case of the pre-school program and possible goals for the program being social versus academic outcomes, although both outcomes were valid for such a program, some parents might choose to tradeoff social skills in favor of academic achievement as an appropriate focus for the program. Tradeoffs are made in situations where more than one outcome is valued, but not to the same degree. In the case of school-based management, such tradeoffs are assumed to be commonplace. Due to the myriad of factors that can potentially impact school operations, teams most certainly make many decisions that involve tradeoffs. Subsequently, these decisions, or tradeoffs, reflect what is most valued by individual team members and by the team as a whole. The following scenario provides an example of how the values inquiry checklist might be used to identify, assess, and address a hypothetical values conflict experienced by a school management team.

Table 1. Values inquiry checklist

Does your school management team: 1=yes, 0=no

include budgets to facilitate new activities and training for participants?
include budgets to enable on-going activities and training for participants?
create new administrative positions to administer school-based management?
involve a plan for the district decentralization of resources that is developed with input from various stakeholder groups?
enable teachers to identify problems and resources needed to solve them?
give the school rather than the district office authority over how school resources are allocated?
include group problem solving strategies/training?
include conflict resolution strategies/training?
incorporate team building?
incorporate training in budgeting?
include interviewing/listening skills?
apply group consensus strategies such as delphi and nominal group techniques, force field analysis, and other brainstorming techniques?
employ data-driven decision-making?
offer training in communication skills for presentations and report writing?
offer training writing mission statements, goals, and objectives for curriculum and instruction?
clarify decision authority (versus influence) between the team and the administrator?
clarify decision authority and influence within the team?
delineate team processes such as the roles, tasks, and responsibilities of team members?
clarify roles/tasks and responsibilities of the administrator?
clarify which decisions will be within the domain of the management team?

Unit 12 School Management 学校管理

> define team goals and identify measurable outcomes?
> establish a consensus on the goals and outcomes?
> define clear purposes for all students' learning?
> take collective responsibility for student learning?
> clearly delineate managerial policies?
> safeguard against bureaucratic administrator control?
> reflect the spirit of participation that views teachers as managing professionals?
> encourage participation from non-management team staff members?
> clarify the role of teacher unions?
> include mechanisms that prohibit administrators from using teacher contracts as a means to exclude teachers from participating?

Most school-based management teams involve subcommittees which address particular school issues and report back to the primary team with recommendations. Within this structure, it is not atypical for subcommittee chairs to be selected by the management team chair. In turn, values held by the team chair are reflected, in part, by his or her choice of subcommittee chairs. For the current scenario, suppose the team chair chooses subcommittee chairs, who are personal friends or who are likely to align with and support the views of the team chair. In this case, it is probable that other team members would see the choice as transparent and perhaps even anticipated. In terms of possible repercussions, most team members likely would not resent the favoritism, but accept it. For others, however, it might be reasonable enough to attempt to sabotage the efforts of the favored members. The team chair would most certainly be aware of ramifications such as this, but, nonetheless, would accept them as tradeoffs—the team chair chose to risk or tradeoff team cohesion in favor of having supporters head the subcommittees. The chair does not know if the possible negative impact on team cohesion will eventually outweigh the benefits of controlling who leads the subcommittees. However, this is the tradeoff. The team chair potentially has sacrificed team cohesion in favor of what he or she seems to be by increased team capacity.

The fundamental problem in the scenario described here is that the chair's authority appeared to go unchecked and, as a result, team cohesiveness likely would be negatively affected. Further, distribution of authority within the team was unclear and consequently impacted not only team cohesion but team capacity as well. Some team members likely would not work cooperatively with the selected subcommittee chairs.

For the management team in this scenario, the values inquiry checklist would be introduced by the administrator as a tool the team could use to examine and to self-evaluate its internal decision-making process. The checklist would be administered, for example, to each team member. The structure of the values inquiry checklist is a simple dichotomous response format("yes =1" or "no =0" to each question). Responses could be summed at the item level across team members and, as such, would represent areas of greatest and least value to the team as a whole. This simple analysis followed by some degree of structured group discussion on answers to the various questions would enable teams to also identify areas of greatest tradeoff. For example, for the questions on team training, it is probable that many teams do not put time and/or resources into team professional development (Turnbull, 2003). As such, the checklist could be used to measure team member values on training and the data could be used as a platform to address the issue and possible associated tradeoffs. Through simple record keeping and periodic application of the checklist, teams could revisit these issues and create benchmarks to gauge progress; all of which would be woven into the day-to-day functioning of the team in a relatively unobtrusive way.

In terms of using the checklist with established versus newly implemented teams, it is appropriate in both contexts. In the case of the team in the scenario, where issues of distribution of authority arose in the early implementation stages, the checklist would be useful as a means for teams to articulate and define decision authority, which ultimately is at the center of team functioning. Distribution of authority within the team and overall team decision authority ultimately impact the degree to which teams can achieve their goals and the expectations of their constituents. Therefore, established teams could use the values inquiry checklist as a means to review their goals and related values. Conversely, the checklist could be used by new teams as a tool to define goals, determine constituent needs and values, and to identify and align their own team values accordingly.

In an effort to move beyond school-based management as a symbolic gesture of democracy in practice, it is not unreasonable to expect that teams be accountable to their school community and the various constituent members. To achieve this, teams must be able to articulate their values and to assess their performance based on these values. The values inquiry checklist was developed to assist teams in achieving these important goals. The checklist is proposed as an unobtrusive and adaptable tool that principals and teams can use to evaluate overall management team effectiveness.

Unit 13 Teaching Methods
教学方法

Text A Refuting Misconceptions about Classroom Discussion

导读：长期以来，小组讨论法被普遍认为是一种能培养学生批判性思维、小组合作精神，提高学生理解能力的有效教学手段。但是，在现实教学情景下，受到一些条件的限制，小组讨论法经常被误用，以至于达不到理想的效果。本文探讨了四个对课堂小组讨论法的错误性认知，并对这些错误观点进行反驳，减少教学者对采用这种教学法的顾虑。

Social studies educators advocate discussion as an influential instructional method to encourage students to apply knowledge and develop higher-order thinking and understanding. Because firstly, telling students about something does not necessarily ensure their comprehension, but discussing a topic helps students strengthen and extend their existing knowledge of the topic and increase their ability to think about it. Secondly, discussion promotes students' involvement and engagement. Researches, as well as the wisdom of experienced teachers, demonstrate that for true learning to take place students must take responsibility for their own learning and not depend solely on a teacher. Using discussion is one means of doing this. It gives students public opportunities to talk about and play with their own ideas and provides motivation to engage in discussion beyond the classroom. Thirdly, discussion is used by teachers to help students learn important communication skills and thinking process. Because discussions are public, they provide a means for a teacher to find out what students are thinking and how they are processing the ideas and information being taught. Discussions thus provide social settings in which teachers can help students analyze their thinking process and learn important communication skills such as stating ideas clearly, listening to others, responding to others in appropriate ways, and learning how to ask good questions.

In classroom reality, however, teachers only use the discussion method sparingly. Instead, teachers predominantly use a quasi-discussion form called recitation to involve students in demonstrating their knowledge of subject matter. The problem is compounded by the fact that teachers generally refer to all major interaction sessions with students in the classroom as "discussions" when, in reality, they are recitations. Although both forms of interaction are effective in achieving their intended purposes, discussion is vastly more appropriate and effective in developing in students the widely endorsed citizenship competencies associated with rational and humane decision making and problem solving necessary for the common good.

Social studies teachers do not use discussion in their classrooms for many reasons, including a lecture-recitation instructional tradition, a long tradition of discipline-based curriculum design, emphasis on speedy and superficial coverage of content, fact-based textbooks and the limited availability of issue-based materials. It is hypothesized that one reason teachers avoid discussion is that they are relying on common misconceptions about the discussion method to make judgments about its use. Those misconceptions diminish the role that discussion can play in the classroom to help achieve the purpose of social studies. Logically, we can further assume that reflective and conscientious teachers might consider using discussion more often if their misconceptions were refuted with accurate and practical information. Possessing reliable and up-to-date information is the first step teachers need to consider when evaluating discussion as a viable instructional method.

Discussion misconception 1: A discussion consists of a teacher asking questions and students answering them.

If we substitute the word recitation in place of discussion, that statement would not be a misconception. A recitation does consist of a teacher asking questions and students answering them, but a discussion is much more. Therefore, a recitation is not a discussion; it is, at the most, a quasi-discussion.

The traditional recitation method emphasizes on finding out whether students know certain facts, often to prepare them for objective tests. As an instructional method, the use of the recitation method is very effective in achieving goals related to knowing content. It has been the dominant interaction form in classrooms throughout the past century, and it is characterized by the interaction pattern of a teacher question, usually at the lower cognitive levels, followed by a student response, and then a teacher evaluation. This procedure is referred as the IRE (teacher initiation, student response, teacher evaluation) pattern. One reason the pattern has persisted in the classroom is that it helps teachers manage and direct the flow of interaction. Teachers continuously need to reaffirm their authority when dealing with groups of twenty to thirty students, many of whom are reluctant learners.

  Discussions physically look and sound different from recitations. Discussion has a different purpose, interaction structure, and cognitive focus. It has as it emphasizes that students should apply what they have read or learned through the oral exploration of ideas, issues, and problems. A teacher's interaction with students aims at encouraging students to make connections between the new content and their past knowledge and perspectives. The general goal is for students to understand the material more fully. Key to achieving that is the use of authentic questions that request new information rather than memorized facts from the text. The interaction pattern is much more variable than the pattern of a recitation with teacher and students asking and answering questions and making comments. A discussion more closely approximates natural conversation than recitation because it is slower paced and not driven by the questions or evaluations of one person. It is an educative conversation with and among students. For example, a teacher might initiate a discussion with a higher cognitive-level question and may redirect that question to several students who have different perspectives on the issue being discussed. The teacher may probe one or more of the students for clarification of their responses and for elaboration or extension of their thinking. Students may converse with one another, sharing or questioning perspectives, and asking for evidentiary support for perspectives. It is not uncommon during genuine discussions for students to assume discussion leadership at various points.

  Discussion misconception 2: Teachers cannot get students involved in discussions if the students do not want to participate.

  This misconception applies to reluctant students, not to those students who adamantly refuse to participate in class for whatever reason. That is an extreme behavior. Teachers can get students involved who appear apprehensive, who do not raise their hands, who say "I don't know." who sit in the back of the room, who appear disinterested, and who are silent most of the time.

  The classroom climate a teacher creates is very important in encouraging student participation. In an international study, Klinzing and Klinzing-Eurich find that teachers tend to control discussions excessively by moving discussions back to themselves. They inadvertently do this by reacting in one way or another to almost every student response, question, or comment. Instead, they should only intervene with a comment or question at key points during the discussion and encourage more student-student interaction. Teachers who use those discussion techniques will give students more freedom to converse.

Teachers can employ many questioning techniques to encourage students to participate, including probing students' initial responses, redirecting questions to several students, and calling on non-volunteering students. During discussions, students sometimes lack the skill and confidence to express themselves at the higher cognitive levels. Resulting responses to questions can be ambiguous and incomplete. Teachers find that probes are useful follow-up questions to encourage students to complete, clarify, expand, or support their answers, especially with younger students as they begin to articulate the basics of reflective thinking during discussions. Questions such as "Why?", "What evidence do you have?", and "How can you support your view?" are common in discussions about societal issues and problems. A teacher leading students in discussion will need to be particularly diligent in listening to students' initial responses to follow-up with appropriate probes. Another useful approach to stimulate student participation in discussion is to direct one question to several students. The redirection could be prompted by an unanswered question or a desire to get additional responses to the same question and can involve volunteering and non-volunteering students.

Another questioning approach to stimulate participation during discussions is to have students formulate questions. Students ask few information-seeking questions so they need to be prompted to formulate questions related to the issue or problem being discussed. For example, a teacher might ask that all students write one question in response to the request, "If you had an opportunity to participate in a presidential press conference, what question would you ask him related to his policy on terrorism?" A question of this type will encourage all students to think and get involved. Having students ask questions of each other is another approach to consider because students tend to respond in more complex ways to each other than to teachers' questions.

The key to encouraging students to get involved in discussions is to create the conditions under which they want to contribute to discussions. The most obvious one is to rearrange students from seating in rows facing the teacher to seating them in a circle or semicircle to face each other, thereby facilitating communication. Another seating arrangement is referred to as the parliamentary style with two sets of rows facing each other. Establishing a positive social-emotional climate where students' responses, comments, and questions are respected, encouraged, and supported by both teacher and students is essential. Rules might be established by the teacher or the students to create discussion-behavioral expectations and guide the development of students' civic behaviors.

Other approaches to encourage participation include "pump priming" techniques such as having students write a response to a question first before answering, using a "think-pair-share" approach to get them to test a response with a peer first rather than with the whole class, or using small groups of two to three students to have them reflect on questions related to issues and problems. The key is getting students to discuss with each other, which they find is much less threatening than having to "be on stage" in front of the whole class. A student's "stage performance" will improve after having presented "off-Broadway" first.

There are many other instructional activities to get students to think and contribute responses to higher-order questions that can then be used as a base for a discussion:

1. Response cards. Pass out index cards and ask for anonymous answers to your discussion questions. Then group the responses to structure a class discussion or identify an issue for the class to explore through discussion;
2. Polling. Use a verbal survey by asking for a show of hands on positions related to an issue. Then follow up the diagnosis of group sentiment with a discussion based on support for positions;
3. Whips. Go around the group and obtain each student's point of view or a random sample of views. Use whips when you want to obtain something quickly from each student. The information might be used to form small groups representing different perspectives on an issue or solutions to a problem;
4. Informal panel. Invite a small number of students to present their views in front of the entire class;
5. Discussion chip. Distribute the same number of chips or pennies (three to five) to each member in a small group of students. Tell them that they are to use one chip for every answer, comment, or question as part of a discussion. Students need to use up all their chips before the discussion is completed or redistribute another equal number of chips for the discussion to continue;
6. Talking ball. Toss a small foam ball to a student with the understanding he or she must provide an answer to the discussion question, make a comment, or ask a question. That student then tosses the ball to another student, and so on.

Discussion misconception 3: Teachers are unbiased when encouraging students to make discussion contributions.

Although social studies teachers claim they take student diversity into account when involving students in discussion, observation of their discussion practices suggests a differentiated approach. In an in-depth study of five social studies teachers, Larson found that student diversity is a factor teachers said they consider when deciding whether to engage their students in discussion. Components of this factor are cultural background, ethnicity, gender, race, learning styles, and ability. Students representing different backgrounds were perceived as potentially valuable for discussion because an opportunity was provided to have a variety of viewpoints represented on an issue.

Evidence had shown that teachers, generally, expose low ability students to an "impoverished curriculum", which translates to limited and repetitive content, emphasis on factual recitation rather than on lesson-extended discussion, stress on drill and practice tasks rather than application and higher-level thinking tasks. In other research, it was also found that male students were given more time to talk in classrooms and received more remediation, praise, and criticism than female students.

Discussion misconception 4: Teachers cannot objectively evaluate students' contributions during classroom discussions.

Through the use of rubrics, teachers can assess more objectively the quantity and quality of students' verbal contributions during classroom discussions. During the past decade, there has been a movement toward integrating assessment of students' learning with instruction. One of the trends is the emphasis on moving away from what have been, until recently, the "tried and true" means of assessing student achievement and skills—traditional objective tests. In the old paradigm, the primary and major evaluation, usually a test was something that followed instruction to determine if students had learned the lesson material. Today, alternative and authentic assessment is more closely linked to instruction so that assessment becomes the means and ends of instruction.

Instruction involves formative and summative assessment of students by using authentic approaches or approaches that reflect the real world. Discussion is considered to be one such alternative and authentic instructional approach because it is how we communicate in many different venues—schools, works, communities, and families, for example. And, we can measure and assess discussion in terms of the content of the discussion and the process of discussing.

Over the past ten years, new techniques can help teachers to assess students' contributions during discussions more objectively. One such technique is a discussion rubric, which is a description of the teacher's requirements for varying degrees of student performance as the students attempt to meet the established criteria for an effective discussion. Harris created a rubric for assessing classroom discourse about civics that is based on standards and criteria. The teacher's goal in assessing each student engaged in a small group discussion of an issue is to judge the extent that a student's contribution to

Unit 13 Teaching Methods 教学方法

clarifying the issue under consideration and assisting the group toward an understanding and resolution of the issue. Students are assessed on substantive criteria aiming at evaluating students' understanding of the issue and procedural criteria that focus on students' ability to engage one another in discussion about the issue. The procedural criteria include positive(e.g. "inviting contributions of others" and "summarizing points of agreement and disagreement") and negative(e.g. "irrelevant distracting statements" and "personal attack") components. Three elements of performance focus the assessment:Whether or not the student has presented accurate knowledge related to the policy issue, employed skills for stating and pursuing related issues, and engaged others in constructive dialogue.

Off-Broadway[在纽约市戏院区以外的戏院上演的戏剧(多半是非主流,制作费较少,或实验剧)]:It is a term for a professional venue in New York City with a seating capacity between 99 and 499, and for a specific production of a play, musical or revue that appears in such a venue, and which adheres to related trade union and other contracts. These theatres are smaller than Broadway theatres.

New Words and Expression

1. compound[ˈkɔmpaund]   vt.   混合,调和,使严重,私了
2. diminish[diˈminiʃ]   vt.   减少,减损,贬低
                         vi.   变少,逐渐变细
3. viable[ˈvaiəbl]   adj.   能生存的,可行的
4. reluctant[riˈlʌktənt]   adj.   不情愿的,勉强的
5. adamantly[ˈædəməntli]   adv.   坚决地,顽固地
6. inadvertently[ˌinədˈvəːtəntli]   adv.   不注意,疏忽的,非故意的
7. ambiguous[æmˈbigjuəs]   adj.   模棱两可的,含糊不清的
8. remediation[riˌmiːdiˈeiʃən]   n.   纠正,补习
9. rubric[ˈruːbrik]   n.   种,类,题目,标题,注释
                      adj.   红色的,用红色写的
10. paradigm[ˈpærədaim]   n.   范例,示范,典范

I Vocabulary.

Fill in the blanks with the most suitable words. Change the form when necessary.

compound   diminish   reluctant   ambiguous   paradigm

1. He's _____ to begin, but when he does you should see him go into action.
2. We were lost into bewilderment due to his intentionally noncommittal or _____ statement.
3. Several unpopular decisions _____ the governor's popularity.
4. The painting provides us with one of the earliest _____ of the use of perspective.
5. He _____ various ingredients into an effective drug.

II Comprehension of the text.

Decide whether the following statements are true (T) or false (F) according to the passage.

1. Instead, teachers predominantly use a quasi-discussion form called recitation to involve students in demonstrating their knowledge of subject matter.
2. A discussion more closely approximates natural conversation than recitation because it is quicker paced and driven by the questions or evaluations of one person.
3. To encourage students to get involved in discussions, it is essential to create the conditions under which they want to contribute to discussions.
4. It was found that male students were given more time to talk in classrooms and received more remediation, praise, and criticism than female students.
5. Response cards, polling, and informal panel are used to help teachers to objectively evaluate students' contributions during classroom discussions.

III Translate the following phrases into Chinese.

communication skills   _____
up-to-date information   _____
substitute A in place of B   _____

integrate...with...
meet criteria

Text B   Brainstorming: a Creative Way to Learn

导读：头脑风暴这一问题解决方法不仅在商业、政府机构、工业等领域大受推崇，也在教育界成为一种教学手段。本文从使用这一教学手段该遵守的原则，以及在课堂实践中实施的具体步骤两方面入手，引导教育工作者最有效率地使用该方法。

Man is a highly creative creature who prefers to learn by doing, exploring, testing, questioning, and modifying ideas. However, the traditional school has not usually found it "economical" to foster learning by a process that is so natural to students. Education for today and the future must be relevant and meaningful. It must equip each student with a process by which he may solve many complex problems that will eventually evolve. Brainstorming is a creative problem solving technique that has been used successfully in business, government, industry, and to a limited degree in the field of education. In the classroom, brainstorming can provide a student the means by which early contact with peers becomes a stimulating and challenging experience. Children might be asked to solve practical problems that arise during the day or to solve problems that might be proposed by the teacher or students during a social studies lesson. Researchers have found that even first grade children can profitably use the brainstorming technique.

Small group interaction has long been cited as an effective teaching technique. This interaction is of importance because the pupil has the opportunity to become actively involved in the process of learning. Developing a positive self-concept by active participation would be one of the major benefits derived from group brainstorming. Educators often promote brainstorming as a useful technique in gifted education. There are many who claim that in a search for ideas there can be no implicit techniques, and rightly so, if the technique means a rigid set of rules. Any attempt to lay down hard-and-fast methods would be nothing but terminology masquerading as technology, but, there can be and are certain principles in the form of guides to procedure.

Brainstorming principles

Alex F. Osborn, the father of modern day brainstorming outlined four basic principles for effective brainstorming:

1. Critical judgment is ruled out; criticism of ideas must be withheld until later. Many creative thoughts have been lost simply because a person doubted that others would think his ideas insignificant and of no value. Many students start out their question with "This may be a stupid question, but…" Education and experience have trained most children and adults think critically rather than creatively, and this preface to a question is an example.

As a result, they tend to impede their fluency of ideas by applying their critical power too soon. By deferring judgment during a brainstorming session, children will be able to conceive a large number of creative ideas.

2. "Free-wheeling" is welcomed. The wilder the idea, the better; it is easier to tame down than to think up.

3. Quantity is wanted. The greater number of ideas, the more likelihood of potential solutions. Practically all the experiences with group brainstorming confirm the principle that quantity helps breed quality.

4. Combination and improvement are sought. In addition to contributing ideas of their own, participants should suggest how ideas of others can be turned into better ideas, or how two or more ideas can be combined to make one.

Steps to successful brainstorming in the classroom

1. Description of brainstorming and statement of instructions. Explain to the children that brainstorming is a way of stating the greater number of ideas in a limited amount of time. Emphasize the idea of spilling out ideas as quickly as possible while applying the deferred judgment principle. A short practice session can be attempted by asking the children to write a list of as many items as possible under the heading, "things we do at school." After several minutes, stop the listing and compile the number of different ideas on the chalkboard. You may wish to discuss with the children the following questions: Did each of you contribute some ideas? Were you able to avoid being critical of each others' contributions? This deferred judgment principle must be accomplished before effective brainstorming can take place.

2. Divide the class into brainstorming groups. Beginning groups seem to function well with 3 to 11 members. The groups can be all boys, all girls, or mixed. An odd number in the group might assure the availability of a majority, and thus avoid the danger of a split between two children of equal number. It will help if the teacher selects a few individuals who serve as self-starters for each group. With proper planning and guidance the whole room can brainstorm a problem or just one individual can use this technique.

Unit 13 Teaching Methods 教学方法

Several groups can be brainstorming at one time within the classroom.

3. Selection of a group leader and secretary. Each group should have a leader who would present the problem and keep the group actively engaged in the brainstorming process. The function of the secretary would be to write in brief form all ideas as they are presented. At times the ideas may tumble out so fast that even a shorthand expert would have difficulty recording them. It may be necessary to have two secretaries, each one jotting down every other idea. A tape recorder can also be utilized with transcription of the tape to the made layer.

4. Selection of the problem. The problem to be brainstormed should be one that will arouse student interest. This may not be easy to do, but a way usually can be found to make the problem relevant to many interests. Many times a functional problem, like what to do during the upcoming party could be used as a starting point. After the technique is refined, problems dealing with academic topics could be brainstormed. Students should assist in the selection process.

5. Statement of the problem. Problems can be presented that will encompass several areas of study. Social studies is a particularly good area in which children can brainstorm. The major objective in selecting a problem and stating the problem properly is to make sure that it is specific, not general.

The guiding principle is that a problem should be simple rather than complex. Failure to narrow the problem to a single target can seriously mar the success of any brainstorming session. Sometimes a session can be conducted to break down broad problems into their specific components. But in the normal course of events, make sure the problem is simple and specific.

Another principle to be considered is that the problem must be one that lends itself to many possible answers. If there are just a few possible solutions to the present one, then it would be wise to select another problem.

6. The brainstorming session begins. The problem should be explained, and the group leader should then discuss the four basic principles. Placards stating these principles could be displayed to act as a constant reminder to the children.

After these preliminaries are completed, the leader then calls for suggestions on how the problem could be solved. What happens if all of the children's hands go up? If this occurs the group leader could simply go around the table and let each person present one idea in turn. One student should present only one idea at a time. The fun is just beginning! If a child has some idea that is directly related to the previous statement, he can snap his fingers to be recognized by the leader. The leader should give priority to the finger snappers and thus make the most of the power of association. The students will find this exciting and challenging! Throughout this entire procedure the secretary should be taking brief notes. However, a tape recorder works very well with elementary school children.

Past experiences indicated the optimum time for beginners using brainstorming is about ten minutes. As their experience in this activity increases so can the time period.

As the children's brainstorming skills become more sophisticated with time, new variations can be tried. After a brief amount of time on a problem, the leader can stop the session and ask the group members to keep the problem on their minds until the next day when they will be asked for their afterthoughts. Maybe you can come up with some new variations.

7. Evaluations of the presented ideas.

After the brainstorming session has been completed, the secretary of the group should prepare a list of all ideas suggested during the session. At this point the teacher has to make a decision: Should the ideas be evaluated by the group of students who think up the ideas or by an entirely different group? It is usually wise to have the final evaluation done by those directly responsible for the problem. This may or may not be the group that does the brainstorming. The teacher has a great deal of latitude when choosing the method of evaluation. To facilitate this evaluation, it is often advisable to prepare a check-list of criteria by which students and teachers can evaluate the ideas. The following criteria could be used to evaluate each idea: Is it feasible? Is the idea simple enough? Is it timely? Is it appropriate? Is it efficient? Is it an improvement?

It is important that the criteria are appropriate for the problem being brainstormed. With each new problem you may need to create a new check-list. The entire class can work together to determine the relative worth of the presented ideas. This evaluation process usually develops into a most effective and meaningful type of group interaction. During the final evaluation, the students should attempt to apply the final ideas to the problem to determine whether or not the ideas are applicable.

If application is not feasible, the children can conduct a debate or continue with class discussion on the relative worth of the ideas.

At this point a very important concept must be noted. In many areas of instruction, particularly in the social studies, there is not a "right" or "wrong" answer. From this type of learning experience students will have the opportunity to discover the dichotomies in our society. It is important that students find out how the real world operates and how to evaluate real problems. The teacher should integrate the final evaluated ideas into his teaching lesson.

Most practitioners of group brainstorming recommend that brainstorming groups be assisted by trained facilitators. These facilitators can ensure that group members follow the rules for effective brainstorming. For example, they might remind group members not to criticize or evaluate each other's ideas. Facilitators can also keep groups from drifting into issues or topics not directly related to the central problem being discussed. Group members who do not actively participate because of fear or lack of motivation can be encouraged to contribute to the group effort. When groups hit dry spells, the facilitator can suggest some areas or angles they have not considered and encourage them to keep trying by mentioning high performance levels attained by other groups. Several studies have shown that facilitators that use these strategies can in fact help brainstorming groups attain relatively high levels of performance.

It is often not feasible to have a facilitator work with each brainstorming group. Teachers who divide their classes into groups for brainstorming sessions cannot effectively monitor and facilitate each one of these groups. It is also difficult and expensive to provide facilitators for group brainstorming sessions in organizations. A more useful strategy is to train students to be effective group brainstormers. Experience in group brainstorming with an effective facilitator greatly enhances group brainstorming in subsequent sessions without facilitators.

Computers also appear to be useful in facilitating group brainstorming. Many corporations and university laboratories employ a group decision support system that allows participants to exchange ideas by means of a computer network. Ideas can be entered in the lower section of the computer screen while ideas generated by others in the group network are shown in the top of the screen. Studies have shown that this type of group brainstorming is as effective as individual brainstorming. It appears to be especially useful when dealing with large groups of 12 or more, in part because participants do not experience the interference of conventional group brainstorming. They can type their ideas at any time and do not have to wait until others have expressed their ideas. Unfortunately, this type of computer-based brainstorming requires equipment and software not easily available in most educational contexts. However, simply having students in a group type their ideas on computers as they share them aloud appear to be an effective alternative. Even though there is still some potential distraction from hearing others generate ideas, one does not have to wait one's turn to generate ideas. Moreover, there is a record of each person's ideas which should minimize the tendency to loaf in groups.

1. **Brainstorming(头脑风暴):** a group creativity technique by which a group tries to find a solution for a specific problem by gathering a list of ideas spontaneously contributed by its members.

2. **Alex F. Osborn (May 24,1888–May 13,1966):** was an advertising executive and the author of the creativity technique named brainstorming.

New Words and Expression

1. foster [ˈfɔstə] vt. 领养,培养,促进,鼓励,抱有(希望等)
2. derive [diˈraiv] v. 获取,得自,起源
3. rigid [ˈridʒid] adj. 严格的,固执的,刻板的
4. impede [imˈpiːd] vt. 妨碍,阻止
5. free-wheeling 单向转动
6. spill out 溢出
7. tumble out 乱七八糟地倒出来
8. encompass [inˈkʌmpəs] vt. 围绕,包围,包括,完成
9. preliminary [priˈliminəri] adj. 初步的,预备的,开始的
   n. 初步行动,准备,初步措施
10. optimum [ˈɔptiməm] adj. 最佳的,最适宜的
11. sophisticated [səˈfistikeitid] adj. 老练的,精密的,复杂的,久经世故的
12. dichotomy [daiˈkɔtəmi] n. 两分,分裂,二分法
13. distraction [disˈtrækʃən] n. 分心,分心的事物,注意力分散

Unit 13　Teaching Methods　教学方法

I　Vocabulary.

Fill in the blanks with the most suitable words. Change the form when necessary.

derive　encompass　rigid　optimum　sophisticated

1. She enjoys doing yoga because she can not only keep fit but also _____ happiness from it.
2. In the _____ college entrance exam, he stood out and was admitted into Peking University.
3. Nowadays, iPhone enjoys immense popularity because it is very _____.
4. Both the weather and also the market offered _____ conditions for the sale of this product.
5. The general arts course at the university _____ a wide range of subjects.

II　Comprehension of the text.

Decide whether the following statements are true (T) or false (F) according to the passage.

1. Brainstorming is a creative problem solving technique that has been used successfully in business, government, and industry, but not in the field of education.
2. Researchers have found that even first grade children can profitably use the brainstorming technique.
3. The greater number of ideas the more likelihood of potential solutions.
4. Beginning brainstorming groups function well more than 11 members.
5. Assisted by trained facilitators, it is more likely that group members will follow the rules for effective brainstorming.

III　Translate the following sentences into Chinese.

1. Man is a highly creative creature who prefers to learn by doing, exploring, testing, questioning, and modifying ideas.
2. Critical judgment is ruled out; criticism of ideas must be withheld until later. Many creative thoughts have been lost simply because a person doubted that others would

think his ideas insignificant and of no value.
3. In addition to contributing ideas of their own, participants should suggest how ideas of others can be turned into better ideas, or how two or more ideas can be combined to make one.
4. The function of the secretary would be to write in brief form all ideas as they are presented. At times the ideas may tumble out so fast that even a shorthand expert would have difficulty recording them.
5. Ideas can be entered in the lower section of the computer screen while ideas generated by others in the group network are shown in the top of the screen.

 Supplementary Reading

Learning Styles and Teaching Styles

Learning styles have profound effects on material processing, exercises designing, teachers' instruction options, and performance assessments. Educators should place emphasis on intuition, feeling, sensing, and imagination, in addition to the traditional skills of analysis, reason, and sequential problem solving. Teachers should design their instruction methods to connect with all learning styles, using various combinations of experience, reflection, conceptualization, and experimentation. Instructors can introduce a wide variety of experiential elements into the classroom, such as sound, music, movement, experience, and even talking. Teachers should employ a variety of assessment techniques, focusing on acquiring the essential language skills.

Students preferentially take in and process information in different ways: by seeing and hearing, reflecting and acting, reasoning logically and intuitively, analyzing and visualizing. Teaching methods also should vary accordingly. How much a student can learn is also determined by the compatibility of the student's learning styles and the teacher's teaching styles. It is important for teachers to know their learners' preferred learning styles because this knowledge will help teachers to plan their lessons to match or adapt their teaching and to provide the most appropriate and meaningful activities or tasks to suit a particular learner group at different stages.

Student-centered methods contain a great number of various instructional methods, for example, project-based learning, problem-based learning, and discussion. All these methods are inductive, based on constructivist approach. In the constructivist approach the present instructive teaching practice is completed by chosen learning problems through creating adequate learning environment. It is necessary to know that knowing is forming—it constructs itself individually and in terms of social relationships. Learning is an active process, for it realizes in multidimensional relationships. From this perspective the learning process is primarily the matter of construction, and learning individuals enter as co-creators of learning process. There are several modern teaching methods that can be used in teaching and learning. These methods focus on students' active work, and are used in various classes by in-service teachers and by pre-graduated teachers.

Project-based learning

Project-based learning is often referred to as the most common method. It is an instructional methodology in which students learn important skills by doing actual projects. The acquisition and structuring of knowledge in project-based learning is thought to work through the following cognitive effects: initial analysis of the problem and activation of prior knowledge through small-group discussion, elaboration on prior knowledge and active processing of new information, restructuring of knowledge, construction of a semantic network, and social knowledge construction.

Problem-based learning

Problem-based learning is often referred to as a form of inquiry-based learning, which describes an environment in which learning is driven by a process of inquiry owned by the student. The problem can be presented in various forms—question, task, or experiment. Some theories suggest that learning occurs as students collaboratively engage with concepts in meaningful problem solving. In this view, knowledge is seen as a tool for thinking and for enabling learners to participate in meaningful activity.

Brainstorming

Brainstorming is a group creativity technique designed to generate a large number of ideas for the solution of a problem. Experts propose that groups can double their creative output with brainstorming.

The most important outcome of brainstorming is improving team work. Brainstorming certainly has disadvantages, for example, students may not feel free to present unusual ideas. The aim of brainstorming is to generate a great number of ideas.

The teacher has to create a criticism-free environment, to present the problem and organize the discussions. The teacher also must be clear about how to measure progress and success. The solution of brainstorming must be clear for all.

Mind map

Mind maps help avoid linearly thinking, the problems are solved more creatively.

You can use a sheet of paper, the central idea is written in the middle of the paper. Then you can add new ideas using words, combine them, and add a structure. It is a visual method, and there are a lot of possibilities of how to create a mind map. Later on you can modify the information.

Heuristic methodology

The heuristic method of learning is based on learning by discovering, constructivism and active interaction of teachers and pupils. The common axes of their philosophy are: use of scientific process, leader guided creativity, use of cheap and non-sophisticated materials. The method includes entertaining activities to stimulate the kids' exposure to the scientific phenomena they meet in everyday environment, to develop the child's curiosity and analytic mind, and to have training effects on the family, scholar and social scales. Seminars and workshops for teachers are organized, and materials and worksheets for interested teachers are prepared.

Interactive methods mentioned above were used as teaching methods. Methodology materials for teachers and worksheets for students were prepared by the pre-service teacher and our research team. Recommended methods were attached to the materials. The effectiveness of several interactive activities was explored. The Interactive teaching methods can help to teach for understanding. But it is necessary to change the role and position of the teacher in the classroom. The teacher in the 21st century has to be a classroom manager. The teacher has to be an expert. Traditional teaching methods are not effective. The goal of the initiative is to apply new methods based on the constructivist learning theory. The learning and teaching process will be more effective, when students can construct their knowledge by their own.

According to the report today's education system faces irrelevance unless we bridge the gap between how students live and how they learn. However, variations of interactive methods are not used. Teachers complain that they don't know the methodology of these methods and that they have not enough time to teach in the new way. Pre-service teachers should be taught these new methods and its methodology and invited to seminars and workshops where they get informed about the methodology. I think it is necessary to prepare more instructional materials for teachers, and in-service teachers complain that it is time consuming for them to prepare a lesson with interactive methods. The research has shown that interactive teaching methods can improve the quality of

Unit 13 Teaching Methods 教学方法

teaching. The main problem is how to get more interested and skilled in-service teachers. Our further activities will be concentrated not only on students or pre-service teachers but also on in-service teachers to improve their knowledge about the methods mentioned above.

Traditionally, teaching is dominated by a teacher-centered, book-centered, grammar-translation method and an emphasis on mechanical memory. These traditional language teaching approaches have resulted in a number of typical learning styles, with visual learning being one of them. A teacher must design her lesson plan around her students. After you know the students learning styles, you should set goals for your teaching strategies. This requires you to differentiate instruction through use of the learning styles. Ideally you want to incorporate all of the learning styles so that each student may learn in a way that suits them best for the day.

Studies show that matching teaching styles to learning styles can significantly enhance student attitude and student behavior. This is not to say that the best thing one can do for one's students is to use their preferred modes of instructions exclusively. A point no educational psychologist would dispute is that students learn more when information is presented in a variety of modes than when only a single mode is used. The following are some techniques employed in teaching practice:

1. Provide a balance of concrete information (data, facts, experiments and results) and abstract concepts (principles, theories);

2. Balance material that emphasizes practical problem-solving methods with material that emphasizes fundamental understanding;

3. Use pictures, graphs and simple sketches liberally, during and after the presentation of verbal material. Show films or provide demonstrations, if possible;

4. Don't fill every minute of class time lecturing and writing on the blackboard. Set aside intervals, however brief, for students to learn what have been told on their own. Raise questions and problems to be worked on;

5. Talk to students about learning styles, both in advising and in class. Students who are reassured to find their academic difficulties may not all be due to personal inadequacies. Explaining to students how they learn most efficiently may be an important step in helping them reshape their learning experiences so that they can be successful;

6. Try to design some activities which involve students' senses as many as possible, using all the senses to help improve English learning. For example, relatively long passage dictations, and games, which require students to write down what they are told by their classmates, who already have learnt that by heart;

7. Encourage students to learn something online. In terms of English learning, students can write assignments through e-mail or read materials given online (the students in the experimental class use the new horizon college English book, a web-assisted textbook);

8. Motivate learning. As much as possible, teaching new material in the context of situation to which students can relate in terms of their personal experiences, rather than simply as more material to memorize.

Teachers confronted with this list of techniques might feel that is impossible to do all that in the class and cover the syllabus and requirements. The idea, however, is not to adopt all the techniques at once but rather to pick several that look feasible and try them on an occasional basis, and try one or two more later in class. In this way a teaching style that is both effective for students and comfortable for teachers will evolve naturally, with a potentially dramatic effect on the quality of learning.

Unit 14　Materials & Test
教材与考试

Text A　Materials and Media

导读：随着社会进步和科学技术的发展，教材与教学媒体也经历着一次次重大的变革。本文从教材与教学媒体的定义和分类，外语教学发展历程中教材与教学媒体的演变和改革，以及教师面临的挑战几方面入手，呼吁教师在使用教材与教学媒体时，要善于扬长避短，结合学习者的学习方式和学习需求，营造一个理想的教学情境。

Throughout the history of foreign language teaching, theorists and practitioners have tried to support the language learning process as best they can. To that end, foreign language teachers and material developers have introduced a variety of aids, materials and media. Whatever supportive means are chosen, their conception and format to a large extent determine the layout of a foreign language course.

Developments in the understanding of what foreign language competence implies and what is required to achieve it, combined with technological innovations and shifts in social demands on education, have entailed changes in the way in which the foreign language teaching process is conceived and supported. Materials and media that were believed to be effective learning tools at one point in time are supplemented with or even supplanted by others, which may in their turn become marginalized.

The gradual increase in diversification of teaching materials and media, with the ensuing danger of overburdening teaching with them for their sheer availability, makes it an absolute necessity that teachers are able to perceive both strengths and weaknesses of available teaching aids, and can make well-considered judgments as to when, how and to what end they can most effectively be harnessed to particular learning or teaching tasks. Often such decisions are influenced by considerations beyond the control of the course designers and procedures. Questions of organization and coordination in any multimedia course will play an important role. In addition, materials and media deliberations must be made with respect to the abilities and needs of particular learner groups.

Definition and classifications

Materials and media are everything that can be used to support the foreign language learning process. In many foreign language classes today these aids will probably include the teacher's voice, a tape-recorder with cassettes, a writing board, the textbook, and a workbook. Many teachers will use additional worksheets, sets of task cards and objects (props, pictures, posters, food tins or labels, maps, wall charts and the like). Some teachers may also have an overhead projector with transparencies or even a video player with videotapes or films at their disposal. In some language classrooms reference materials, such as dictionaries, grammar or phrase books, may also be permanently available. Schools may have foreign newspapers, periodicals, magazines, cultural background books or supplementary readers in their library. The large majority of teachers may not yet consider computers with foreign language learning software, CD-ROMs, DVDs or an internet connection common teaching aids. A minority of specialized language schools may have at their disposal a self-access centre, where a large variety of the above-mentioned media and materials are freely accessible to learners for self study. Still other materials and media which have at some point in time been introduced into foreign language teaching with more or less success could be mentioned here. They include the language laboratory, the flannel board, the epidiascope, the flipchart, flashcards, radio, television and even puppets.

This broad spectrum of teaching aids can be classified according to various perspectives. An obvious way to do so is to distinguish between aural, visual and audio-visual aids, with the last category having the advantage of combining sound and image. Another common way to classify materials and media is to do so according to their function. Thus a distinction can be made between teaching and learning materials, or between data, instruction, process and reference materials. Data materials are chunks of language that are presented to learners for exploration. Instruction materials typically include workbooks, exercise books and other materials designed for language practice. Process materials are those parts of a language course that mediates to learners how the course is to proceed. Reference materials and media may be referred to as either basic or supplementary, with the first category comprising materials and media that are considered essential parts of a particular language course, and the latter that can but need not be used on top of the basic materials to assist students to meet the requirements of a particular course or to further improve their language competence. Whereas course books, workbooks and course-related cassettes are now typically considered basic course materials, computer packages, slides and transparencies, videos, additional listening materials, set of games, simplified readers and the like, tend to be considered supplementary, although many multimedia courses attempt to integrate a large variety of different media and materials, and, consequently, might consider these aids to be basic, not supplementary. Fourth, materials may either be designed for use in the classroom or for self study. A final commonly used procedure is to classify materials and media according to the language components or skills they aim to practice. Thus, listening materials are distinguished from, for example, reading, writing, speaking or grammar practice materials. Some media are considered better suited to practice particular skills or deal with particular requirements of foreign language course than others. Thus, learners' listening skills may benefit most from aural aids, such as tapes, radio broadcasts or the teachers' voice. Cultural background information, on the contrary, may best be presented over video, television, films, transparencies, posters or pictures, or it may be taught via the internet or with the help of CD-ROMs.

Materials and media in the history of foreign language education

When looking at the history of foreign language education from the point of materials, a number of evolutions in their selection and design are noticeable. At various stages in the development of foreign language teaching, new media and teaching aids have been introduced, of which some have managed to establish themselves firmly, and continue to be used to date, whereas others have become marginalized or seem to have gradually disappeared from mainstream teaching altogether.

Shifts in the selection and conception of media and materials seem to have been dependent on a number of interrelated factors. Developments in the understanding of what competence in a foreign language entails and what is required to reach it, in theories about the nature of the language learning process and how it is best supported, combined with technological developments and the commercial exploitation of particular "teaching and learning machines", have to a large extent determined the way in which materials and media have been used in foreign language instruction. Thus, the need for the pupil to hear himself when practicing pronunciation was recognized early. No effective way of meeting the problem was found until the tape recorder was invented. The popularity of drill exercise in the audio-lingual foreign language teaching can in part be explained by the commercialization of a machine that was capable of doing these monotonous, unnatural and inhuman activities, i.e. the language laboratory. Television and video were acclaimed by foreign language education theorists of the communicative era for their capability of bringing "real life" into the language learning classroom and of communicating the total situation of language to the learner. Insights from cognitive psychology, notably that people learn best when several senses are simultaneously addressed, triggered efforts of the teaching profession to introduce all kinds of visual, audio-visual and even tangible aids into foreign language teaching, so as to complement or replace the predominantly written and aural materials.

Teaching practice and teachers' and learners' experiences with particular materials and media, too, contributed to their refinement and adaptation to particular educational needs. Thus, following teachers' unsatisfactory experiences with films and videos which tended to be quite long when they were first introduced into the foreign language classroom, a clear evolution towards shorter films has been noticeable replacing the input of large amounts of aural and visual data with shorter sequences, say of about four minutes, followed by careful exploitation. Learners' frustrating experience with monolingual dictionaries containing long entries formulated in a language too far above their level of competence incited publishers and researchers to develop learner dictionaries with clear definitions written in simple language, highlighting active words to be learnt first, providing study pages and grammar help boxes focusing on vital grammar points, building in a workbook section to develop students' dictionary skills, providing colorful illustrations with corresponding vocabulary practice exercises or usage notes designed to help learners avoid common errors.

Teacher frustration at the impracticability of certain media and materials proposed by theorists further determined their lifecycle. Whereas textbooks are very user-friendly "packages" of materials, because they are light, easily scanned, easily stacked and do not need hardware or electricity. Slide projectors or video machines are less so, also because in many institutions and schools the rooms where they are available have to be booked well in advance, which makes course planning more difficult. Some media can also be considered more flexible than others because they can be used for a variety of language practice activities, with various age groups and working arrangements. Thus, transparencies can not only be used by the teacher to capture class attention, they may also be used by pupils to report on group work results. They are easily wiped off and can be used in the context of almost any thinkable language practice activity. The language laboratory, on the contrary, appears more static and limited in use, seeming suitable foremost for individual pronunciation and drill practice, albeit those communicative group activities are not wholly excluded.

The selection of teaching materials and media is also partly dependent on the demands made by society at a given period in time. Computer literacy is now put forward as one of the aims which all teaching should pursue. In view of the explosion of knowledge and the fastness with which it is distributes, over the information highway and other media, society also demand that teachers and schools educate their children for independent, lifelong learning, providing them with the skills to find and evaluate information next to passing a body of well-structured knowledge on to them which can serve as a guiding framework. Since computers use language, it would seem logical to take advantage of them for language learning. Computers, moreover, enable independent individual work, since learners can progress at their own pace and many programs include a self-check facility, automatic contextualized feedback, the possibility to use reference materials in the screen, to listen to the spoken language, to watch pieces of video, to record one's own voice, or to interact on real time with native speakers of a foreign language, to name only a few advantages. The fact that young and adolescent learners in particular find the use of computers attractive and motivating is an added benefit.

These social demands urge a change in teachers' and learners' roles. Teachers have to become coaches rather than providers of information, since pupils can find their own texts and language data. Coaching entails the need to redesign many of the materials that have been developed for teacher-guided instruction and to consider seriously how individual differences in learning styles, needs, abilities and interests can best catered for in integrated powerful multimedia learning environments.

Debates and perspectives

With the boom of teaching media, interdisciplinary groups of social scientists, psychologists, educationists and technically oriented researchers started studying "educational technology". One of their major concerns was to investigate the possible surplus value of particular media over others in particular learning environments. A major problem facing this field of study is the fact that it is next to impossible to prove empirically the excess value of one medium over another, since each language learning situation is shaped by a complex whole of situational, relational, educational, cognitive and affective variables, which are hard to control and make a reliable comparison of two groups of learners-one working with a particular media remain largely based on assumptions, not on general facts. It follows that authors, course designers and teachers alike have very little evidence upon which they can base any improvements to exciting media, materials or multimedia programs, or suggestions for new approaches in new materials.

It seems that, partly as a consequence of this, teachers have become skeptical and critical toward the hyperbole created around new teaching media. They tend to prefer to stick to what is familiar and most practicable, being ill-disposed toward devoting energy to changing teaching approaches that may well not lead to more effective learning. The fact that theorists and researchers often overlook the practical institutional or organizational constraints every teacher has to live with may further undermine teachers' belief in proposals made by non-practitioners.

On top of this, teachers may be afraid that new media may come to replace them as teachers, and therefore prefer not to cooperate in what to them seems a self-destructive process. However, since it is only when media and materials are used in a meaningful and pedagogically well-considered manner that they may make the learning process more effective, and since the teacher best qualifies for designing appropriate learning environments, the chance that teachers will disappear altogether is small. Certainly, if learners are to be provided with a large variety of learning experiences that promote independent learning, teacher's whole-class instruction time may well have to be reduced. Rather than supplanting the teacher and the textbook, however, newer teaching aids will supplement and support them.

In view of the challenges that await teachers, teacher training intuitions have the responsibility to prepare teachers for an informed selection, adaptation and integration of available media and materials. It will be vital for teachers to perceive both the strengths and weaknesses of teaching media and materials, and to find ways to overcome shortcomings. The dangers that threaten teachers are those of over-burdening teaching with media for their sheer availability, and of falling prey to a naive belief in media's inherent capacities, without devoting sufficient attention to the quality of data input and instruction and process materials, or carefully considering learners' needs, learning styles, abilities, interests and levels of competence in designing learning environments.

1. **Epidiascope**(幻灯机片): a device which displays opaque materials by shining a bright lamp onto the object from above. A system of mirrors, prisms and/or imaging lenses is used

Unit 14   Materials & Test   教材与考试

to focus an image of the material onto a viewing screen.

2. **Flipchart**(活动挂图): a stationery item resembling a whiteboard, typically supported on a tripod or four-legged easel.

3. **Cognitive psychology**(认知心理学): a sub-discipline of psychology exploring internal mental processes. It is the study of how people perceive, remember, think, speak, and solve problems.

New Words and Expression

1. entail [in'teil]	vt.	使必需,带来,限定继承
	n.	限定继承权
2. supplement ['sʌplimənt]	n.	增刊,补充物
	vt.	增补,补充
3. supplant [sə'plɑːnt]	v.	取代,排挤
4. harness ['hɑːnis]	vt.	利用,管理,控制
5. cassette [kə'set]	n.	盒式磁带,暗盒
6. periodical [ˌpiəri'ɔdikəl]	n.	期刊
	adj.	定期的
7. epidiascope [ˌepi'daiəskəup]	n.	幻灯机
8. spectrum ['spektrəm]	n.	系列,幅度,范围,光谱,[科]频谱
9. chunk [tʃʌŋk]	n.	厚块(片),相当大的量
10. tangible ['tændʒəbl]	adj.	可触摸的,实际的,有形的,确凿的
11. surplus ['səːpləs]	n.	过剩,顺差,盈余
	adj.	过剩的,多余的
12. empirically [im'pirikli]	adv.	经验主义地
13. prey [prei]	n.	牺牲者,被掠食者
	vi.	掠夺,捕食,使……苦恼

I Vocabulary.

Fill in the blanks with the most suitable words. Change the form when necessary.

| entail | supplement | harness | periodical | chunk |
| tangible | supplant | surplus | spectrum | prey |

1. The project would _____ a huge increase in defense spending.
2. He retired, and was free. Every day he spent the whole morning reading _____.
3. Nowadays, solar energy _____ to better serve us.
4. The policy of apartheid is only a political _____ to an economic policy that depends on cheap native labor.
5. Instead of falling a _____ to the enemy, he committed suicide.
6. To better pursue his dreams, he spent _____ of time studying and finally became a scientist.
7. An efficient government should serve the people and bring more _____ benefits to common people.
8. The Commercial Press published a wide _____ of book.
9. I hate this writer's writing because his works is always heavy with _____ phrasing.
10. Machinery has largely _____ hand labor in making shoes.

II Comprehension of the text.

Decide whether the following statements are true (T) or false (F) according to the passage.

1. The broad spectrum of teaching aids can be classified according to various perspectives.
2. At various stages in the development of foreign language teaching, some media and teaching aids have managed to establish themselves firmly, and continue to be used to date, whereas others seem to have gradually disappeared from mainstream teaching altogether.
3. No valid facts have shown that people learn best when several senses are

simultaneously addressed.

4. Computers support independent individual work because learners can progress at their own pace.

5. Teachers may be afraid that new media may come to replace them as teachers, and therefore prefer not to cooperate in what to them seems a self-destructive process.

III Complete the following sentences according to the text.

1. An obvious way to classify teaching aids is to distinguish between aural, visual and audio-visual aids, with _____ _____ having the advantage of combining sound and image.

2. In terms of _____ _____ _____ _____ listening materials are distinguished from reading, writing, speaking and grammar practice materials.

3. When looking at the history of foreign language education from the point of materials, a number of _____ in their selection and design are noticeable.

4. With the boom of teaching media, _____ _____ is studied by groups of social scientists, psychologists, educationists and technically oriented researchers.

5. Textbooks are very _____ "packages" of materials, because they are light, easily scanned, easily stacked and do not need hardware or electricity.

Text B In Defense of Teaching "Outdated" Material

导读：虽然欧几里得几何学并不能完全解释我们生存的空间，但是许多学校仍然教授这一课程，因为如果不能了解欧几里得几何学，研究三角学、微积分则很困难。要想精通一门课程，了解这些所谓的"过时"的教材是非常有必要的。不能掌握一门课程的发展史，则充其量也只能是个门外汉。本文在呼吁重视一些经典教材时，要求教育者们培养学生在先前知识基础上，学会构建新知识的能力，而不只是做一个普通的信息接受者。

We all know that Euclidean geometry does not adequately explain the space in which we live. Our world is not that of the plane, as found in Edward Abbott's *Flatland*. Why, then, is Euclidean geometry still taught in schools? I suggest that without an understanding of Euclidean geometry, one would have difficulty understanding advanced concepts, such as trigonometry or calculus. As my college calculus teacher noted, calculus is just addition done with lines. Advanced concepts build on previous knowledge.

During my rhetorical criticism course, students sometimes wonder why we cover so much history. A similar issue is also raised in my rhetorical theory course, a survey course that begins with the pre-Socratics and ends with postmodern rhetorical theory. I openly state that some of the material that we cover is no longer useful from a methodological standpoint, but that there are reasons for teaching the material. I explain to the students that it is important to recognize not only current rhetorical theory and methods of criticism, but also the controversies, dead ends, and landmarks that brought us to the place we are today. Innovation is often the result of recognition of suboptimal processes or ideas. If we help students see where these shifts in method or theory occurred and what spawned these insights, and, more importantly, why previous generations held inaccurate understandings, we are more likely to have students who will likewise improve the discipline because they, too, can see potential ways to improve their craft.

In this essay, I will draw on the idea of time-binding in order to make a case for teaching supposedly "outdated" material. My focus is primarily toward educators, but the idea can also be applied by anyone who wishes to more fully understand his or her craft. Knowledge does not spring forth exnihility, and current knowledge is built on previous knowledge. But it is not enough to simply teach history. We must teach students how to use history. If we can teach students how to bind together previous knowledge with current knowledge, there will be little in any discipline that can truly be considered outdated.

Every subject has a history, including biology, physics, mathematics, literature, music and art... To teach, for example, what we know about biology today without also teaching what we once knew, or thought we knew, is to reduce knowledge to a mere consumer product. It is to deprive students of a sense of the meaning of what we know, and of how we know.

Too often we seek the most up-to-date material at the expense of the monumental works that defined a discipline. This is also structural. Publishers stop publishing groundbreaking books because there is no longer sufficient demand for them. For example, when I ordered Postman's Teaching as a Conserving Activity as part of the readings for my graduate pedagogy course, I was informed by the university bookstore that the book was out of stock indefinitely with the publisher and no longer available (despite the many potential sellers on Amazon and other such sites). Groundbreaking works in my field of rhetorical criticism, such as Edwin Black's Rhetorical Criticism: A

Study in Method, are only recently available through print-on-demand. With a seemingly constant flood of new books and knowledge, it is difficult enough to simply keep up, let alone delve into the archives.

We must, of course, stay up-to-date on current trends in our field. However, we must also remember that the insights of tomorrow are dependent on the knowledge of the past. Alfred Korzybski observed: The simple steel structure of a bridge, familiar to us in every day life, is a clear reminder to us all of the arts of Hephaestus and the bound-up knowledge of countless generations of smiths and mechanics, metallurgists and chemists, mathematicians and builders, teachers and engineers who toiled for many thousands of years to make possible the riveted steel beams which are the elements of modern structure. Korzybski referred to this process as time-binding, defining it thus: Human beings possess a most remarkable capacity which is entirely peculiar to them — I mean the capacity to summarize, digest and appropriate the labors and experiences of the past; I mean the capacity to use the fruits of past labors and experiences as intellectual or spiritual capital for developments in the present; I mean the capacity to employ as instruments of increasing the accumulated achievements of the all-precious lives of the past generations spent in trial and error, trial and success; I mean the capacity of human beings to conduct their lives in the ever increasing light of inherited wisdom; I mean the capacity in virtue of which man is at once the heritor of the by-gone ages and the trustee of posterity.

S. I. Hayakawa describes it more succinctly as "the ability to organize social cooperation at a distance and to accumulate knowledge over generations of time through the use of symbols" (emphasis in original). The simple fact that I am writing this essay using a system of symbols that I did not develop, and drawing on ideas created by a man who is now dead, is an example of time-binding. As Harry Weinberg observes, each of us "stands on the shoulders of the dead to peer into the future".

Yet, time-binding is not simply a matter of constantly revising and discarding the past. As Hayakawa notes, "The greater the area of cooperation between the living and the dead in the interests of those yet unborn, the better; the more people embraced in the cooperative enterprise, the better." We must make use of the past if we are to become effective time-binders ourselves and teach our students how to use the past if we are to also help them to become effective time-binders. Herein lays the problem with most uses of history: Rather than teaching the student to use history, many of us teach the student the history itself, as if it stood apart from contemporary practice. Perhaps the key term in time-binding is not time, so much as binding, at least where pedagogical practice is concerned. We must recognize that we are building knowledge from disparate elements and binding them together. Milton Dawes reminds us that "Whatever we think, say, feel, do, expect, plan for, want, or theorize about, is incomplete, because we have not included all." And we never can say it all. Michael McGee notes, "The only way to say it air in our fractured culture is to provide readers and audiences with dense, truncated fragments which cue them to produce a finished discourse in their minds. In short, text construction is now something done more by the consumers than by the producers of discourse". We must help students to become active participants in the construction of knowledge, rather than simply consumers of information.

Henry Giroux writes, "This is what the pedagogical struggle is all about—opening up the material and discursive basis of particular ways of producing meaning and presenting ourselves, our relations with others, and our relation to our environment so as to consider the possibilities not yet realized." But to help students recognize the possibilities not yet realized, we must inculcate a consciousness of their own time-binding nature. Dawes suggests: With time-binding consciousness we shift our notion of time-binding from a definition and classification, to a verb representing an action. We recognize time-binding as a psychological tool—a tool we can use to improve ourselves in any area we choose. With time-binding consciousness, we move from simply repeating "each generation can start where the former left off" to "self-consciously appreciating ourselves as time-binders". By helping students to make the connections between past and present understandings of the topic at hand, we can help them learn how to use the past. In other words, we can help them to become the self-conscious time-binders that Dawes proposes.

When we teach, we are not merely teaching content. We are teaching an orientation to a discipline, especially in upper-division courses and certainly in graduate programs. To know the current literature without an understanding of how we arrived there is much like entering a conversation at a bar and immediately joining in an ongoing heated debate. Without an understanding of the controversies and issues within a discipline, the student will likely have only a surface understanding of the material. The student will have a much greater understanding of the intricacies of a topic if he or she is aware of the ground that has already been covered by those before. This will help students avoid the pitfalls and dead ends that others may have already encountered. More importantly, the controversies in a field often persist and shape present understanding; knowing the contours of these arguments is an essential part of becoming a member of the discipline rather than simply an outside observer. Teaching the history of a discipline—any discipline—provides students with a greater understanding of how we have collectively arrived at the knowledge we currently hold. But we must teach this history with an eye focused on building conscious time-binders—those who can effectively use the history of a discipline to drive forward our understanding of the problems that face the world as a whole. After all, the ability to transmit knowledge across time and space is worth little if we are unable to use it well. Teaching students without providing a context in which to understand the discipline may well doom them to repeat the mistakes of those before them.

Despite our best efforts, many teachers still hold a bias toward current material, sloughing off old readings as we bring our reading lists and syllabi "up-to-date". Yet, recency of the scholarship does not necessarily equal relevance. After all, Plato has been read for almost 2500 years and his insights are still useful. Moreover, in our quest to teach current research, it is easy to lose sight of ideas to which we can bind that current scholarship. In the words of Ziggy Marley, "If you don't know your past, you don't know your future." But it is not enough to simply teach the insights that are still valid. A biologist teaching students that people used to believe that geese were generated from gooseneck barnacles not only teaches a historical anecdote in biology, but also helps students understand how misguided thinking led to incorrect conclusions. Just because one thing looks similar to another does not mean that one becomes the other or that they have similar properties. It is just as important for the biologist of today to continually evaluate his or her patterns of thought that may likewise lead to incorrect conclusions. Such is the aim of general semantics.

History must also be critically assessed. After all, our representations of history are never as accurate as one may hope. Thus, we must take care when concerning how we transmit knowledge to students. Ben Hauck writes, "When the future listens, its understanding and success depend on our reports from the present. Time-binding is done individually and now, but the minutest choice of word can have cultural impacts and implications now and later." The practice of teaching is an exercise in creating the future out of the past. Gerald Savage notes that educators should transcend mere instrumental teaching and help students begin to reconceive the profession as one that can be practiced in alternative ways that would permit them greater autonomy and professional integrity. This seems to be good advice for educators in any discipline.

New Words and Expression

1. methodological [ˌmeθədəˈlɔdʒikəl]   adj.   方法的,方法论的
2. landmark [ˈlændmɑːk]   n.   陆标,地界标,里程碑,划时代的事
3. suboptimal [sʌbˈɔptiməl]   adj.   未达最佳标准的,非最理想的,非最适宜的,非最满意的
4. spawn [spɔːn]   vt.   产生,造成
5. nihility [naiˈhiliti]   n.   虚无,不存在,无效
6. pedagogy [ˈpedəgɔgi]   n.   教育学,教授法
7. delve [delv]   vi.   探究,挖掘,搜索
8. archives [ˈɑːkaivz]   n.   档案,档案馆
9. metallurgist [meˈtælədʒist]   n.   冶金家,冶金学者
10. peculiar [piˈkjuːljə]   adj.   奇怪的,特殊的,独特的,古怪的
11. succinctly [səkˈsiŋktli]   adv.   简明地,简洁地
12. disparate [ˈdispərit]   adj.   不同的,异类的
13. truncated [trʌŋˈkeitid]   adj.   被截的,缩短的
14. discursive [diˈskəːsiv]   adj.   散漫的;不得要领的
15. pitfall [ˈpitfɔːl]   n.   陷阱,隐患,想不到的困难
16. contour [ˈkɔntuə]   n.   周线,轮廓,等高线,概要,电路
17. slough [slau]   v.   蜕皮,摆脱

1. **Euclidean geometry(欧几里得几何)**: a mathematical system attributed to the Alexandrian Greek mathematician Euclid, which he described in his textbook on geometry: *The Elements*. Euclid's method consists in assuming a small set of intuitively appealing axioms, and deducing many other propositions from these.

2. **Trigonometry(三角学)**: a branch of mathematics that studies triangles and the relationships between their sides and the angles between these sides.

3. **Plato(柏拉图)**: a Classical Greek philosopher, mathematician, student of Socrates, writer of philosophical dialogues, and founder of the Academy in Athens, the first institution of higher learning in the Western world. Along with his mentor, Socrates, and his student,

Unit 14   Materials & Test   教材与考试

Aristotle, Plato helped to lay the foundations of Western philosophy and science.

I Vocabulary.

Fill in the blanks with the most suitable words. Change the form when necessary.

| landmark | spawn | nihility | archive | suboptimal |
| disparate | truncated | discursive | contour | slough |

1. The invention of internet is a _____ in the development of human history.
2. His sudden resignation _____ many rumors.
3. Though the sweater and the coat are of _____ styles, he managed to wear in a fashionable way.
4. She could _____ off sadness and replace it by a hope.
5. He is a man of imagination and often thinks in a _____ style.
6. They were allowed to stay in the _____ to look for the information that they want.
7. He was angry because his original report had become a badly _____ one because of some trenchant but true words.
8. Nothing happens because of _____, and it happens of reasons.
9. I don't think now it is _____ for your investment, and the best time is yet to come.
10. Even having a glimpse of the _____ of Mount Tai is breathtaking.

II Comprehension of the text.

Decide whether the following statements are true (T) or false (F) according to the passage.

1. Innovation is often the result of recognition of suboptimal processes or ideas.
2. Time-binding is simply a matter of constantly revising and discarding the past.
3. Time-binding consciousness enables us to move from simply repeating that "each generation can start where the former left off" to "self-consciously appreciating ourselves as time-binder".
4. Students can learn how to use the past if they know the connections between past

understandings and the present ones.

5. Recency of the scholarship always equals relevance.

III Choose the word or expression that has the similar meaning of the underlined word or expression.

1. To finish his paper, he <u>delved</u> in many libraries for that book and finally got it.
   A. searched   B. probed   C. read   D. questioned
2. The workers in that factory were exploited by the boss and <u>toiled</u> all through the night.
   A. worked hard   B. stayed up late   C. carried on   D. labored
3. His remarks are always <u>succinct</u> and pointed.
   A. complicated   B. easy   C. long   D. simple
4. Be careful. Don't fall into the <u>pitfalls</u> set up by the enemy.
   A. holes   B. traps   C. caves   D. wells
5. Teachers shouldn't <u>have a bias towards</u> these excellent students. They should treat them as equal.
   A. be fond of   B. be strict with
   C. have partiality for   D. admire

Supplementary Reading

Using Examinations and Testing to Improve Educational Quality

Academic achievement affects the eventual economic benefits of education. In industrialized countries, family socioeconomic background and other factors external to the school heavily influence the level of academic achievement. However, in low-income countries, the quality of the school influences student achievement as much as these factors, especially in science and mathematics. School quality includes the amount of instructional resources available per student and how these resources are used and managed. Rising population growth rates, slowed economic growth, and mounting foreign debt in developing countries mean that there are more children to educate and less money with which to educate them. The effect on the quality of schooling varies from region to region and from country to country. The poorest countries in the Third World have less money to invest in items that boost learning such as textbooks, instructional materials, good teachers, and teacher training. Although some middle-income countries in Asia, Latin America, and the Middle East are experiencing slight increase in school quality, the gap between them and countries belonging to the Organization for Economic Cooperation and Development continues to widen. As a result, educator and economists alike are intensifying the search for an inexpensive means of improving the quality of education in developing countries.

Examinations can be a powerful, low-cost means of influencing the quality of what teachers teach and what students learn in school. Examination agencies have an important role to play in increasing the effectiveness of schools. They can act not only as ex post evaluators of educational achievement but also takes responsibility for making good teaching and learning happen. Examination agencies should improve the quality of tests they design, in which an appropriate distribution of questions involving recall, application, synthesis, and evaluation is included.

The examinations rely heavily upon recall of factual, sometimes esoteric information. The emphasis in the classroom is on rote learning to pass classroom and the national examinations. There is very little incentive to pay attention to developing reasoning, imagination, and independent inquiry. Graduates thus are not usually prepared for the demands of reasoning ability and initiative in the workplace. The majority of students may not even achieve the basic literacy and numeracy skills needed to improve farming, family nutrition, or health practices.

Achievement also varies significantly from region to region within the same country depending on the type of community and school. Sometimes private schools are of higher quality and have higher achievement scores than public ones. Urban schools often score higher than rural ones, largely because scores are also higher in higher per capita income areas where classroom resources are more abundant.

When school performance is inadequate it weakens the future skills, adaptability, and competitiveness of a country's labor force. New pressures on already restricted education budgets have made making better use of scarce resources and maintaining acceptable standards of quality a high priority for educational officials in developing countries. Reforms in the area of examinations are valued as uniform mechanism for identifying talent and measuring achievement. Especially in environments where education resources are limited or unequally distributed among schools, examinations can help to ensure that society is investing in those who will in turn make the most useful contributions to society. A well-designed examination system can monitor and measure achievement and, occasionally, aptitude; provide performance feedback to individual districts, schools, and students; and inform education officials about the overall strengths and weaknesses of their education systems and suggest directions for change and improvement. However, the most important aspect of examinations is the degree to which teachers, administrators, students and parents think of them as important. Selection examinations are one of the most powerful motivational levers in the education sector. The question is whether their influence is positive or negative.

Deteriorating standards, high dropout and repletion rates, labor shortages in certain fields, high youth unemployment, and the demands of ambitious development plans are the main factors motivating educational and examination reform. Such reforms are usually aimed at making the curriculum more relevant to development needs or at redressing regional imbalances in the quality and opportunity for education. If reforms are contrary to public or parental aspirations, officials use the power of examinations to make reforms acceptable. However, if examinations do not fulfill parental aspirations for social and economic advancement, reforms are likely to fail.

Attitudes toward testing have changed. In the 1960s, many educators viewed tests as antithetical to creative thinking, as unreliable predictors of future academic success, and as unfair to disadvantaged groups. In the United States, many people thought that teaching the basic skills was only a part, and perhaps a lesser part, of schooling's mission. Schools, it was said, should respond to pupil interests and needs to make learning more attractive and productive. Those who held such views tended to deny the educational value of tests. Newly independent countries sometimes considered testing an unwanted colonial legacy, irrelevant for building new national identities. In some countries, such as Tanzania, education officials replaced standardized tests with school-based assessments and experimented with other criteria for selection and certification, such as political attitudes or quotas based on socioeconomic, geographic, and ethnic origins or on gender. Unforeseen problems arose. With school-based assessments it is difficult to ensure that all teachers are judging on the same criteria. Since parents judge teachers on their abilities to get their children ahead, teachers tend to inflate grades. Judging a child's potential on political attitudes is not reliable since attitudes can be faked. Though quotas are sometimes necessary to ensure equal utilization of facilities, making selection decisions solely on ethnic or geographic criteria can lead to abuse and can also create resentment among groups not selected. However, whether criteria are academic or political, the need for some fair and efficient mechanism to recognize and reward ability is indisputable. Examinations are thus reemerging as instruments of educational and occupational selection. The challenge is how to make such a mechanism reinforce the teaching and learning of skills that are useful to a society.

Especially in the context of scarce resources, with declining educational standards and the ever-increasing demand for better-qualified manpower, education officials are looking for low-cost ways to improve their education systems. What makes testing powerful is its use to allocate life's chances. This is especially the case in developing countries where rates of returns from education are higher and where in some instances high income-earning opportunities are available almost exclusively to those with access to postsecondary education.

When examinations determine a child's advancement through school and his or her later life's opportunities, parents understandably put pressure on teachers to ensure that their child succeeds. They hold the school system and particularly teachers accountable for their child's results on examinations. The consequence or backwash effect of their public expectation is that teachers adjust their teaching to what the examination will cover to ensure that their students score the highest marks. Teachers are less concerned with whether the test measures the full range of competencies set out in the official curriculum or whether the knowledge, concepts, and skills tested are of as much use to students who will enter the work force as to those who will continue to be the next level of education. If examinations fail to test useful skills, teachers will have little incentive to teach them. The backwash effect of the examination thus restricts what is taught and learned in school. How can officials tell the extent to which their examinations measure the mastery of relevant skills and, therefore, have a positive impact on teaching and learning?

One means of making the backwash effects of tests positive is to improve the content of examinations. The content of examinations should correspond to the many functions they perform. In developing countries, one examination is often used to serve several functions. Examinations are used to select students to secondary and higher education and to certify mastery of the primary or secondary school curriculum. Rarely are they used to diagnose learning problems, place students at different levels of ability, or to help teachers plan what to teach. Usually the content of the examination is determined much more by its function as a selection instrument. This enhances the importance of the knowledge tested in the examination and consequently of what is taught and learned in the classroom. Ideally, one should test separately for selection, certification, and monitoring functions; however, resources do not permit this in many developing countries. Another means of making backwash effects positive is to set up a good feedback mechanism to analyze and interpret student errors. Explaining the thought processed behind wrong answers and making performance results public give school and testing officials incentive to do their jobs better. A third means is to make sure that the examination body is financed and managed in such a way that it can set questions and provide the necessary feedback on student performance.

What makes a good test item? Good examination questions should test more than the ability of the candidate to recall isolated facts. They should test the ability to observe, experiment, and interpret, to understand concepts and draw reasonable conclusions, to use knowledge and skills to solve problems, and to make decisions in new situations and contexts both in and out of school. Good test questions require the mastery of knowledge and skills that when applied in everyday life improve the quality of life and help families use their limited resources better. Anthony Somerset, who worked on improving the quality and relevance of test questions for the Kenya primary school-leaving examination, suggests eight criteria for enabling an examination agency to design the right balance of test questions:

1. Most questions should require students to restructure information rather than simply reproduce it;

2. Many questions should require candidates to understand and use information they have not seen before, in new situations and contexts;

3. Knowledge-based questions drawn from the official curriculum should test understanding of causes or consequences of interventions rather than familiarity with specific facts. Questions should ask "why", "how", rather than "who", "when", "where", and "what". Tests should emphasize understanding the world as a prerequisite to changing it;

4. The knowledge elicited should require integrating with a new knowledge explicitly related to the competent performance of some target behavior;

5. A high proportion of items, especially in science, health, agriculture, and geography, should draw upon both in-and out-of-school experience;

6. When an examination is given in languages other than the mother tongue, test designers should carefully monitor questions for language loading. Test questions should not contain idiomatic expressions or the use of "registers" not accessible to all. Good questions should measure mastery of knowledge and skills rather than mastery of the language of the test;

7. Though they are more expensive, some proportions of the questions should be open ended. Candidates should generate answers as well as select them. In the world outside of school, one is rarely presented with possible solutions to a problem from which

the correct response is chosen;

8. Some questions should test the creative, imaginative skills of learners—that is, to be based upon giving an unusual response, despite the problems associated with marking such responses.

If test questions measure the acquisition of knowledge useful to school leavers as well as to those continuing to the next level of education, the resulting positive backwash effects can benefit the entire school system. To tap these benefits, examination agencies must first inform teachers and students, well ahead of time, of changes in the content of examination questions and of the nature of the skills being tested. Second, they have to analyze performance on individual questions to determine what errors students are making and why. Third, the examination body has to suggest ways to improve the teaching of skills that require mastery of difficult concepts.

In addition to teachers and students, the audience for such feedback on test results includes teacher training institutes—so that future teachers will learn to teach difficult cognitive skills; curriculum development institutes and textbook designers—so that they can improve the way concepts and principles are identified and explained; and in-service training programs for inspectors, education officers, and head teachers—so that they can better focus their attention on managing the most crucial function of the education system.

Examination bodies can provide different levels and depths of feedback. They can report only individual performance as a general mean and standard deviation, or they can break mean scores and standard deviations down by subject, type of skill, and individual test item. They can report these, in turn, for the country as a whole, each region, each district, each school, and ideally, each classroom or each individual student. Any testing agency that can do all this has a strong feedback system. Unfortunately, few agencies even in OECD countries provide this level and depth of feedback. Most agencies see their task of explaining past performance as supplementary to their main function of grading individuals. Thus they rarely report more than general means and standard deviations for the country as a whole or for each region and seldom go into detail more specific than subject-by-subject results.

What are the aims of feedback system? They help reduce performance gaps between different schools or districts by showing where differences in performance occur and why. They encourage better educational management by identifying specific cognitive skills that need to be strengthened. They also suggest what type of investments in schools—for example, more and better teachers, better textbooks, and better administrators—influences achievement.

  A good examination body acts not only as an evaluator of educational achievement but also takes responsibility for making good teaching and learning happen. It does this by constructing tests that have a positive backwash effect on teaching and learning and by showing school systems the sources of children's learning problems. To provide high-quality feedback, an examination agency should analyze the pattern of errors made in past performance and break those patterns down to the lowest-possible unit of analysis—ideally that may even be down to the level of specific questions and to the level of the individual school or classroom. However, a testing agency cannot design good test items and set up a good feedback system if it is not efficient, credible, and autonomous. To be efficient it must produce tests on time, within its budget, and within its competence. To be credible it must maintain professional standards when setting and marking tests and not succumb to political pressures to test inappropriately. To be autonomous it must be managed as an entire entity separate form the Ministry of Education and be able to hire the technical expertise necessary at competitive salary levels and to purchase the technical equipment necessary independent of public-sector regulations. It, therefore, requires a budget separate from the normal rises and falls typical of most public-sector enterprises—that is, it will most probably have to be self-financed. It must create a demand for its services, for which clients are willing to pay. Once self-financed, a testing agency can pursue its professional responsibilities without political interference.

  Some issues in the area of examinations and testing have no hard and fast answers. They include dilemmas such as: test coverage of the curriculum versus fairness of the examination, mother tongue versus metropolitan language as the language of testing, professionalism of examination bodies versus political influence, and well-constructed test questions versus socioeconomic advantages.

  The content to which the national examination covers the official curriculum varies from country to country. Tests and the curriculum influence what teachers teach in the classroom and what students actually learn. Discrepancies between test content and the taught curriculum pose a dilemma since tests are supposed to choose and certify individuals on the basis of their knowledge of the common curriculum. If testing experts intend to draw conclusion from test results about the quality of teaching and learning, the match between what is actually taught and test content must be a close one. In Africa, for example, where schools are poorly equipped and learning materials scarce, teachers are typically able to cover only a small portion of the curriculum. The implications of this are particularly serious in countries where outside influences such as previous learning and home and social environment are less a factor and where achievement may be more directly traceable to school quality.

The amount of the curriculum covered varies enormously—rich schools cover more, poor schools less. What should the test designers do in case where the quality of schools varies? Should they set questions on the intended curriculum even though some parts may have been taught in only 10 to 15 percent of the schools? If that is done, the test will not reflect what has been learned but rather who had opportunity to learn. Alternatively, should the test emphasize those parts of the curriculum for which it can be shown that a wide proportion of students had an opportunity to learn—non-laboratory sciences instead of laboratory techniques, for instance, since typically only wealthy schools can afford the laboratory materials to teach that portion of the science curriculum. If this is done, the test will be a truer reflection of what has been learned by the student population, but it will not accurately reflect the intended curricular objectives.

National tests are designed to measure commonly taught knowledge, and since the ability to teach that knowledge is shrinking, the portion that can be fairly tested is also shrinking. Schools that wish to do well must teach the knowledge and skills identified as important for pupils to learn. Better equipped schools, with well-trained teachers and active head masters are more likely to cover the curriculum than poorer, ill-equipped schools. If test content is based on the official curriculum rather than on what is actually covered in the classroom, it will favor students from schools that are better able to cover the curriculum and thus will risk measuring students' opportunity to learn rather than what they have actually been taught. If tests measure more than what is covered in the classroom they can be unfair and unjust.

The language of assessment poses many questions for testing and instruction. In multilingual societies, the rationale for using international languages such as English, French, or Spanish for teaching and testing is that they do not favor any particular linguistic group. How adequately is achievement measured in the second language? How does the tester of mathematics rather than what they understand of the English-based mathematics questions? Does the language of the test determine how exam items are constructed—that is, do test questions measure understanding of concepts and underlying principles or rather the language-based recognition of the correct answers? Tests in languages other than the mother tongue may be measuring the ability to understand the concepts themselves. There is more evidence of problem solving and other higher-order abilities when students are tested in their mother tongue. Particularly in science subjects, testing in the second language may discourage the use of concepts and principles of modern science in everyday life. The existing literature suggests a larger role for indigenous languages in testing on the grounds that testing in an international language may confuse subject knowledge with comprehension of the language of the test.

The primary goal of learning should be understanding concepts and principles in order to make inferences from that knowledge and to apply it in daily life. Tests should accurately measure students' achievement of these competencies. Do tests in a second language elicit meaningful evidence of student achievement of competencies in a subject area? A good test should measure language in a particular subject area, not understanding of the language of the test. If a language other than the mother tongue is the medium of the test, children with more access to the language of the test will do better regardless of whether they know subject matter better. A testing agency must ensure that the language bias of test questions is minimized. In multilingual environments testing agencies can handle the language question in two ways. They can make sure that tests are free of language experience and that test questions are accurately measuring subject-matter competence. In other words, they can pretest the language of the test item thoroughly and satisfy themselves ahead of time that there are no differences between performance of mother-tongue and non-mother-tongue students. Alternatively, they can use the mother tongue in testing to ensure that those who perform poorly in the second or international language, but well in subject matter, are not discriminated against. A testing agency that chooses the second option will probably run into political problems with those who have a vested interest in testing in one or the other language. They will also face the high costs and logistical complexity of setting questions, administering, marking, and analyzing results of subject matter tests in several languages.

Unit 15 Educational Evaluation
教育评价

Text A Integration of Technology and Educational Assessment

导读：随着科学技术的发展，教育评价也走上了现代化的道路。对于学生评价体系也由单一向多维度转变。技术的发展让设计复杂的评价体系成为可能。

Across the disciplines, technologies have expanded the phenomena that can be investigated, the nature of argumentation, and the use of evidence. Technologies allow representations of domains, systems, models, data, and their manipulation in ways that previously were not possible. Models of population density permit investigations of economic and social issues. This movement from static to dynamic models has changed the nature of inquiry among professionals as well as the way that academic disciplines can be taught. Correspondingly, a new generation of assessments is well on its way to transforming what, how, when, where, and why assessment occurs and its linkages to teaching and learning. Powered by the ever-increasing capabilities of technology, these 21st century approaches to assessment expand the potential for tests to both probe and promote a broad spectrum of human learning, including the types of knowledge and competence advocated in various recent policy reports on education and the economy.

Although early uses of technology in large-scale testing have focused on relatively straightforward logistical efficiencies and cost reductions, a new generation of innovative assessments is pushing the frontiers of measuring complex forms of learning. Computers' abilities to capture student inputs permit collecting evidence of processes such as problem-solving sequences and strategy use as reflected by information selected, numbers of attempts, approximation to solutions, and time allocation. Such data can be combined with statistical and measurement algorithms to extract patterns associated with varying levels of expertise. Research in the learning sciences is simultaneously informing the design of innovative, dynamic, interactive assessment tasks and powerful scoring, reporting, and real-time feedback mechanisms. When coupled with technology, such knowledge has propelled various advances in adaptive testing, including knowledge and skills diagnosis, the provision of immediate feedback to teachers and students accompanied by scaffolding for improvement, and the potential for accommodations for special populations. Technology also supports movement toward the design of more balanced sets of coherent, nested assessments that operate across levels of educational systems.

Information and communications technologies such as Web browsers, word processors, editing, drawing, simulations, and multimedia programs support a variety of research, design, composition, and communication processes. These same tools can expand the cognitive skills that can be assessed, including the processes of planning, drafting, composing, and revising. For example, the National Assessment of Educational Progress(NAEP) writing assessment in 2011 will require use of word processing and editing tools to compose essays.

In professional testing, architecture examinees use computer-assisted design programs as part of their licensure assessment. The challenge that such technology-based presentation and data capture contexts offer now lies in the design principles for eliciting complex learning, the analysis of complex forms of data, and their meaningful interpretation relative to models of the underlying components of competence and expertise. The area of science assessment is perhaps leading the way in exploring the presentation and interpretation of complex, multifaceted problem types and assessment approaches. In 2006, the Program for International Student Assessment pilot tested a Computer-Based Assessment of Science to test knowledge and inquiry processes not assessed in the paper-based booklets. The assessment included such student explorations as the genetic breeding of plants. At the state level, Minnesota has an online science test with tasks engaging students in simulated laboratory experiments or investigations of phenomena such as weather or the solar system.

Recently, a distinction has been made between assessments of the outcomes of learning, typically used for grading and accountability purposes(summative assessment), and assessments for learning, used to diagnose and modify the conditions of learning and instruction(formative assessment). Research has repeatedly shown the formative use of assessment to significantly benefit student achievement. Such effects depend on several classroom practice factors, including alignment of assessments with state standards, quality of the feedback provided to students, involvement of students in self-reflection and action, and teachers making adjustments to their instruction based on the assessment results. Technologies are well suited to support many of the data-collection, complex analysis, and individualized feedback and scaffolding features needed for the formative use of assessment.

In addition to assessment of student knowledge and skills in highly structured problems with one right answer, technology can also support the design of complex, interactive tasks that extend the range of knowledge, skills, and cognitive processes that can be assessed. For example, simulations can assess and promote understanding of complex systems by superimposing multiple representations and permitting manipulation of structures and patterns that otherwise might not be visible or even conceivable. Simulation-based assessments can probe basic foundational knowledge such as the functions of organisms in an ecosystem, and, more important, they can probe students' knowledge of how components of a system interact along with abilities to investigate the impacts of multiple variables changing at the same time. When well designed and implemented, classroom assessments that are used during instruction to monitor and improve progress and that are also administered following instruction to document learning and identify remaining needs can become credible components of a multilevel state assessment system. Technology-enhanced formative assessments during instruction can provide immediate, contingent feedback and adaptive coaching for reteaching of problematic knowledge and skills. Benchmark assessments following instruction can provide summative classroom-based assessments with technical quality that could be aggregated into the state accountability system. Moreover, because simulations use multiple modalities and representations, students with diverse learning styles and language backgrounds may have better opportunities to demonstrate their knowledge than are possible in text-laden print tests.

It is an exciting time in the field of assessment for several reasons. First, individuals have realized that there are multiple roles for assessment to play in the educational process and that one of the most valuable roles is the formative function of assisting student learning. Second, cognitive research and theory have provided us with rich models and representations of how students understand many of the key principles in the curriculum, how students develop knowledge structures, and how to analyze and understand simple and complex aspects of student performance. Third, technology makes possible more flexible, tailored presentations to students of a much wider and richer array of tasks and environments where students can learn and where they can show us what they know and how they know it. Thus, there is an interesting and powerful confluence among theory, research, technology, and practice, especially when it comes to the integration of curriculum, instruction, and assessment.

In numerous areas of the curriculum, information technologies are changing what is taught, when and how it is taught, and what students are expected to be able to do to demonstrate their knowledge and skill. These changes in turn are stimulating people to rethink what is assessed, how that information is obtained, and how it is fed back into the educational process in a productive and timely way. This situation creates opportunities to center curriculum, instruction, and assessment around cognitive principles. With technology, assessment can become richer, timelier, and more seamlessly interwoven with multiple aspects of curriculum and instruction. As discussed earlier, the most useful kinds of assessment for enhancing student learning emphasize knowledge integration and extended reasoning, support a process of individualized instruction, allow for student interaction, collect rich diagnostic data, and provide timely feedback. The demands and complexity of these types of assessment can be quite substantial, but technology makes them feasible. Diagnostic assessments of individuals' learning, for example, must involve collecting, interpreting, and reporting significant amounts of information. No educator, whether a classroom teacher or other user of assessment data, could realistically be expected to handle the information flow, analysis demands, and decision-making burdens involved without technological support. Thus, technology removes some of the constraints that previously made high-quality formative assessment of complex performances difficult or impractical for a classroom teacher.

Clearly, we are just beginning to see how to harness technology to support the formative and summative functions of assessment. We still need to learn a great deal about the quality and efficacy of systems operating at both the large-scale level and the small-scale level. Not the least of the concerns facing us is the integration of assessment tools and practices into the educational system and teachers' practices. But we must also take note of the fact that extremely powerful information technologies are becoming as ubiquitous in educational settings as they are in other aspects of people's daily lives. Technologies are almost certain to continue to provoke fundamental changes in learning environments at all levels of the education system. Many of the implications of technology are beyond people's speculative capacity. Little more than 15 years ago, for example, few could have predicted the sweeping effects of the Internet and social networking on education and other segments of society. The range of computational devices and their applications is expanding exponentially, fundamentally changing how people think about communication, collaboration, problem solving, connectivity, information systems, educational practices, and the role of technology in society.

We can, therefore, imagine a future in which the audit function of assessments external to the classroom would be significantly reduced or even unnecessary because the information needed to assess students, at the levels of description appropriate for various monitoring purposes, could be mined from the data streams generated by students in and out of their classrooms. A metaphor for such a radical shift in how one does the business of educational assessment exists in the world of retail outlets, ranging from small businesses to supermarkets to department stores. No longer do these businesses have to close down once or twice a year to take inventory of their stock. Rather, with the advent of automated checkouts and barcodes for all items, these enterprises have access to a continuous stream of information that can be used to monitor inventory and the flow of items. Not only can business continue without interruption, but the information obtained is far richer, enabling stores to monitor trends and aggregate the data into various kinds of summaries. Similarly, with new assessment technologies, schools would no longer have to interrupt the normal instructional process at various times during the year to administer external tests to students, nor would they have to spend significant amounts of time preparing for specific external tests peripheral to the ongoing activities of teaching and learning.

The design and deployment of even simple technology tools must ultimately rely on a technology infrastructure that connects the classroom to powerful database management and information retrieval systems that operate within and across schools and systems. This is especially true when the classroom assessment data are viewed as part of a coordinated system of assessment data that would potentially include curriculum-embedded assessment information, unit and end-of-course benchmark assessment data, interim cross-unit summative status checks, and state-level test data. Further work addressing issues of technology and the design of a comprehensive assessment system involves consideration of information and how it needs to flow through this system. For example, who needs to use assessment data? What questions need to be answered? In what timeframe do they need to be answered? What actions might they take based on these answers?

Extensive technology-based systems that link curriculum, instruction, and assessment at the classroom level might enable a shift from today's assessment systems, which use different kinds of assessments for different purposes, to a balanced design that would ensure the three critical features of comprehensiveness, coherence, and continuity. In such a design, for comprehensiveness, assessments would provide a variety of evidence to support educational decision-making, for coherence, the information provided at differing levels of responsibility and action would be linked back to the same underlying conceptual model of student learning, and for continuity, it would provide indications of student growth over time.

Technological advances will allow for the attainment of many of the goals that educators, researchers, policymakers, teachers, and parents have envisioned for assessment as a viable source of information for educational improvement. When we implement powerful technology-based systems in classrooms, rich sources of information about intellectually significant student learning will be continuously available across wide segments of the curriculum and for individual learners over extended periods of time. This is exactly the kind of information we now lack, making it difficult to use assessment to truly support learning. The major issue is not whether this type of innovative assessment design, data collection, and information analysis is feasible in the future. Rather, the issue is how the world of education anticipates and embraces this possibility, and how it will explore the resulting options for effectively using assessment information to meet the multiple purposes served by current assessments, and most important, to enhance student learning.

1. **Summative assessment(or Summative evaluation) (终结性评价)**: is the assessment of the learning and summarizes the development of learners at a particular time. After a period of work, e.g. a unit for two weeks, the learner sits for a test and then the teacher marks the test and assigns a score.

2. **Formative assessment (形成性评价)**: is a reflective process that intends to promote student attainment. Cowie and Bell define it as the bidirectional process between teacher and student to enhance, recognize and respond to the learning.

Unit 15 Educational Evaluation 教育评价

New Words and Expression

1. manipulation [məˌnipjuˈleiʃən] n. 操纵,控制
2. algorithm [ˈælgəriðəm] n. 算法
3. simultaneously [saiməlˈteinjəsli] adv. 同时地
4. propel [prəˈpel] v. 推进,驱使
5. cognitive [ˈkɔgnitiv] adj. 认识的,认知的,有认识力的
6. elicit [iˈlisit] vt. 引出,诱出,探出
7. alignment [əˈlainmənt] n. 排成直线,直线性;结盟
8. interactive [intərˈæktiv] adj. 相互作用的,交互的
9. seamless [ˈsiːmlis] adj. 持续的,无缝的
10. interwoven [ˌintəˈwəuvn] adj. 交织的,混合的(动词 interweave 的过去分词)
11. audit [ˈɔːdit] n. 审计,查账
    vt. 旁听,审计
12. aggregate [ˈægrigeit] adj. 合计的,总的
    n. 总计,进球总数,集料
    v. (使)聚集,总计
13. envision [inˈviʒən] vt. 想象,设想
14. segment [ˈsegmənt] n. 部分,弓形,瓣,段,节
    vt. 分割

I Vocabulary.

Fill in the blanks with the most suitable words. Change the form when necessary.

| manipulate | simultaneous | cognitive | alignment | interactive |

1. Hearing the good news, the crowds burst into applause _____.
2. Practice is based on the _____ elements of perception.
3. Intimate friends always have _____ effect on each other.
4. Having been in China for 4 years, Mr. Smith was able to _____ chopsticks with great dexterity.
5. A new _____ is rising in Mideast.

II Comprehension of the text.

Decide whether the following statements are true (T) or false (F) according to the passage.

1. Planning belongs to the rank of cognitive skills, while revising is not.
2. Assessment used to diagnose and modify the conditions of learning and instruction is called summative assessment.
3. Technology can now support the design of complex and interactive tasks that can assess students' learning.
4. Technology information is changing the way in which knowledge is taught and the content of teaching.
5. Technology removes some of the constraints that previously made high-quality formative assessment of complex performances difficult or impractical.

III Choose the word or expression that has the similar meaning of the underlined word or expression.

1. Chop the stalks into short segments so that the animals can digest them easily.
   A. parts   B. sticks   C. circles   D. chunks
2. Though his plan is seamless, he still failed and got caught by the police.
   A. good   B. plain   C. tight and close   D. clever
3. People in war all envision peace and a bright future.
   A. desire   B. look forward to C. call   D. fight for
4. Propelled by greed, he took away a large sum of money and went abroad.
   A. Stimulated   B. Seduced   C. Tormented   D. Asked
5. The audiences aggregated a million people.
   A. were less than B. were more than C. totaled   D. added

Text B Sustainable Assessment and Evaluation Strategies for Open and Distance Learning

导读：随着互联网的兴起，远程教育的发展方兴未艾。和传统的教育评价相比，远程教育的评价则比较棘手。本文列出了远程教育评价的一些策略，如创建题库、设计计算机化的考试系统等。

Unit 15 Educational Evaluation 教育评价

Distance Learning (DL) is the fastest growing form of domestic and international education today. In addition to the challenges of assessment in conventional institutions, distance learners are spread out geographically and physically from each other and from the instructor. Moreover, class sizes for DL courses are generally larger than those for traditional classes. These large numbers of students and numerous courses make assessment and evaluation very difficult and administrative nightmare at DL institutions. Yet, given large class sizes and their physical separation from students, many distance learning instructors feel they have few options for assessing students' performance.

Assessment is a systematic basis for making inferences about the learning and development of students. It is the process of defining, selecting, designing, collecting, analyzing, interpreting and using information to increase students' learning and development. In education, assessment may be thought of as occurring whenever one person, in some kind of interaction, direct or indirect, with another is conscious of obtaining and interpreting information about the knowledge and understanding, or abilities and attitudes of that other person. There are two distinct interpretations of assessment. The first is interpretation of assessment in terms of the routine tasks that students undertake in order to receive feedback on their learning and a mark or grade signifying their achievement. The second interpret assessment is applied to processes at the institutional level, for example, program evaluation.

There are various methods of assessment. The commonly used ones are objective questions, short answer questions, long answer questions and presentation. The method of assessment named objective questions derives its name from objectivity employed in marking the answers to the questions. The marking which is a simple mechanical process can be done by an individual or by a computer. Examples of objective type questions are true/false items; fill in the blanks item; multiple choice items; completion items and matching items. Short answer questions may take different forms of answers such as one word/phrase; one sentence; completing a table/diagram; preparing a list or writing a paragraph. Long answer questions may also take various forms such as essay; reports or dissertations. The method of presentation is used to assess presentation skills. It requires appropriate assessment criteria for assessing the appearance of presenter; introduction of self; introduction of presentation; content of presentation; logic and order of presentation; eye contact; audibility; handling questions and use of visual aids. This method of assessment has high validity when the presentation is assessed by a group.

Assessment in ODL, unlike in the conventional system where students have a range of opportunities to demonstrate their learning periodically, depends on formal assessment tasks. The major characteristics of assessment in both settings are: For the conventional system, the learners are known through lectures, tutorials and individual consultations. They have a range of opportunities to demonstrate their learning—their interest, motivation, questioning and interaction. Moreover, they have opportunities to diagnose their errors before they go for formal assessment tasks and assessment activities have some flexibility.

On the other hand, ODL learners are at a distance, thus they rarely enjoy varied opportunities to communicate their learning depending much on formal task as they have less opportunity in which to diagnose their errors or mistakes before formal assessment task. Accordingly, assessment must be thoroughly planned, communicated and managed.

Validity is the extent to which an assessment measure does the job for which it is intended. The validity of an assessment can only be determined by reference to the assessment's stated purposes and its design specifications. For validity to be high the assessment must analyze student's performance on each objective and the assessment should provide the appropriate situation possible for measuring the specific abilities being measured. Reliability refers to consistency or precision or dependability of the assessment measurement and how consistent results are from one to another. The assessment is reliable if the results would be replicated on a subsequent occasion. Reliability is maximized when the assessment items are many, the items are not too easy or too difficult for the candidates and the marking is consistent.

Educators generally work with learners to review and support learning, and to make judgment regarding their merits and their achievements. In ODL, Self Assessment Questions, Tutor Marked Assessments and End of Semester Examinations are used. There is no immediate feedback and reinforcement. Self Assessment Questions embedded in the course material enable distance learners to evaluate their progress frequently. Tutor Marked Assessments serve as the continuous assessment and the marks obtained carry about 25% to 30% weight which count in the final result of the course. End of Semester Examinations carries about 70% to 75% weight age of the final results. Distance learners are usually free to appear at any of these examinations either for specific courses or for all the registered courses provided that the minimum period of study prescribed for the relevant course is completed. Like in the conventional system, assessment in ODL can be both formative and summative. Formative assessment takes the form of Tutor Marked Assessments. It helps to identify the weaknesses and strengths in learning. It also helps to improve upon the process and the attainment of learning. Grading or scoring may be done in formative assessment. Summative Assessment takes the form of End of Semester Examinations.

A question bank is a planned library of test items pooled through cooperative efforts under the protection and support of an institution for the use of evaluators, academics and students in partial fulfillment of the requirements of the teaching learning process.

It is designed to fulfill certain pre-determined purposes namely to enrich the instructional aspect and to judge the distance learner. It offers a utility service with an inbuilt feedback mechanism for improvement of its questions. The number of questions needed for a course or a program which runs for a number of years is very large in a distance education institution. The academic staff are accordingly supposed to prepare a large number of quality questions on different topics of the prescribed courses or programs for Learners' Self Assessment, Tutor Marked Assessments and End of Semester Examinations. Most of these academics lack the adequate skill in test development and the time at their disposal is limited and they cannot be expected to develop a question pool of reasonable magnitude and quality within a specific time.

In the absence of a stock of ready made questions, the quality of question papers is liable to suffer. This necessitates the entrusting the preparation of quality items in different subjects to experienced teachers who are well conversant with the content and techniques of framing questions.

This strategy helps to build up ready-made stock of items for Learners' Self Assessment, Tutor Marked Assessments and End of Semester Examinations. Such pool of item is of immense use if developed according to predetermined objectives. The types of questions making up a question bank are to depend entirely on the total framework of reference envisaged at the planning stage.

Running a question bank efficiently to sustain assessment necessitates careful planning. The objectives of such a bank should clearly be visualized and include: to increase the value of measurement; to increase the pedagogical value of evaluation; and more detailed specific objectives on special need for the question bank. The question bank should be located in such a place that it should be managed properly to provide utility services to all those who are interested. The planning of a question bank should take care of suitable place and equipment for storing, vetting and screening of items before depositing them in the bank, sorting and classifying items in the question bank, arrangement for subject wise assistance for efficient maintenance and an academic manager for question bank to direct the activities of the question bank. Carefully selected questions from the question bank can be used for instructional purposes. Various types of questions may be selected from the question bank for pre-testing, review and revision of a lesson. A question pool from a question bank can be utilized in the preparation of textual material and review exercises in course materials.

Learners can also use questions from question bank for self-assessment of their learning outcomes for specific units or modules of a course since outline answers are provided in such questions. A question bank is evaluated at regular intervals at least once in three years, the questions are screened and the obsolete ones are discarded. As old and obsolete materials are discarded, new materials are continually added in line with the revision of course materials. Enrichment of questions by updating, replacing, discarding, modifying, adding new ones, regrouping and classification is an ongoing process aimed at giving the question bank a dynamic look. A well developed and efficiently used question bank is an asset to sustainable assessment.

Computer-based tests are defined as test or assessments that are administered by computer in either alone or networked configuration or by other technology devices linked to the internet or World Wide Web (WWW). Computer-based testing is recognized as a sustainable strategy for sustainable assessment for ODL because it can be more responsive to the needs of both the test provider or institution and distance learners. Where "on demand" testing of examinees is needed, the use of computer-based testing is more helpful. Computer-based testing works on a completely different model than paper and pencil administration and offers the benefits that the later cannot match. Smaller number of candidates can be tested throughout the year rather than large numbers several times a year. Study centers can offer different tests at the same time since examinations may be delivered on personal computers using local area network, and the computer selects test questions from a pool, so candidates taking the same examination will not be answering identical questions, which would enhance test security.

Computer-based assessment allows for a diverse range of question types which is a better test of candidates competency. It can be offered at different times, locations or even different tests to different students. The computer selects test question from a pool, so candidates taking the same examination will not be answering identical questions. It eliminates the need for test booklets and answer sheets that increase the security levels. Self paced tutorials show candidates how to use a mouse and other testing tools, ensuring that even those without computer experience are comfortable. Candidates can use either paper and pencil or word processing for essay questions depending on their own preference. It improves the link between instruction and assessment, providing a profile of candidates' strengths and weaknesses, and matches questions and the order in which they are presented to the ability of each test taker.

Computer-based examination system reduces the large proportion of workload on examination, training, grading and reviewing. The set of questions mostly used in computer-based examination system are multiple choice tests that can be formally and easily evaluated online. Emphasis is now shifting to computer-based tests and on-screen marking of essay questions in the developed world. Computer-based tests are scored immediately or shortly after administration unlike the paper and pencil test result that takes several months to process. Fast scoring helps for publishing results quickly. It can be used to control inadequate examination halls.

Limitations of computer-based testing attempts to grade students' essays online are now being explored in the on-screen marking is already being practiced by Cambridge Assessment. On-screen marking is much better than paper scripts. Although this process is already practiced by some institutions in the developed world, it is still at the fundamental stage. It is necessary that the question bank should be large enough to prevent high levels of repetition. Computer crashes sometimes occur. Hence, there is need for contingency plan in case there are any technical faults in the middle of the examination period that may prevent student from completing the examination and disadvantage their results. Other limitations are related to resources required—a sufficient numbers of computers, a room to install them, appropriate software and adequate technology expertise.

University of Cambridge Local Examinations Syndicate (UCLES) (剑桥大学考试委员会): is a non-teaching department of the University of Cambridge and is a not-for-profit organization. Cambridge Assessment is the brand name of UCLES.

New Words and Expression

1. replicate ['replikeit]   v.   复制, 模拟, 折叠
2. reinforcement [ˌriːinˈfɔːsmənt]   n.   增强, 加固, 强化物, 增援力量
3. embed [imˈbed]   v.   (使)插入, (使)嵌入, 深留脑中

4. magnitude['mægnitjuːd]　　　n. 大小,重要,光度,(地震)级数,(星星)等级
5. entrust[in'trʌst]　　　　　　vt. 信赖,信托,交托
6. immense[i'mens]　　　　　　adj. 巨大的,广大的,〈口〉非常好的
7. envisage[in'vizidʒ]　　　　　vt. 面对,想象
8. pedagogical[pedə'gɔdʒikəl]　adj. 教学(法)的
9. configuration[kənˌfigju'reiʃən]　n. 结构,布局,形态,格式塔心理完形,[计算机]配置
10. responsive to　　　　　　　对……起反应,对……敏感
11. contingency[kən'tindʒənsi]　n. 偶发事件,偶然

I　Vocabulary.

Fill in the blanks with the most suitable words. Change the form when necessary.

| replicate　　magnitude　　configuration　　pedagogical　　envisage |

1. The board of this company _____ that there will be a high profit in producing this kind of new product.
2. To be an excellent teacher, one should learn _____ techniques.
3. Due to the lack of space, the designer has to reduce the _____ of the building.
4. Twenty-four _____ texts are carried out to obtain reasonable statistics.
5. Though it is a small business computer system in its simplest _____, it managed to produce large quantities of products efficiently.

II　Comprehension of the text.

Decide whether the following statements are true (T) or false (F) according to the passage.

1. Teaching assessment is the process of defining, selecting, designing, collecting, analyzing, interpreting and using information to increase students' learning and development.

2. ODL learners enjoy varied opportunities to communicate their learning and have more opportunity to diagnose their errors or mistakes before formal assessment task.
3. In the absence of a stock of ready made questions in question bank, the quality of question papers is liable to suffer.
4. Computer-based assessment can be offered at different times, locations or even different tests to different students.
5. Computer-based testing is recognized as a sustainable strategy for sustainable assessment for ODL because it can be more responsive only to the needs of distance learners.

III Choose the word or expression that has the similar meaning of the underlined word or expression.

1. I have reinforced the elbows of the jacket with leather patches.
   A. intensified B. changed C. minimized D. beautified
2. Self Assessment Questions embedded in the course material enable distance learners to evaluate their progress frequently.
   A. excluded B. list C. covered D. included
3. I entrusted him to sign the contract for me.
   A. authorized B. asked C. told D. invited
4. China, as a trading market with immense potential and endless opportunities, has attracted many foreign funds.
   A. profound B. huge C. extensive D. little
5. In case of future contingencies, one should get well prepared.
   A. problems B. incidents C. accidents D. cases

 Supplementary Reading ◄◄◄◄◄────

Broadening Our Approach to Teaching Evaluation

Although evaluative judgments are part of everyday living, knowing we are about to be evaluated tends to send a shiver down our spine. In our hearts we know that evaluation can be good for us because it can provide useful insights that help us do things differently and better. Yet most of us hate to be evaluated, whether it is in our personal, social, or working lives. And this is especially true when important decisions hinge on the results of the evaluation, such as when we take a final examination or a driving test. This is certainly the case with the evaluation of teaching—an activity where a good deal of self-esteem is involved.

Just as the assessment of students is perhaps the task that faculty like least, the evaluation of teaching performance can be fraught with unpleasantness, even controversy. Student ratings of university teachers have been common for at least thirty years, but it is a rare campus where they are accepted with equanimity. It is now also increasingly common to review teaching quality in entire departments and programs, but these assessments are often resisted as simply invalid and inaccurate time wasters. Yet evaluation—of teaching and of our other professional and personal activities—is inevitable. We go through each day making thousands of evaluations. We are even content to quantify our evaluations; we enjoy the star system for restaurants and movies and the points awarded to products in Consumer Reports. Most evaluative judgments are subjective, even though we may make use of quantitative data to help with our decisions. What's important to recognize is that such judgments will be made even in the absence of good data. Just as many of us feel we know that University X is good and University Y is outstanding, students and colleagues quickly form impressions of a professor's teaching abilities, as well as the quality of instruction in different academic departments. Evaluation will take place, even in the absence of solid evidence, based on such sources as hearsay and gossip. And teaching is such an important activity for universities that we would be well advised to make the process as informed and helpful as possible. How can this best be done?

Criteria for evaluation

One good starting point is to decide on our goals and criteria for the evaluation of teaching, which in turn means having some consensus on what we understand "good teaching" to be. Yet it is surprising that either this is often not done or such criteria are implicit and never openly discussed. Even in the case of prestigious teaching awards offered by national bodies and individual institutions, the basis for judgment may be obscure, which can lead to controversy and skepticism.

When we put a general statement on an evaluation form such as, "On the whole, how good was this teacher?" we are, in effect, asking students to use their own definition and criteria for good teaching on the assumption that worth is in the eye of the beholder. And by including questions about organization, fair grading, quality of feedback, enthusiasm, and concern for students' needs, we are imposing criteria, even if we might not recognize the fact.

Unit 15 Educational Evaluation 教育评价

Whose criteria should count the most: those of the students (the recipients of teaching), the faculty (who presumably have more expertise in pedagogy), some external agency such as the government, some professional association, or an employer? Or, is there a body of evidence to which we might turn to show that certain characteristics of teaching are related to particular learning outcomes to tackle the question in a different way? If so, this evidence would be helpful in guiding the choice of dimensions and processes for evaluation.

Even here, though, complications arise, due to the general purposes of education. For example, if we believe that the goal of higher education is to train students for jobs, which dictates one set of outcomes. In this case the outcomes of job placement or lifetime salary are relatively easy to measure and are frequently used by higher education institutions to justify the excellence of their teaching programs. However, the belief that higher education exists primarily to prepare students for citizenship or help them develop as lifelong learners would suggest another set of outcomes.

Despite these caveats, having information about the relationship between teaching processes and their effects on learning would certainly be useful in helping design evaluation schemes. In the case of lectures, for example, there is some evidence that exam performance is helped by such factors as teacher clarity, organization, enthusiasm, and rapport with students. In practice, performance on exams in a single course is of less importance over the long term than the impact of an entire program of study on students' values, attitudes, and the learning habits they will take with them into other aspects of their lives. This is clearly a much trickier issue, but there is emerging evidence about the effects of teaching programs and academic climate on student learning approaches.

For example, the extensive research by some researchers has examined aspects of teaching that influence cognitive development in students. Their findings are rather surprising for the large number of factors that apparently have no effect at all, which might indicate that students themselves have more to do with successful learning than the influence of particular teachers or courses. The classic study by Ramsden and Entwistle (1981) identifies a number of factors that encourage deep learning approaches in students, including workload, use of active learning methods, and type of assessment tasks that are set, interpersonal contact between teacher and students. The Course Experience Questionnaire (CEQ), now used routinely in Australian universities to evaluate teaching effectiveness at the departmental and institutional level, is an approach to evaluation built on this research. Along similar lines, Kember has shown links between university teachers' approach to teaching and changes in the learning approaches of their students. In particular, teachers who adopt more learner-centered methods, more active learning tasks and less reliance on didactic lectures tend to foster deeper learning.

Although the linking of evaluation methods to specific and agreed-upon educational and learning goals is time consuming and difficult, it is certainly worth the effort, not just because it produces better evaluation but because the whole process helps stimulate debate about the university's central mission: teaching and learning. Some colleges have become this kind of institution that embeds ongoing evaluation into its programs. Moreover, they have done so in a consultative manner, involving both faculty and students in the process. Here evaluation is seen as an essential component of learning, not simply something tacked on at the end of a course for largely bureaucratic reasons. Their linking of institutional goals to both the assessment of students and the evaluation of learning outcomes is an example of Biggs' notion of alignment.

One other aspect of the goals of evaluation concerns the formative versus summative distinction. As more and more faculty in North American universities have become unionized, the evaluation of individual performance has been increasingly seen as part of the terms of employment and thus negotiable as part of a collective bargaining agreement. This in turn has tended to sharpen the distinction between evaluation for accountability purposes and evaluation that is intended primarily to give feedback that can serve as a basis for reflection about teaching and possible changes or improvements.

Although it has become a cliche that evaluation methods well suited for one purpose are often much less appropriate for another, there is considerable overlap between these two types of evaluation. Similarly, undertaking a departmental review, although it may be intended primarily for administrative or accountability purposes, will stimulate reflection and debate about goals and priorities in all but the most moribund and cynical academic unit. At the same time, there is no question that before institutions, units, or individuals undertake an evaluation of teaching, they should carefully consider the motives for evaluating, the purpose the information will serve, and what actions might be taken as a result to undertake possible future change. If these questions have not been considered and satisfactorily answered, it is doubtful that the evaluation will achieve anything of value.

The changing context for evaluation

University teaching has been largely unscrutinized, perhaps because it is done in private—or, at least, out of the sight of colleagues and administrators. In medieval universities, students voted with their feet, either by stamping them to show disapproval or by simply abandoning the class altogether. In more recent times, evaluation has relied primarily on student questionnaires. This has always been problematic in the sense that effective learning (presumably the main goal of teaching) is dependent on far more than an individual instructor or course. For example, learning also depends on the motivation, prior knowledge, values, and attitudes of students, as well as the amount of independent work they undertake. This, in turn, is affected by demographic, social, and institutional factors, in particular the academic climate in the university and home department. Yet teaching evaluation has traditionally focused on individuals, not organizations.

Although there is a long history of reviewing academic departments and entire institutions, the attention paid to teaching in these exercises has generally been superficial and has relied mainly on describing curriculum content and the qualifications of faculty, perhaps supplemented by evidence of student performance on exams.

One recent change is the broadening of evaluation from a focus on individuals to a scrutiny of larger units and the widening of the scope and methods used, often including both qualitative appraisals and quantitative data. It is increasingly being recognized that evaluation methods used in the past are inappropriate at a time when many profound changes are affecting higher education. For example, we now have a much more diverse student population, and there is concern to provide equal opportunities for students of different backgrounds and abilities to learn and succeed in college. The last decade has seen a rapid growth of educational technology, distance education, and on-line learning. The role and influence of an individual instructor in these approaches may be much less clear than in a traditional lecture course. Technology has, in fact, changed the way evaluation itself takes place. Other factors are political and financial. Students in many universities pay much higher fees than they did in the past and have started to regard themselves as "consumers" of an educational "product". This, in turn, is part of a move toward market-driven higher education in which the purpose of a university seems largely to fulfill strategic objectives, often dictated by business interests. All these issues affect approaches to the evaluation of teaching; in particular, they reinforce the importance of accountability, both internal and external.

The questionnaire-based teacher ratings that date back to at least the 1960s were initiated by students, primarily as an aid to selecting courses and teachers (hence the criticism of student evaluations as a popularity contest). To this day, a number of student governments publish "anti-calendars" that summarize the results of student ratings.

A powerful stimulus for the development of teaching portfolios was the aim of having individual faculty members take control of the evaluation process by broadening the basis of teaching appraisal. Not only are faculty members the focus of most teaching evaluation but they play a major role as evaluators, especially through service on tenure, promotion, and appointment committees. Other potential stakeholders in the evaluation of teaching include university administrators, employers, parents, and the government. This has led to externally imposed evaluation systems such as the academic audits and collection of performance indicators of teaching. This has led to interesting debates about teaching standards and criteria, appropriate training for new entrants to the profession, and methods of evaluating their effectiveness. It is interesting that the preferred method of documenting and appraising teaching is an expanded version of the teaching portfolio.

With multiple stakeholders, one challenge is to devise an approach to evaluation that can serve different and possibly conflicting needs. This is an almost impossible task and often produces acrimonious disagreements between representatives of the different constituencies. For example, information that is useful for one purpose (for example, a student selecting a college or a department head assigning teaching loads) may be unhelpful or even harmful for other purposes, such as providing feedback to a beginning teacher. Negotiating a balance of interests among stakeholders can be a delicate matter and requires extensive compromise. In my own university a committee of faculty, students, and administrators devised a system of evaluation based on a combination of student ratings and teaching portfolios. Each agreed to sacrifice elements of evaluation that they would like to have kept. For example, department heads and students wanted to see the open-ended comments written on the rating forms, but this was thought to be undesirable from the point of view of the individual teacher (especially in the case of beginning teachers). The latter would have preferred the ratings be confidential, but student government representatives naturally wished to have publicly available data for purposes of accountability. Although the committee reached a delicate consensus, and the system put in place worked reasonably well, the original process leading to this balance of interests was soon forgotten, and political pressures subsequently led to changes in the system that pleased no one.

A decade ago a monograph about university teaching evaluation would have been primarily concerned with the reliability and validity of student ratings. Student evaluations are certainly discussed in these pages, but the broad range of alternative approaches dealt with in later chapters indicates how much evaluation has changed. The contributions that follow not only reflect the interest of a much broader range of stakeholders but introduce alternative evaluation processes that are already changing practice. Some of these methods have been borrowed from other sources (for example, outcomes assessment, performance indicators, and academic audits); others, such as the teaching portfolio, have been devised specifically for academic purposes. This broader and more eclectic approach to evaluation is, in my view, a good thing, as is the increased attention being paid to underlying goals and the interests of different stakeholders. Although this makes evaluation more complex, it forces us back to first principles and makes us examine not just the criteria and rationale for evaluation but the goals of higher education itself and the question of whose interests we serve. From the point of view of the individual faculty member, the new emphasis on outcomes and accountability may seem threatening. However, if university teaching is to be a professional activity (as Beaty describes), the honest appraisal of ourselves and our peers is surely an inherent part of our role and obligations as a teacher. And it is an essential component of the scholarship of teaching, if we are to gather data that can improve our own practice and inform a more general understanding of effective teaching strategies. It is not a matter of whether we evaluate teaching but rather a question of how we do it. What ends do we have in mind, and who controls the process. If academics fail to take responsibility for evaluation of teaching, it is clear that others will be eager to do so.

Keys to Exercises
练习答案

Unit 1

Text A

I. 1. corporal 2. hallmarks 3. monastery 4. slam 5. truancy
   6. reluctance 7. rampart 8. preliminary 9. compulsory 10. principality
II. compulsory education; convince; material/physical comfort; spiritual needs; supervise
III. 1. F 2. F 3. F 4. T 5. T

Text B

I. 1. E 2. A 3. H 4. C 5. F 6. I 7. D 8. B 9. G 10. J
II. freshmen; sophomore; junior sophister; senior sophister; academic institution; administrative regulations; unexpected changes; be destined to; be immune to; residential college
III. 1. F 2. T 3. F 4. F 5. T 6. F 7. T 8. F 9. T 10. F

Unit 2

Text A

I. 1. comprehensive 2. optimal 3. aptitude 4. encompass 5. inculcate
   6. compromised 7. interpret 8. integrate 9. disseminate 10. initiative
II. human capital; sustainable development; natural resources; rational thinking; take into account; living condition; physical infrastructure; consistent with; life long learning; social justice
III. 1. F 2. F 3. T 4. F 5. T

Keys to Exercises 练习答案

Text B

I. 1.B 2.E 3.H 4.F 5.C 6.A 7.I 8.D 9.J 10.G

II. Knowledge-based Society; bring light into; exclusive right; tertiary education; be bound to; vocational colleges; cultural norm; quality assurance; quality audit; cultural diversity; adapt to

III. 1.T 2.T 3.F 4.T 5.F 6.F 7.T 8.F 9.T 10.F

Unit 3

Text A

I. 1. cluster   2. probe   3. crucial   4. elucidate   5. intertwined
   6. perception   7. thrive   8. propensity   9. intriguing   10. idiosyncratic

II. individual differences; educational environment; developmental process; academic potential; genetically identical; be aware; learning profiles; lay out; take up the challenge; build on

III. 1.T 2.T 3.F 4.T 5.F 6.F 7.F 8.T 9.T 10.F

Text B

I. 1.D 2.H 3.F 4.B 5.I 6.A 7.E 8.G 9.J 10.C

II. social skills; carry out; unconditional love; addict to; student-centered teaching method; be conscious of; secondary education; struggle for; obey rules; self-discipline

III. 1.T 2.F 3.T 4.T 5.F 6.F 7.T 8.T 9.T 10.F

Unit 4

Text A

I. 1. E-learning

2. Doing is the best learning way and E-learning is suitable for the modern educational system.

3. 听而易忘,见而易记,做而易懂。

4. Learning is a process of achieving certain competences that can be defined as a dynamical combination of cognitive and meta-cognitive skills, knowledge and understanding, as well as the development of social skills and growth in ethical values.

5. E-learning enhances the quality of educational process by enabling the practice of new

roles in the process of learning. In addition, during this process, lifelong learning technologies are used.

Through E-learning, a new educational environment can be set and an environment can be constructed in the direction of interaction, processing information, researching and problem-solving. The students are asked to actively get involved, and often work in teams. The role of the professor is to design the methods of learning and help the student develop their talents and capabilities.

Ⅱ. 1. B 2. D 3. C 4. B 5. D
Ⅲ. 1. F 2. F 3. T 4. T 5. F

Text B

Ⅰ. 1. A 2. C 3. B 4. B 5. B 6. B 7. A 8. C 9. D 10. A
Ⅱ. 1. F 2. F 3. F 4. T 5. F
Ⅲ. 1. 尽管联合国正在为到2015年实现全球儿童普遍基础教育而奋斗,但教育的不公平性一直存在,并且对全球的教育决策人、学者以及从业人员都是重大的挑战。
   2. 关于义务教育的法规,在中国,法律在决策制定中是一种解决特定教育问题的实用手段,也是对各级的政府负责提高教育的最终手段。
   3. 比尔顿证明,教育机会的平等需要确保让在学校的机会对每个相同能力的人都是一样的,无论其性别、种族、社会经济背景如何。
   4. 在《世界人权宣言》中,联合国声明每个人都有教育的权利,而教育至少在基础和基本阶段应该是免费义务教育。
   5. 结果,尽管一些如性别差异的问题存在,但世界儿童进入小学率从1999年到2005年增加了6%至688 000 000,而2005年儿童辍学率从1999年的96 000 000降低到72 000 000。

Unit 5

Text A

Ⅰ. 1. C 2. D 3. A 4. D 5. B
Ⅱ. 1. exert   2. flourish/flourished   3. equipped   4. intuitive   5. priority
   6. abide   7. normative   8. talented   9. egalitarian 10. emphasized
Ⅲ. 1. 教育应该使孩子们成为自主、自立的个体,能够对如何过自己的生活和如何为自己适应复杂的现代生活有很好的判断。
   2. 教育应该为孩子们提供必要的技能和知识,使他们在经济中是有效的参与者,这样他们在劳动力市场中有大量不同的选择,必要的收入所得来繁荣市场经济。
3. 教育应该为孩子的成长发挥作用,使之成为独立参与经济活动的成年人。
4. 教育应该使孩子们成为好的公民——在政治生活中有责任感、能有效参与政治。
5. 当你对比有着同样才能、同样意愿努力的孩子们时,直觉告诉你说,当他们得到同样水平的教育资源,教育的公平会是令人满意的。

Text B

I. 1. C 2. D 3. D 4. A 5. B 6. B 7. C 8. A 9. D 10. B
II. 1. elusive   2. ample   3. upsurge   4. equitable   5. variations
    6. evading   7. straightforward 8. boost   9. warrant   10. assess
III. 1. T 2. F 3. F 4. F 5. T

Unit 6

Text A

I. 1. D 2. B 3. A 4. C 5. D
II. 1. ethnocentric   2. underscore   3. dogmatic   4. orthodox   5. attacked
    6. inculcate   7. articulate   8. constitute 9. filial   10. conquered
III. 1. Xunzi underscored the realistic and materialistic aspects of Confucian thought, stressing that morality was inculcated in society through tradition and in individuals through training.
2. He had many Confucian scholars killed and their books burned.
3. Zhu Xi
4. The works of Confucius were translated into European languages through the agency of Jesuit scholars stationed in China.
5. This passage talks about the development of Confucius thought.

Text B

I. 1. B 2. A 3. D 4. D 5. C 6. D 7. A 8. B 9. C 10. D
II. 1. T 2. T 3. F 4. F 5. F
III. 1. 教育是灌输自律的过程,这样思想和身体都会从对生活的关注中解放出来。
2. 以上天为中心和以尘世为中心的两种教育都在实践中作用于正规的教育系统,正规教育强迫儿童通过死记硬背记住古代作品,而年长的学生如学徒般或不拘小节地聚集在他们老师周围。

3. 希腊哲学思想认识到教育的目的是使人都要对无穷的,还有地球上的日常事务保持敏感。
4. 因此,他精确的教育设计被剥夺了强有力的目标,那些服务目标是在早期所使用的。
5. 从最广义上讲,作为地球上的生命的人放弃他的好奇心和寻求压倒一切可能未知的欲望是要认真地培育的。

Unit 7

Text A

I. 1. B 2. A 3. D 4. E 5. C
II. 1. F 2. T 3. F 4. T 5. F
III. 1. pre-independence system   2. expression through word and act
    3. social content and social goals   4. optimism and secularism
    5. the individual in society; the society.

Text B

I. 1. B 2. A 3. D 4. E 5. C
II. 1. F 2. T 3. F 4. F 5. T
III. 1. affective and psychomotor   2. demonstrable and measurable
    3. The sequencing of objectives   4. institutional or course goals
    5. Educational Objectives

Unit 8

Text A

I. 1. illiteracy   2. nonsensical   3. shudder   4. captivating   5. onus
   6. provoke   7. courtesy   8. zealously   9. trivial   10. blemish
II. 1. F 2. F 3. F 4. T 5. T
III. 1. The student   2. encourage   3. facilitator
    4. the absence   5. Building a foundation

Text B

I. 1. compelling   2. hostility   3. abhor   4. manifest   5. Concurrently

Keys to Exercises 练习答案

    6. assertiveness   7. maladaptive 8. assert   9. morale   10. hinder

II. 1. F 2. F 3. T 4. T 5. T

III. (1) negative teacher-student interactions

    (2) attachment

    (3) warmth and understanding

    (4) their behavior towards students

    (5) cognitive

Unit 9

Text A

I. 1. comprehensive   2. necessity   3. supervision   4. prescribe   5. contemporary

   6. priority   7. parental   8. intellectual   9. ethic/ethics 10. Admittedly

II. 1. F 2. T 3. T 4. T 5. T

III. 1. family

   2. cooperation between school and family

   3. disappointment and misunderstandings

   4. the family

   5. the district and state

Text B

I. 1. D 2. B 3. E 4. A 5. C

II. 1. F 2. T 3. T 4. F 5. T

III. 1. peer victimization   2. increases   3. developmental outcomes

   4. reduce   5. prosocial behaviors

Unit 10

Text A

I. 1. anthology   2. arbitrary   3. conspicuous   4. ethos   5. capstone

II. 1. F 2. F 3. T 4. T 5. F

III. Omitted.

Text B

I. d-b-c-a
II. 1. F   2. T   3. T   4. F   5. T
III. Omitted.

Unit 11

Text A

I. 1. correspond   2. Insofar   3. estimate/estimation   4. derived/derives   5. propensity
II. 1. F   2. T   3. F   4. T
III. 1. 因此，学生和毕业生们了解课外活动的影响，评估其在从高等教育到就业这一转变时期所可能扮演的角色是非常重要的。
2. 因此，被认为是高离职率人群的求职者面临着更为严格的就业标准，较低的工资，较少的面试机会；即使和其他的求职者一样的条件，他们也可能在招聘流程中被完全的排除在外。
3. 共涉及五个解释变量：课外活动的参与度，活动类型，参与活动花费的时间，参与的强度，以及活动情景。
4. 然而，整个的课外活动量应该控制在一个合理范围内；因为活动时间越长，获得管理职位的机会越少。
5. 此外，重新审视高等教育中课外活动的地位和认可度以及它和常规课程之间的联系可能对在高等教育市场中面临竞争的教育机构有莫大的好处。

Text B

I. 1. sedentary   2. validate   3. respectively   4. Degenerative   5. inferable
II. 1. F   2. T   3. F   4. T
III. 1. 在意大利，现在没有一个现行的个人 SES 分类，区域性数据来自于个人经济消费水平，而不是收入和教育水平。
2. 关于对待体育活动的态度，主要调查体育活动在减肥，社会交往，性格形成方面是否有益。
3. 母亲的受教育水平也似乎相当大地影响学生体育活动的选择和每周课外体育锻炼总时间数。
4. 关于体育活动和父母受教育水平之间关系的研究显示，父母受教育水平的高低是孩子选择体育活动的决定性因素。
5. 从这个意义上讲，此次研究的结果对学校管理者如何去弥补贫富学生之间的隔阂是非常有用的。

Unit 12

Text A

I. 1. auxiliary   2. marginalize   3. spectrum   4. caveat   5. incentive

II. 1. F   2. F   3. F   4. F   5. T

III. 1. School-based Management is a strategy which decentralizes education decision-making by increasing parental and community involvement in schools. it is the decentralization of authority from the central government to the school level. SBM programs transfer authority over one or more of the following activities: budget allocation, the hiring and firing of teachers and other school staff, curriculum development, the procurement of textbooks and other educational material, infrastructure improvements, and the monitoring and evaluation of teacher performance and student learning outcomes.

2. First of all, SBM helps to improve student achievement and other outcomes as these local people demand closer monitoring of school personnel, better student evaluations, a closer match between the school's needs and its policies, and a more efficient use of resources. Secondly, it reduces opportunities for corruption. In addition, it gives parents and stakeholders opportunities to increase their skills.

3. First, the SBM model must define exactly which powers are vested in which individuals or committees and how these powers are to be coordinated to make the plan workable within both the school culture and the available resources.

    Second, SBM requires supports from the various school-level stakeholders, local and national governments. The support from parents and other community members is also needed.

4. The caveat is that the specific type of SBM introduced in any given country depends (or should ideally depend) on the political economy of the particular country.

Text B

I. 1. D   2. B   3. A   4. C   5. E

II. 1. The education system in Turkey is centralized, which means that the policy-making function is in the hands of the Ministry of Education that has power over all educational matters. The Ministry determines the personnel policy and arranges training, certifying, appointment and salary schedules of teachers. On the other hand the public school system in the US is governed by an open decentralized system. State legislatures are responsible for public education. Their task is to authorize funding and give legislative support for the schools. All states have state boards of education, which deal with policy development, personnel recruitment, budgeting and the law.

2. Because centralized structure forms barriers to it, on one hand, it is said that the principal administers the school. On the other hand, the principle is deprived of autonomy. To say the least, whatever the principle wants to do, he needs to get permission from the central authorities. Some teachers related this situation to the bureaucratic structure of the Turkish education in which administration was seen as the powerbase that can override participative decisions.

3. Most teachers agreed that although SIP was mandated by the district office, schools had autonomy in designing the organization and the components of their own improvement plan. But the principal said that the SIP was strategic planning developed by the district, so each school's plan had to fit in with the district's strategic planning. One teacher said that, outside the SIP, the school was involved in other activities which also contributed to school improvement.

Unit 13

Text A

I. 1. reluctant   2. ambiguous   3. diminish   4. paradigms   5. compounded
II. 1. T   2. F   3. T   4. T   5. F
III. 沟通技能；最新信息；将 A 替换成 B；使结合，使合并；达到标准

Text B

I. 1. derive   2. rigid   3. sophisticated   4. optimum   5. encompasses
II. 1. F   2. T   3. T   4. F   5. T
III. 1. 人类是具有高度创造性的生物，喜欢通过对想法进行实践、探索、试验、质疑、纠正而学习。

2. 批判的评论必须略去，对别人想法的批评也应当延至最后。许多创造性地想法没有提出主要是因为提出者怀疑别人会认为他的想法不重要，或者毫无价值。

3. 除了提出自己的想法，成员们应当提出建议：其他人的想法怎样才能变得更好，两个或多个想法如何合并成一个？

4. 书记员的任务是把所有提出的想法简单地记下来。有时候组员们提出想法太快，即使是速记专家，记下这些想法也会有困难。
5. 成员们可以将自己的想法输入并显示在计算机屏幕的下方，而由其他成员提出的想法显示在屏幕的上方。

Unit 14

Text A

I. 1. entail   2. periodicals   3. is harnessed   4. supplement   5. prey
   6. chunks   7. tangible   8. spectrum   9. surplus   10. supplanted
II. 1. T   2. T   3. F   4. T   5. T
III. 1. audio-visual aids   2. what skills are practiced   3. evolutions
     4. educational technology   5. user-friendly

Text B

I. 1. landmark   2. spawned   3. disparate   4. slough   5. discursive
   6. archives   7. truncated   8. nihility   9. suboptimal   10. contour
II. 1. T   2. F   3. T   4. T   5. F
III. 1. A   2. A   3. D   4. B   5. C

Unit 15

Text A

I. 1. simultaneously   2. cognitive   3. interactive   4. manipulate   5. alignment
II. 1. F   2. F   3. T   4. T   5. T
III. 1. A   2. C   3. B   4. A   5. C

Text B

I. 1. envisage   2. pedagogical   3. magnitude   4. replicated   5. configuration
II. 1. T   2. F   3. F   4. T   5. F
III. 1. A   2. D   3. A   4. B   5. C

References
参考文献

[1] ABIDIN R R, KMETZ C A. 1997. Teacher-student interactions as predicted by teaching stress and the perceived quality of the student-teacher relationship//The Annual Meeting of the National Association of School Psychologists. Anaheim, CA.

[2] ADELMAN H S, TAYLOR L. 1998. Reframing mental health in schools and expanding school reform. Educational Psychologist, 33:135 -152.

[3] AIKEN L S, WEST S G. 1991. Multiple regression: testing and interpreting interactions. Newbury Park, CA: Sage.

[4] ALTBACH P G. 2008. Globalization and forces for change in higher education. International Higher Education, 50:2 -4.

[5] ARROW K. 1973. The theory of discrimination//ASHENFELTER O, REES A. Discrimination in labor markets. Princeton, NJ: Princeton University Press:3 -33.

[6] BADDELEY A. 2003. Working memory: looking back and looking forward. Nature Reviews Neuroscience, 4:829 -839.

[7] BAGGEN P, TELLINGS A, VAN HAAFTEN W, et al. 1998. The university and the knowledge society.

[8] BAKER J A, TERRY T, BRIDGER R, et al. 1997. Schools as caring communities: a relational approach to school reform. School Psychology Review, 26:586 -602.

[9] BAKEWELL E B. 1988. Object, image, inquiry: the art historian at work. Santa Monica, CA: Getty Trust Publications.

[10] BEMMEL, BELL D. 1968. The measurement of knowledge and technology//SHELDON E B, MOORE W E. Indicators of social change. Concepts and Measurements Hartford, Connecticut: Russell Sage Foundation:145 -246.

[11] BEREITER C. 1999. Education and mind in the knowledge age [EB/OL]. http://csile.oise.utoronto.ca/edmind/edmind.html.

[12] BERNHARD A. A knowledge-based society needs quality in higher education. London, Paris: Concorde Publishing House.

[13] BLAU F D, KAHN L M. 1981. Race and sex differences in quits by young workers.

Industrial and Labor Relations Review, 34(4):563 –577.
[14] BOER. 2002. Academia in the 21st century: an analysis of trends and perspectives in higher education and research. Den Haag: AWT, 28.
[15] BOGLER R. 2001. The influence of leadership style on teacher job satisfaction. Educational Administration Quarterly, 37(5):662 –683.
[16] BOTSFORD D. 1993. Compulsion versus Liberty in education//Education Note: 5. London: Libertarian Alliance.
[17] BRATTESANI K, WEINSTEIN R, MARSHALL H. 1984. Student perceptions of differential teacher treatment. Journal of Educational Psychology, 76:236 –247.
[18] BREHM J W. 1966. A theory of psychological reactance. New York: Academic Press.
[19] BRENNAN J. 2004. The social role of the contemporary university: contradictions, boundaries and change//Ten Years On: Changing Education in a Changing World. Milton Keynes: The Open University:22 –26.
[20] BRIGHOUSE H. 2007. Educational justice and socio-economic segregation in schools. Journal of Philosophy of Education, 41(4).
[21] BROUILLETTE L. 1997. Who defines "democratic leadership"? Three high school principals respond to school-based reforms. Journal of School Leadership, 7:569 –591.
[22] BROWN A. CAMPIONE J. 1994. Guided discovery in a community of learners// MCGILLY. Classroom lessons: integrating cognitive theory and classroom practice: 229 –270.
[23] BUTERA F, MUGNY G. 2001. Social influence and social reality. Seattle: Hogrefe & Huber Publishers.
[24] CALVIN J. 1962. Institutes of Christian religion. BEVERIDGE, trans. London: James Clarke.
[25] Canadian School Boards Association. 1999. Poverty intervention profile: partners in action.
[26] CENTRA J A. 1993. Reflective faculty evaluation: enhancing teaching and determining faculty effectiveness. San Francisco: Jossey-Bass.
[27] CHALL J S. 1996. Stages of reading development. 2 ed. Fort Worth: Harcourt Brace College Publishers.
[28] CHIAPPETTA E L, KOBALLA R Jr. 2002. Science instruction in the middle and secondary schools. Merrill Prentice Hall: Ohio.
[29] CHRISTMANN U, MISCHO C. 2000. The efficacy of communicative fairness and rhetorical aesthetics in contributions to argumentation. Language and Speech. 43:229 –259.
[30] COHEN L, MANLON L, MORRISON K R B. 2000. Research methods in education.

London: Routledge.

[31] COLDING A, MEEK V L. 2006. Twelve propositions on diversity in higher education. Higher Education Management and Policy, 18(3): 31-54.

[32] COLTHEART M, RASTLE K, PERRY C, et al. 2001. DRC: A dual route cascaded model of visual word recognition and reading aloud. Psychological Review, 108: 204-256.

[33] CROWELL J A, FELDMAN S S. Mothers' internal models of relationships and children's behavioral and developmental status: a study of mother-child interaction. Child Development, 59: 1273-1285.

[34] DAMON. 2002. Bringing in a new era in character education. Stanford, CA: Hoover Institution Press.

[35] DAY C, ELLIOT B, KINGTON A. 2005. Reform, standards and teacher identity: challenges of sustaining commitment. Journal of Teaching and Teacher Education, 21: 563-577.

[36] DE DREU C K W, DE VRIES N K. 2001. Group consensus and minority influence implications for innovation. Oxford: Blackwell.

[37] DESJARDINS S L, DUNDAR H, HENDEL D D. 1999. Modeling the college application decision process in a land-grant university. Economics of Education Review, 18(1): 117-132.

[38] DFEE. 1996-2003. Pupil absence and truancy in England. London: the National Statistics, IIMSO.

[39] DOISE W. 1982. L'explication en psychologie sociale. Paris: Presses Universitaires de France.

[40] DRVFOOS J G. 1990. Adolescent at risk: prevalence and prevention. New York: Oxford University Press.

[41] DUNCAN, G, BROOKS-GUNN J, KLEBANOV P. 1994. Economic deprivation and early childhood development. Child Development, 65: 296-318.

[42] ECCLES J S, BARBER B L, STONE M, et al. 2003. Extracurricular activities and adolescent development. Journal of Social Issues, 59(4): 865-889.

[43] ECCLES J S, GRUSEC J E, HASTINGS P D. 2007. Families, schools, and developing achievement related motivations and engagement. New York: Guilford Press.

[44] EHRI L C, SNOWLING M J, HULME C. 2005. Development of sight word reading: phases and findings//SNOWLING M J, HHLME C. The science of reading: a handbook. Oxford, UK: Blackwell Publishing. 135-154.

[45] EIDE E R, RONAN N 2001. Is participation in high school athletics an investment or a consumption good? Economics of Education Review, 20(5): 431-442.

[46] EL-KHAWAS E, DEPIETRO-JURAND R, HOLM-NIELSEN L. 1998. Quality assurance in higher education: recent progress; challenges ahead. Washington, D. C.: World Bank.

[47] ENDY D, BRENT R. 2001. Modelling cellular behavior. Nature, 409: 391 –395.

[48] ENTWISLE D R, ASTONE N M. 1994. Some practical guidelines for measuring youth's race/ethnicity and socioeconomic status. Child Development, 65: 1521 –1540.

[49] ERDOGAN I. 2002. Turkish education system towards a new millenium. Ankara: Sistem Publishing.

[50] EWELL P. 2007. The "quality game": external review and institutional reaction over three decades in the United States//WESTERHEIJDEN D F. Quality assurance in higher education: trends in regulation, translation and transformation. Dortrecht: Springer: 119 –153.

[51] FEIGENBAUM H B. 1997. Centralization and national integration in France. Mediterranean Quarterly, 8(1): 60 –76.

[52] FISCHER K W. 1980. A theory of cognitive development: the control and construction of hierarchies of skills. Psychological Review, 87: 477 –531.

[53] FISCHER K W, BIDDELL T R. 2006. Dynamic development of action and thought.// DAMON W, LERNER R M. Theoretical models of human development. Handbook of child psychology: Vol. 1. 6th ed. New York: Wiley: 313 –399.

[54] FISHER D, KENT H B. 1998. Associations between teacher personality and classroom environment. Journal of Classroom Interaction, 33(1): 5 –13.

[55] FRITH U. 1986. A developmental framework for developmental dyslexia. Annals of Dyslexia.

[56] GAGER C T, COONEY T M., CALL K T. 1999. The effects of family characteristics and time use on teenagers' household labor. Journal of Marriage and the Family, 61 (4): 982 –994.

[57] GEORGE J M, JONES G R. 1996. Understanding and managing organizational behavior. TX: Texas A & M University.

[58] GERBER S B. 1996. Extracurricular activities and academic achievement. Journal of Research and Development in Education, 30(1): 42 –50.

[59] GIBBONS M. 1994. The new production of knowledge: the dynamics of science and research in contemporary societies. London: Sage Publications.

[60] GIL R M. 2001. Human values and personal development: tutorships of secondary education and schools of parents. Madrid, Spain: Spanish School.

[61] GLEMAN. 1995. Emotional intelligence: why it can matter more than IQ. New York:

Bantam Books.

[62] GOEDEGEBUURE L, MEEK V L. 1997. On change and diversity: the role of government influences. Higher Education in Europe, 22(3):309-319.

[63] GOLDSWORTHY R, SCHWARTZ N, BARAB S, et al. 2007. Evaluation of a collaborative multimedia conflict resolution curriculum. Educational Technology Research and Development, 55(6).

[64] GORNITZKA A, MAASSEN P. 2000. Hybrid steering approaches with respect to European higher education. Higher Education Policy, 13(3):267-285.

[65] GRAHAM P A. 2005. Schooling America: how the public schools meet the nation's changing needs. New York: Oxford University Press.

[66] GROSS, JUVONEN, GABLE. 2002. Internet use and well-being in adolescence. Journal of Social Issues, 58(1):75-90.

[67] HALL. 1995. The convergence of means. Educom Review, 30(4):42-45.

[68] HAMMOND L D. 1993. Reframing the school reform agenda: developing capacity for school transformation. Phi Delta Kaplan, 74(10):753-761.

[69] HANISH L D, GUERRA N G. 2000. Predictors of peer victimization among urban youth. Social Development, 9:521-543.

[70] HARTELMAN P A, VAN DER MAAS H L J, MOLENAAR P C M. 1998. Detecting and modeling developmental transitions. British Journal of Developmental Psychology, 16:97-122.

[71] HARTUP W W. 1996. The company they keep: friendships and their developmental significance. Child Development, 67:1-13.

[72] HARVEY L, GREEN D. 1993. Defining quality. Assessment and Evaluation in Higher Education, 18(1):9-34.

[73] HAWLEY P H. 2002. Social dominance and prosocial and coercive strategies of resource control in preschoolers. International Journal of Behavioral Development, 26:167-176.

[74] HEYNEMAN, STEPHEN P, RANSOM, et al. 1990. Using examinations and testing to improve educational quality. Educational Policy, 4:177-192.

[75] HIGH J, ELLIG J. 1988. The private supply of education: some historical evidence//COWEN. The theory of market failure. Fairfax, VA: George Mason University Press.

[76] HINDSON B, BYRNE B, FIELDING-BARNSLEY R, et al. 2005. Assessment and early instruction of preschool children at risk for reading disability. Journal of Educational Psychology, 97:687-704.

[77] HLEBOWITSH P, TELLEZ K. 1997. American education: purpose and promise.

California: Wadsworth Publishing.

[78] HOLUBOVÁ. 2010. Improving the quality of teaching by modern teaching methods. The 21st century, 25:59.

[79] http://education.stateuniversity.com/pages/2246/Moral-Education.html.

[80] http://tigger.uic.edu/~lnucci/MoralEd/overview.html.

[81] http://en.wikipedia.org/wiki/Confucius.

[82] KACZMANREK P. 2002. Follow the leader. Washington D.C.: Education Reform Network, World Prosperity Ltd.

[83] KAZAMIAS A, EPSTEIN E H. 1968. Schools in transition. Massachusetts: Allyn & Bacon.

[84] KENDALL S, WHITE R, KINDER K, et al. Bedford, N. 2004. School attendance and the prosecution of parents: effects and effectiveness: final report. Slough: NFER.

[85] KENNEDY J H, Kennedy C E. 2004. Attachment theory: implications for school psychology. Psychology in the Schools, 41(2): 247-259.

[86] KNAPPER. 2001. Broadening our approach to teaching evaluation. New Directions for Teaching and Learning, Winter.

[87] KNIGHT C C, FISCHER K W. 1992. Learning to read words: individual differences in developmental sequences. Journal of Applied Developmental Psychology, 13: 377-404.

[88] KOZMA R. 1991. Learning with media. Review of Educational Research, 61(2): 179-212.

[89] KOZMA R. 1994. Will media influence learning? Reframing the debate. Educational Technology Research and Development, 42(2): 7-19.

[90] LANGFORD. 2010. Educational policy, housing policy, and social justice. Prospero, 16(2): 33-36.

[91] LAUGLO J, MCLEAN M. 1985. The control of education: international perspectives on the centralization-decentralization debate. London: Kogan Page.

[92] LAW, PAN SUYAN. 2009. Legislation and equality in basic education for all in China. Interchange, 40(4): 337-372.

[93] LAW. 2007. Major continuities and changes in the basic education law. Education and the Law, 19(12): 177-199.

[94] LEAHY S, LYON C, THOMPSON M, et al. 2005. Classroom assessment: minute by minute, and day by day. Educational Leadership, 63(3): 18-24.

[95] LESLIE N K, LO. 2002. The development of youth discussion on the educational role and functions of out-of-school education. Youth Studies(7): 29-38.

[96] LJOSA E, MANN K. 1995. EDEN: a growing garden. European Journal of Engineering Education,20(2):239 -241.

[97] LUNCEFORD. 2009. In defense against outdated materials. Institute of General Semantics, Inc.

[98] LUNENBURG F C, ORNSTEIN A C. 2004. Educational administration: concepts and practices. California: Wadsworth/Thomson Learning.

[99] LUTHER M. 1962. To the councilmen of all cities in Germany that they establish and maintain Christian schools. Steinhaeuser A, Tr. Philadelphia: Fortress Press: 347 -378.

[100] LUTHER M. 1967. Sermon on keeping children in school. JACOBS, Tr. Philadelphia: Fortress Press: 209 -258.

[101] LYONS M. 1994. Napoleon Bonaparte and the legacy of the French revolution. New York: St. Martin's Press.

[102] MACCOBY E E. 1990. Gender and relationships: a developmental account. American Psychologist,45: 513 -520.

[103] MANTON. 2001. Filling bellies and brains: the educational and political thought of Frederick James Gould. History of Education,30(3):273 -275.

[104] MARGINSON S, VAN DER WENDE M. 2007. Globalisation and higher education. OECD Education Working Paper(8).

[105] MARKWARDT J. 1997. Peabody individual achievement test-revised: normative update: manual. Circle Pines: American Guidance Service.

[106] MARSHALL C, ROSSMAN G B. 1999. Designing qualitative research. 3rd ed. California: Sage.

[107] MARTIN E, FEMFINDEZ I, ANDRS S., et al. 2003. The intervention for the improvement of the conviviality in the educational centers: models and areas. Infancy and Learning, Journal for the Study Education and Development,26(1):79 -95.

[108] MASTEN A S, COATSWORTH J D. 1998. The development of competence in favorable and unfavorable environments: lessons from research on successful children. American Psychologist,53:205 -220.

[109] MATTHEWS. The origins of distance education and its use in the United States. T H E Journal,27(2):54.

[110] MCLOYD V C. 1998. Socioeconomic disadvantage and child development. American Psychologist,53,185 -204.

[111] MEANS B, OLSON K. 1997. Technology's role in education reform: findings from a national study of innovating schools. Washington, D. C. U. S. Department of Education, Office of Educational Research and Improvement.

References 参考文献

[112] MILLER C, SMITH C, TILSTONE C. 1998. Professional development by distance education: does distance lend enhancement?. Cambridge Journal of Education,28(2): 221 – 230.

[113] MORRIS C G, MAISTO A A. 2005. Psychology: an introduction. New Jersey: Pearson, Prentice Hall.

[114] MOSS C M, BROOKHART S M. 2009. Advancing formative assessment in every classroom: a guide for the instructional leader. Alexandria, VA: ASCD.

[115] NEAVE G. 1988. On the cultivation of quality, efficiency and enterprise: an overview of recent trends in higher education in western Europe, 1986 – 1988. European Journal of Education, 23(112): 7 – 23.

[116] NEWTON J. 2002. Views from below: academics coping with quality. Quality in Higher Education, 8(1): 39 – 61.

[117] NEWTON J. 2007. What is quality? //Bollaert L. 2006. Embedding quality culture in higher education. A Selection of Papers from the 1st European Forum for Quality Assurance, 23 – 25 November 2006, hosted by the Technische Universität München. (EUA Case Studies 2007).

[118] NICKELS L. 2002. Theoretical and methodological issues in the cognitive neuropsychology of spoken word production. Aphasiology, 16: 3 – 19.

[119] NOWOTNY H, SCOTT P, GIBBONS M. 2001. Re-thinking science: knowledge and the public in an age of uncertainty. London: Polity Press.

[120] O'CONNELL J, PEPLER D, CRAIG W. 1999. Peer involvement in bullying: insights and challenges for interventions. Journal of Adolescence, 22: 437 – 452.

[121] OKONKWO. 2010. Sustainable assessment and evaluation strategies for Open and distance learning. Turkish Online Journal of Distance Education(10).

[122] OWENS R G. 2000. Organizational behaviour in education: instructional leadership and school reform. Massachusetts: Allyn & Bacon.

[123] PATTON M G. 1987. How to use qualitative methods in valuation. California: Sage.

[124] PEDHAZUR E J. 1997. Multiple regression in behavioral research: explanation and prediction. New York: Harcourt Brace College.

[125] PELLEGRINO, QUELLMALZ. 2010. Perspectives on the integration of technology and assessment. Journal of Research on Technology in Education.

[126] PELLERT A. 1997. Die universität in der wissensgesellschaft zum verhältnis von forschung und lehre. Innsbruck/Wien: Studienverlag.

[127] PERRY K E, WEINSTEIN R S. 1998. The social context of early schooling and children's school adjustment. Educational Psychologist, 33: 177 – 194.

[128] ROBERT W. 2001. Brainstorming: a creative way to learn. Project Innovation, Inc.

[129] RUTTER M. 2000. Psychosocial influences: critiques, findings, and research needs. Development and Psychopathology, 12: 375 - 405.

[130] SANTIAGO P, TREMBLAY K, BASRI E, et al. 2008. Tertiary education for the knowledge society. OECD Thematic Review of Tertiary Education: Synthesis Report, 2.

[131] SCARDIMALIA M, BEREITER C. 1994. Computer support for knowledge-building communities. Journal of the Learning Sciences, 3(3): 265 - 384.

[132] SCOTT P. 2007. Back to the future? The evolution of higher education systems. // KEHM B. Looking back to look forward: analyses of higher education after the turn of the millennium. Kassel: INCHER: 13 - 27.

[133] SEIDLE T, RIMMELE R, PRENZEL M. 2005. Clarity and coherence of lesson goals as a scaffold for student learning. Learning and Instruction, 15: 539 - 556.

[134] SERCU. 2004. Language teaching and learning. London: Routledge.

[135] SIMONS R I, JOHNSON C, BEAMAN J J, et al. 1996. Parents and peer groups as mediators of the effect of community structure on adolescent behavior. American Journal of Community Psychology, 24: 145 - 171.

[136] SPENCER L M Jr, SPENCER S M. 1993. Competence at work: models for superior performance. New York: John Wiley & Sons.

[137] STEIN S, BOOK H. 2006. The EQ edge. Hoboken, NJ: John Wiley & Sons.

[138] STERNBERG R J. 1985. Beyond IQ: a triarchic theory of human intelligence. New York: Cambridge University Press.

[139] STIGGINS R J, ARTER J A, CHAPPUIS J, et al. 2009. Classroom assessment for learning: doing it right: using it well. Columbus, OH: Allyn and Bacon.

[140] STIGLITZ J E. 1999. Knowledge as a global public good. // KAUL I, GRUMBERG I, STERN M A. Global public goods. International cooperation in the 21st century. New York: Oxford University Press: 308 - 325.

[141] SUN C P. 2004. Reflections on moral education from the dimensions of morality new thinking for the study of moral education in the context of social diversity. Journal of East China Normal University: Education Science Edition, 22(4). 17, 24, 37.

[142] SWANER L E. 2007. Linking engaged learning, student mental health and well-being, and civic development: a review of the literature. Liberal Education, 93(1): 16 - 25.

[143] TAYLOR S N. 2006. Why the real self is fundamental to intentional change. Journal of Management Development, 25(7): 643 - 656.

[144] TAYLOR, WARD. 1998. Literacy theory in the age of the internet. New York:

Columbia University Press.

[145] THORNDIKE R L, STEIN S. 1937. An evaluation of the attempts to measure social intelligence. The Psychological Bulletin, 34(5):275-285.

[146] THORNDIKE E L. 1920. Intelligence and its uses. Harper Magazine, 140:227-235.

[147] TOMASEGOVIC, ELIAS, BARACIC, MRVAC. 2011. E-learning and evaluation in modern educational system. US-China Education Review, 8(2):198-203.

[148] TROW M. 1973. Problems in the transition from elite to mass higher education. Berkley: Carnegie Commission on Higher Education.

[149] TROW M. 1976. Elite higher education: an endangered species? Minerva, 14(3): 355-376.

[150] TROW M. 1979. Elite and mass higher education: American models and European realities. //Research into Higher Education: Processes and Structures. Stockholm: National Board of Universities and Colleges:183-219.

[151] TROW M. 1981. Comparative perspectives on access. //FULTON O. Access to higher education. Guildford: SRHE:89-121.

[152] TROW M. 1994. Managerialism and the academic profession: quality and control. QSC Higher Education Report, 2.

[153] TROW M. 2000. From mass higher education to universal access: the American advantage. Research and Occasional Paper Series, CSHE, 1:1-17.

[154] TROW, M. 2006. Reflections on the transition from elite to mass to universal access: forms and phases of higher education in modern societies since WWII. International Handbook of Higher Education, 18:243-280.

[155] TUCKER M L, SOJKA J Z, BARONE F J, et al. 2000. Training tomorrow's leaders: enhancing the emotional intelligence of business graduates. Journal of Education for Business, 75:331-338.

[156] VITARO F, BRENDGEN M, PAGANI L, et al. 1999. Disruptive behavior, peer association, and conduct disorder: testing the developmental links through early intervention. Development and Psychopathology, 11:287-304.

[157] WARDEN R. 1995. Metaphor made real with an open mind. Times Higher Education Supplement(1197).

[158] WATTS W D, SHORT A P. 1990. Teacher drug use: a response to occupational stress. Journal of Drug Education, 20(11):47-65.

[159] WERNER E E. 1993. Risk, resilience, and recovery: perspectives from the Kauai longitudinal study. Development and Psychopathology, 5:503-515.

[160] WILLIAM W. 2004. Refuting misconceptions about classroom discussion. Heldref

Publications.

[161] WILLIAMS W M, STERNBERG R. 1988. Group intelligence: why some groups are better than others. Intelligence, 12: 351-377.

[162] WORLD BANK. 2002. Constructing knowledge societies: new challenges for tertiary education. Washington, D. C. : World Bank.

[163] WORLD BANK. 2003. Lifelong learning in the global knowledge economy: challenges for developing countries. Washington, D. C. : World Bank.

[164] WÖβMANN. 2008. Efficiency and equity of European education and training policies. International Tax and Public Finance, 2: 200-201.

[165] YOON J S. 2002. Teacher characteristics as predictors of teacher-student relationships: stress, negative affect, and self-efficacy. Social Behavior and Personality, 30(5): 485-494.

[166] ZHANG M. 2004. Time to change the truancy laws? Compulsory education: its origin and modern dilemma. UK: Blackwell Publishing.

[167] ZIMMERMAN B J. 2001. Theories of self-regulated learning and academic achievement: an overview and analysis. //ZIMMERMAN B J SCHUNK D H. Self-regulated learning and academic achievement: theoretical perspectives. Mahwah, NJ: Erlbaum: 1-65.